Visible Learning for Teachers

John Hattie's ground-breaking book *Visible Learning* synthesized the results of more than 15 years research involving millions of students and represented the biggest ever collection of evidence-based research into what actually works in schools to improve learning.

Visible Learning for Teachers takes the next step and brings those ground-breaking concepts to a completely new audience. Written for students, pre-service and in-service teachers, it explains how to apply the principles of *Visible Learning* to any classroom anywhere in the world. The author offers concise and user-friendly summaries of the most successful interventions and offers practical step-by-step guidance to the successful implementation of visible learning and visible teaching in the classroom.

This book:

- links the biggest ever research project on teaching strategies to practical classroom implementation;
- champions both teacher and student perspectives and contains step-by-step guidance including lesson preparation, interpreting learning and feedback during the lesson and post lesson follow up;
- offers checklists, exercises, case studies and best practice scenarios to assist in raising achievement;
- includes whole school checklists and advice for school leaders on facilitating visible learning in their institution;
- now includes additional meta-analyses bringing the total cited within the research to over 900;
- comprehensively covers numerous areas of learning activity including pupil motivation, curriculum, meta-cognitive strategies, behaviour, teaching strategies and classroom management.

Visible Learning for Teachers is a must read for any student or teacher who wants an evidence-based answer to the question: 'how do we maximize achievement in our schools?'

John Hattie is Professor and Director of the Melbourne Education Research Institute at the University of Melbourne, Australia and honorary Professor at the University of Auckland, New Zealand. He is the author of *Visible Learning* and co-author of *Intelligence and Intelligence Testing*, both published by Routledge.

D0082266

Visible Learning for Teachers

Maximizing impact on learning

John Hattie

Routledge
Taylor & Francis Group

LONDON AND NEW YORK

First published 2012
by Routledge
2 Park Square, Milton Park, Abingdon, Oxon OX14 4RN

Simultaneously published in the USA and Canada
by Routledge
711 Third Avenue, New York, NY 10017

Routledge is an imprint of the Taylor & Francis Group, an informa business

British Library Cataloguing in Publication Data
A catalogue record for this book is available from the British Library

Library of Congress Cataloging in Publication Data
Hattie, John.
    Visible learning for teachers : maximizing impact on learning / John Hattie.
        p. cm.
    Includes bibliographical references and index.
    1. Visual learning. I. Title.
    LB1067.5.H37 2012
    370.15′23—dc23   2011032967

ISBN: 978–0–415–69014–0 (hbk)
ISBN: 978–0–415–69015–7 (pbk)
ISBN: 978–0–203–18152–2 (ebk)

Typeset in Bembo
by Swales & Willis Ltd, Exeter, Devon

Printed and bound in the USA by
Edwards Brothers, Inc.

Contents

Preface

Elliot is now aged 10. When *Visible Learning* was being completed, Elliot was diagnosed with leukaemia. Since then, he has completed the four-year regime of chemotherapy; now, his own system is being asked to take over. He has started school, is learning to read and write, and is becoming a happy, adventurous pre-teen – having retained his sparkly personality throughout the arduous hospitalization. The scripts that the doctors decided to follow have been successful and the interventions have had major positive consequences. Throughout the treatment, the impact of the interventions was monitored, changed, and led to the critical decisions that now allow Elliot to shine in touch rugby and BMX riding, and to be a peer mediator at his school. He has been a part of a community of doctors, nurses, teachers, friends, and family – so many were involved. The impact of the dosage and treatment was constantly monitored to ensure that it was leading to the criteria of success. Decisions were made in light of the monitoring; teams worked to understand the consequences of treatments; and evidence was the key to adaptive professional decision-making – all aiming to maximize the impact not only on the medical, but also the social and family, aspects. We all truly knew their impact. Again, Elliot is the inspiration for the major message of this book: know thy impact!

For many years of my career, I have worked in schools, met many stunning teachers who have evidence of their impact on student learning, and worked with some of the best in the world in researching teaching expertise. In the past few years, my team has run workshops for over 3,000 teachers and school leaders, and worked in more than 1,000 schools, mainly in New Zealand and Australia. We have learned much from these schools about the implications from *Visible Learning*. The message certainly is not ticking off the top ten in the league table! The most common question is: 'Where do I start?' The argument in this book is that the starting place is the way in which you think about your role – it is to know, on a regular basis, the nature and magnitude of your impact on the learning of your students. The next most common question is 'What does visible learning look like in a school?' – hence one of the themes in this book of 'visible learning inside'. There is no program, no single script, no workbook on how to implement visible learning; instead, I have provided a set of benchmarks that can be used to create debates, to seek evidence, and to self-review to determine whether a school is having a marked impact on all of its students. This highlights the importance of educators as evaluators of their impact.

Both questions ('Where do I start?'; 'What does visible learning look like?') beg the next question, 'What is the nature of the learning that you wish to impact?', and my hope is that it is more than passing surface-level tests. It involves impacting on the love of learning, inviting students to stay in learning, and seeing the ways in which students can improve their healthy sense of being, respect for self, and respect for others — as well as enhancing achievement. What achievement is to be valued needs to be a major debate in schools, communities, and societies; right now, such curricular questions seem more determined by the test specifications than by such lively debate.

I could have written a book about school leaders, about society influences, about policies — and all are worthwhile — but my most immediate attention is more related to teachers and students: the daily life of teachers in preparing, starting, conducting, and evaluating lessons, and the daily life of students involved in learning. Note the plural: it is a community of teachers that is needed to work together to ask the questions, evaluate their impact, and decide on the optimal next steps; it is the community of students who work together in the pursuit of progress. Such passion for evaluating impact is the single most critical lever for instructional excellence — accompanied by understanding this impact, and doing something in light of the evidence and understanding.

Throughout *Visible Learning*, I constantly came across the importance of 'passion'; as a measurement person, it bothered me that it was a difficult notion to measure — particularly when it was often so obvious. But it is a particular form of passion — a passion based on having a positive impact on all of the students in the class. This book starts with a discussion of the attributes of such passionate teachers who have major impacts on students. It then uses the evidence from the synthesis of meta-analyses to elaborate on major messages for teachers as they go about their daily tasks. The book concludes by noting the major mind frames that underline these passionate and inspired educators. A major claim is that it is these mind frames that are the precursors of success in schools, these mind frames that need to be developed in teacher education programs. These mind frames require nurturance and resourcing, and these mind frames are the professional being of those we call 'effective' teachers and school leaders.

As I noted in the preface to *Visible Learning*, the message about schools is a positive one. Both *Visible Learning* and this book are based on the story of many real teachers whom I have meet, seen, and some of whom have taught my own sons. Many teachers already think in the ways for which I argue in both this (and the earlier) book; many are always seeking to improve and constantly monitoring their performances to make a difference to what they do; and many inspire the love of learning that is one of the major outcomes of any school. I ended *Visible Learning* where this book now starts, by citing my friend and colleague Paul Brock (2004: 250–1):

> I want all future teachers of my Sophie and Millie to abide by three fundamental principles that I believe should underpin teaching and learning in every public school.

> First, to nurture and challenge my daughters' intellectual and imaginative capacities way out to horizons unsullied by self-fulfilling minimalist expectations. Don't patronize them with lowest-common-denominator blancmange masquerading as knowledge and learning; nor crush their love for learning through boring pedagogy. Don't bludgeon them with mindless 'busy work' and limit the exploration of the world of evolving knowledge merely to the tyranny of repetitively churned-out recycled worksheets. Ensure that there is legitimate progression of learning from one day, week, month, term and year to the next.

Second, to care for Sophie and Millie with humanity and sensitivity, as developing human beings worthy of being taught with genuine respect, enlightened discipline and imaginative flair.

And third, please strive to maximize their potential for later schooling, post-school education, training and employment and for the quality of life itself so that they can contribute to and enjoy the fruits of living within an Australian society that is fair, just, tolerant, honorable, knowledgeable, prosperous and happy.

When all is said and done, surely this is what every parent and every student should be able to expect of school education: not only as delivered within every public school in NSW, but within every school not only in Australia but throughout the entire world.

Know thy impact.

John Hattie
University of Melbourne, 2011

Acknowledgements

The team in the visible learning lab at the University of Auckland have been a major inspiration for this book. We have all worked in an open space, sharing ideas, problems, and successes. Over the past 12 years, we have developed a major assessment and reporting system for all New Zealand elementary and high schools, have worked in many schools implementing the ideas relating to visible learning, and have conducted many studies relating to the major themes of visible learning. Over 1,000 teachers have worked with us in developing the assessment system; over 100 people have worked in our lab; we have had many visitors (academics and students) spend time with us – and it has made coming to work a pleasurable experience. Gavin Brown, Annette Holt, Earl Irving, Peter Keegan, Andrea Mackay, and Debra Masters have all led this team, and their thoughts, prompts, and feedback are ever-present in these pages. I thank all involved in this place of fun, learning, and valuing.

Many have read and commented on drafts of this book, and they are acknowledged for their suggestions for improvement, although I accept responsibility for the remaining errors. Thanks to Kristin Anderson, Janet Clinton, Steve Dinham, Michael Fullan, Patrick Griffin, John Marsden, Brian McNulty, Roger Moses, Geoff Petty, Doug Reeves, Ainsley Rose, Julie Schumacher, Carol Steele, and Greg Yates for their input, critique, and valuable advice. I am most grateful for the nine reviewers who provided reports to the publishers: Ann Callander; Rick DuFour; Michael Fullan; Christopher Jones; Geoff Petty; Andrew Martin; Elaine Smitheman; Sebastian Suggate; and Huw Thomas. I am especially indebted to Debra Masters and Janet Rivers for their attention to the details, to Earl Irving for permission to use his student evaluation survey, and to Steve Martin from Howick College for allowing me to use the SOLO lesson plan in Chapter 4. The team at Routledge, headed by Bruce Roberts, have made completing this book a pleasure, and the Australia MacMillan team headed by Lee Collie and Col Gilliespie have made it enjoyable to travel around talking about the messages. I also thank the team at my new academic home, the Melbourne Graduate School of Education at the University of Melbourne, for their welcoming of me to my next set of challenges.

But, most of all, I thank: my family – Janet, Joel, Kyle, Kieran, Billy (deceased), Bobby, and Jamie – who are my inspirations for living; my sisters and brothers; and all those passionate teachers who have invited me into their classrooms over the past 12 years.

Visible learning inside

When we buy a computer, there is often a label proclaiming that it has 'Intel inside'. While most of us might not know exactly what this means, the label acts as a seal of approval indicating that what we are buying is good quality and will work. Indeed, it does indicate this: 'Intel inside' refers to the processor, or brain, in the computer – and it is the key to the success of the software and other hardware that makes up the 'workings' of the computer. In many ways, our schools have emphasized the 'software' (the programs in schools) and the 'hardware' (buildings, resources), rather than the 'Intel inside' (the core attributes that make schools successful). The 'software' and 'hardware' have been the major marketing tools of schooling used by politicians and principals, and they are also the topics that we most love to debate. Raise the question of class size, grouping in class, salaries and finance, the nature of learning environments and buildings, the curriculum, assessment, and the ensuing debate will be endless and enjoyable. These are *not*, however, the core attributes of successful schooling.

This book is about those core attributes – about the 'Intel inside'. It discusses not the software or hardware of schooling, but instead asks what are the attributes of schooling that truly make the difference to student learning – the 'processing' attributes that make learning visible, such that we might say that the school has 'visible learning inside'?

The 'visible' aspect refers first to making student learning visible to teachers, ensuring clear identification of the attributes that make a visible difference to student learning, and *all* in the school visibly knowing the impact that they have on the learning in the school (of the student, teacher, and school leaders). The 'visible' aspect also refers to making teaching visible to the student, such that they learn to become their own teachers, which is the core attribute of lifelong learning or self-regulation, and of the love of learning that we so want students to value. The 'learning' aspect refers to how we go about knowing and understanding, and then doing something about student learning. A common theme throughout this book is the need to retain learning at the forefront and to consider teaching primarily in terms of its impact on student learning.

The arguments in this book are based on the evidence in *Visible Learning* (Hattie, 2009), although this book is not merely a summary. *Visible Learning* was based on more than 800 meta-analyses of 50,000 research articles, about 150,000 effect sizes, and about 240 million students (Chapter 2 gives an outline of this evidence). A further 100+ meta-analyses completed since *Visible Learning* was published have been added in Appendix A of this book – but they have not changed the major messages.

This book also builds on perhaps the most significant discovery from the evidence in *Visible Learning*: namely, that almost any intervention can stake a claim to making a difference to student learning. Figure 1.1 shows the overall distribution of all of the effect sizes from each of the 800+ meta-analyses examined in *Visible Learning*. The *y*-axis represents the number of effects in each category, while the *x*-axis gives the magnitude of effect sizes. Any effect above zero means that achievement has been raised by the intervention. The average effect size is 0.40, and the graph shows a near normal distribution curve – that is, there are just as many influences on achievement above the average as there are below the average.

The most important conclusion that can be drawn from Figure 1.1 is that 'everything works': if the criterion of success is 'enhancing achievement', then 95 per cent[+] of all effect sizes in education are positive. When teachers claim that they are having a positive effect on achievement, or when it is claimed that a policy improves achievement, it is a trivial claim, because virtually everything works: the bar for deciding 'what works' in teaching and learning is so often, inappropriately, set at zero.

With the bar set at zero, it is no wonder every teacher can claim that he or she is making a difference; no wonder we can find many answers as to how to enhance achievement; no wonder there is some evidence that every student improves, and no wonder there are no 'below-average' teachers. Setting the bar at zero means that we do not need any changes in our system! We need only more of what we already have – more money, more resources, more teachers per students, more . . . But this approach, I would suggest, is the wrong answer.

Setting the bar at an effect size of $d = 0.0$ is so low as to be dangerous.[1] We need to be more discriminating. For any particular intervention to be considered worthwhile, it needs to show an improvement in student learning of at least an average gain – that is, an

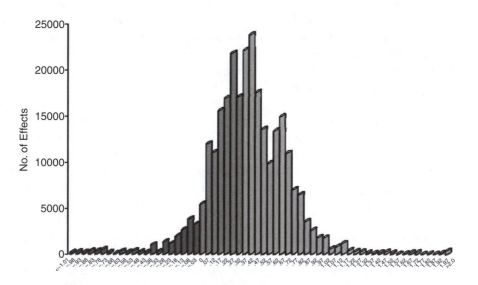

FIGURE 1.1 Distribution of effect sizes across all meta-analyses

[1] *d* is shorthand for 'effect size'.

effect size of at least 0.40. The *d* = 0.40 is what I referred to in *Visible Learning* as the *hinge-point* (or h-point) for identifying what is and what is not effective.

EFFECT SIZE

An effect size is a useful method for comparing results on different measures (such as standardized, teacher-made tests, student work), or over time, or between groups, on a scale that allows multiple comparisons independent of the original test scoring (for example, marked out of 10, or 100), across content, and over time. This independent scale is one of the major attractions for using effect sizes, because it allows relative comparisons about various influences on student achievement. There are many sources for more information on effect sizes, including: Glass, McGaw, and Smith (1981); Hattie, Rogers and Swaminathan (2011), Hedges and Olkin (1985); Lipsey and Wilson (2001); and Schagen and Hodgen (2009).

Half of the influences on achievement are above this hinge-point. This is a real-world, actual finding and not an aspirational claim. That means that about half of what we do to *all* students has an effect of greater than 0.4. About half of our students are in classes that get this effect of 0.40 or greater, while half are in classes that get less than the 0.4 effect. *Visible Learning* told the story of the factors that lead to effects greater than this hinge-point of 0.40; this book aims to translate that story into information that teachers, students, and schools can put into practice. It translates the story into a practice of teaching and learning.

Outcomes of schooling

This book is concerned with achievement; we require much more, however, from our schools than mere achievement. Overly concentrating on achievement can miss much about what students know, can do, and care about. Many love the learning aspect and can devote hours to non-school-related achievement outcomes (in both socially desirable and undesirable activities), and love the thrill of the chase in the learning (the critique, the false turns, the discovery of outcomes). For example, one of the more profound findings that has driven me as a father is the claim of Levin, Belfield, Muennig, and Rouse (2006) that the best predictor of health, wealth, and happiness in later life is *not* school achievement, but the number of years in schooling. Retaining students in learning is a highly desirable outcome of schooling, and because many students make decisions about staying in schooling between the ages of 11 and 15, this means that the school and learning experience at these ages must be productive, challenging, and engaging to ensure the best chance possible that students will stay in school.

Levin et al. (2006) calculated that dropouts from high school have an average income of US$23,000 annually, while a high-school graduate earns 48 per cent more than this, a person with some college education earns 78 per cent more, and a college graduate earns 346 per cent more. High-school graduates live six to nine years longer than dropouts, have better health, are 10–20 per cent less likely to be involved in criminal activities, and are

20–40 per cent less likely to be on welfare. These 'costs' far exceed the costs of demonstratively successful educational interventions. Graduating from high school increases tax revenue, reduces taxes paid into public health, and decreases criminal justice and public assistance costs, plus there is clear justice in providing opportunities to students such that they can enjoy the benefits of greater income, health, and happiness.

That the purposes of education and schooling include more than achievement have been long debated – from Plato and his predecessors, through Rousseau to modern thinkers. Among the most important purposes is the development of critical evaluation skills, such that we develop citizens with challenging minds and dispositions, who become active, competent, and thoughtfully critical in our complex world. This includes: critical evaluation of the political issues that affect the person's community, country, and world; the ability to examine, reflect, and argue, with reference to history and tradition, while respecting self and others; having concern for one's own and others' life and well-being; and the ability to imagine and think about what is 'good' for self and others (see Nussbaum, 2010). Schooling should have major impacts not only on the enhancement of knowing and understanding, but also on the enhancement of character: intellectual character, moral character, civic character, and performance character (Shields, 2011).

Such critical evaluation is what is asked of teachers and school leaders. This development of critical evaluation skills requires educators to develop their students' capacity to see the world from the viewpoint of others, to understand human weaknesses and injustices, and to work towards developing cooperation and working with others. It requires educators to develop in their students a genuine concern for self and others, to teach the importance of evidence to counter stereotypes and closed thinking, to promote accountability of the person as responsible agent, and to vigorously promote critical thinking and the importance of dissenting voices. All of this depends on subject matter knowledge, because enquiry and critical evaluation is not divorced from knowing something. This notion of *critical evaluation* is a core notion throughout this book – and particularly in that teachers and school leaders need to be critical evaluators of the effect that they are having on their students.

Outline of the chapters

The fundamental thesis of this book is that there is a 'practice' of teaching. The word *practice*, and not *science*, is deliberately chosen because there is no fixed recipe for ensuring that teaching has the maximum possible effect on student learning, and no set of principles that apply to all learning for all students. But there are practices that we know are effective and many practices that we know are not. Theories have purposes as tools for synthesizing notions, but too often teachers believe that theories dictate action, even when the evidence of impact does not support their particular theories (and then maintaining their theories becomes almost a religion). This rush by teachers to infer is a major obstacle to many students enhancing their learning. Instead, evidence of impact or not may mean that teachers need to modify or dramatically change their theories of action. Practice invokes notions of a way of thinking and doing, and particularly of learning constantly from the deliberate practice in teaching.

This book is structured about the big ideas from *Visible Learning*, but presented in a sequence of decisions that teachers are asked to make on a regular basis – preparing, starting, conducting, and ending a lesson or series of lessons. While this sequence is not intended to imply that there is a simple linear set of decisions, it is a 'coat hanger' to present the ways of thinking – the mind frames – which are the most critical messages.

The first part of the practice of teaching is the major mind frames required by the school leaders or teachers. The source of these ideas is outlined in Chapter 2, explored in more detail in Chapter 3, and returned to in the final chapter, Chapter 9. The second part of the practice of teaching is the various phases of the lesson interaction between teacher and students, each of which is discussed in a separate chapter:

- preparing the lessons (Chapter 4);
- starting the lessons (Chapter 5);
- the flow of the lessons – learning (Chapter 6);
- the flow of the lessons – feedback (Chapter 7); and
- the end of the lesson (Chapter 8).

Figure 1.2 sums up the high-level principles argued throughout this book. I do note that there may seem to be 'too much' at times, but then our enterprise of teaching and learning is never straightforward. The big ideas in Figure 1.2 are expanded in each chapter and can

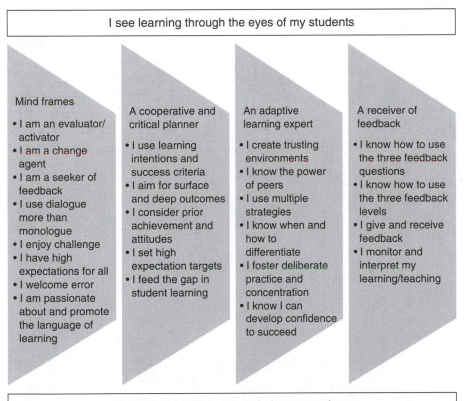

FIGURE 1.2 Know thy impact

serve as an advance organizer, and the aim of the chapters is to convince you of the merits of this program logic.

Each chapter develops a set of checklists for schools to evaluate whether they have 'visible learning inside'. These checklists are not meant as tick lists of 'yes' or 'no', but as guidelines for asking and answering questions about the way in which a school knows about the effect it is having on the students in that school. Atul Gawande (2009) has detailed the power of such checklists, most often used in the airline industry and in his case translated into the medical domain. He shows how checklists help to achieve the balance between specialized ability and group collaboration. He does comment that while most surgeons resist checklists (finding them too confining and unprofessional), more than 90 per cent would require them if a member of their family were to be under the surgeon's knife. The set of checks aims to ensure that critical matters are not overlooked, to give direction to debates in staff rooms, and to provide an outline for assessing whether there are good evaluation processes in the school. Michael Scriven (2005) also has been a long-time advocate of checklists. He has distinguished between the many types, from the laundry list, the sequential list, flow charts and, most usefully, the merit checklist. It is the merit checklist that is suggested for each chapter here. These consist of a series of criteria that can each be considered; those reviewing the evidence for each criterion can then make an overall decision about merit and worth (see http://www.wmich.edu/evalctr/checklists for further examples of checklists). The merit checklists in each chapter are more DO–CONFIRM not READ–DO, because this allows for much flexibility in providing evidence and acting to ensure that a school is working towards making learning visible.

The source of ideas and the role of teachers

2

The source of the ideas

In 2009, *Visible Learning* was published. This was the culmination of many decades of work – finding, reading, and analysing meta-analyses. I recently spoke in Seattle to a group of educators about this work. It was like a return to the beginning: my search began there in 1984, when I was on sabbatical at the University of Washington. In many cases, as part of researching the meta-analyses, I went back to the original articles, wrote separate articles on themes, and spoke to many groups about the meaning of these analyses. Always, the question was: 'So, what does all of this *mean*?' Addressing this question is the reason the book had a long gestation. The aim of *Visible Learning* was to tell a story, and in most cases the reviews and reactions indicate that the story has been heard – although, as expected, not always agreed with.

The *Times Educational Supplement* was first to review it. Mansell (2008) argued that *Visible Learning* was 'perhaps education's equivalent to the search for the Holy Grail – or the answer to life, the universe and everything'. Mansell recognized that the 'education Grail' was most likely to be found in the improvement in the level of interaction between pupils and their teachers. (Please note that we have yet to find the 'real' Holy Grail – despite the efforts of Dan Brown, *Lord of the Rings*, and *Spamalot*!)

It was not the aim of *Visible Learning* to suggest that the state of teaching is woeful; indeed, the theme was the opposite. The majority of effects above the average were attributable to success in teaching, and there is no greater pleasure than to visit schools and classrooms in which the ideas in *Visible Learning* are transparently visible. As I wrote in the conclusion to *Visible Learning*:

> I have seen teachers who are stunning, who live the principles outlined in this book, and demonstrably make a difference. They play the game according to the principles outlined here. They question themselves, they worry about which students are not making appropriate progress, they seek evidence of successes and gaps, and they seek help when they need it in their teaching. The future is one of hope as many of these teachers exist in our schools. They are often head-down in the school, not always picked by parents as the better teachers, but the students know and welcome being in their classes. The message in this book is one of hope for an excellent future for teachers and teaching, and based on not just my explanation for 146,000+ effect sizes but on the comfort that there are already many excellent teachers in our profession.
>
> (Hattie, 2009: 261)

So what was the story and what was the evidence base? This chapter introduces the main implications from *Visible Learning* and, most importantly, introduces the course of ideas for this book. The next chapter, Chapter 3, will provide more about the evidence on which this story is based – although it is not intended to be a substitute for detailed discussion of the evidence presented in *Visible Learning*.

The evidence base

The basic units of analysis are the 900+ meta-analyses. A meta-analysis involves identifying a specific outcome (such as achievement) and identifying an influence on that outcome (for example, homework), and then systematically searching the various databases: mainstream journals and books (such as ERIC, PsycINFO); dissertations (for example, ProQuest); grey literature (material such as conference papers, submissions, technical reports, and working papers not easily found through normal channels). It involved contacting authors for copies of their work, checking references in the articles found, and reading widely to find other sources. For each study, effect sizes are calculated for appropriate comparisons. In general, there are two major types of effect size: comparisons between groups (for example, comparing those who *did* get homework with those who *did not* get homework), or comparisons over time (for example, baseline results compared with results four months later).

Take, for example, Cooper, Robinson, and Patall's (2006) meta-analysis on homework. They were interested in the effect of homework on student achievement based on research over the past twenty years. They searched various databases, contacted the deans of 77 departments of education (inviting them also to ask their faculties), sent requests to 21 researchers who have published on homework, and letters to more than 100 school districts and directors of evaluation. They then examined each title, abstract, and document to identify any further research. They found 59 studies, and concluded that the effect size between homework and achievement was $d = 0.40$; effects of homework were higher for high-school students ($d = 0.50$) than for elementary-school students ($d = -0.08$). They suggested that secondary students were less likely to be distracted while doing homework and more likely to have been taught effective study habits, and could have better self-regulation and monitoring of their work and time investment. Like all good research, their study suggested the most important questions that now needed to be addressed and reduced other questions to being of lesser importance.

As I have noted, more than 800 of these meta-analyses formed the basis of *Visible Learning*. For each meta-analysis, I created a database of the average effect size plus some related information (for example, standard error of the mean). A major part of the analyses was looking for a moderator: for example, did the effects of homework on achievement differ across ages, subjects, types of homework, quality of the meta-analyses, and so on?

Consider my synthesis of five meta-analyses on homework (Cooper, 1989, 1994; Cooper et al., 2006; DeBaz, 1994; Paschal, Weinstein, & Walberg, 1984). Over these five meta-analyses, there were 161 studies involving more than 100,000 students that investigated the effects of homework on students' achievement. The average of all of these effect sizes was $d = 0.29$, which can be used as the best typical effect size of the influence of homework on achievement. Thus, compared to classes without homework, the use of homework was associated with advancing students' achievement by approximately one year, or improving the rate of learning by 15 per cent. About 65 per cent of the effects were positive (that is, improved achievement), and 35 per cent of the effects were zero or negative. The average achievement level of students in classes that prescribed homework exceeded 62 per cent of the achievement levels of the students not prescribed homework. However, an effect size of $d = 0.29$ would not, according to Cohen (1977), be perceptible to the naked eye, and would be approximately equivalent to the difference in height between someone measuring 5'11" (180 cm) and someone 6'0" (182 cm).

The 800+ meta-analyses analysed for *Visible Learning* encompassed 52,637 studies – about 240 million students – and provided 146,142 effect sizes about the influence of some program, policy, or innovation on academic achievement in school (early childhood, elementary, high, and tertiary). Appendices A and B (taken from *Visible Learning*) sum up this evidence. The appendices include 115 additional meta-analyses discovered since 2008 (an extra 7,518 studies, 5 million students, and 13,428 effect sizes). There are a few additional major categories (going from 138 to 147), and some minor changes in the rank order of influences, but the major messages have not changed.

Since *Visible Learning* was published, I have continued to add to this database, locating a further 100 meta-analyses – added in Appendix A. The overall ranking of the influences, however, has negligibly changed between this and the previous version ($r > 0.99$ for both rankings and effect sizes). The underlying messages have certainly not changed. The estimated total sample size is about 240 million+ students (the 88 million below is only from the 345 meta-analyses that included sample size).

The overall average effect from all meta-analyses was $d = 0.40$. So what does this mean? I did not want to simplistically relate adjectives to the size of the effects. Yes, there is a general feeling that $d < 0.20$ is small, 0.3–0.6 is medium, and > 0.6 is large – but often specific interpretations make these adjectives misleading. For example, a small effect size that requires few resources may be more critical than a larger one that requires high levels of resourcing. The effect of reducing class size from 25–30 students to 15–20 students is 0.22 and the effect of teaching specific programs to assist students in test-taking is about 0.27. Both are smallish effects, but one is far cheaper to implement than the other. The relatively better return on cost from the latter is obvious – thus, the relative effect of two smallish effects can have different implications.

Almost everyone can impact on learning if the benchmark is set at $d > 0.0$ – as is so often the case. Most interventions with a modicum of implementation can gain an effect

TABLE 2.1 Average effect for each of the major contributors to learning

ACROSS DIMENSIONS	NO. OF META-ANALYSES	NO. OF STUDIES	NO. OF PEOPLE	NO. OF EFFECTS	ES	SE
Student	152	11,909	9,397,859	40,197	0.39	0.044
Home	40	2,347	12,066,705	6,031	0.31	0.053
School	115	4,688	4,613,129	15,536	0.23	0.072
Teacher	41	2,452	2,407,527	6,014	0.47	0.054
Curricula	153	10,129	7,555,134	32,367	0.45	0.075
Teaching	412	28,642	52,611,720	59,909	0.43	0.070
Average	**913**	**60,167**	**88,652,074**	**160,054**	**0.40**	**0.061**

of 0.20, and on average we can have an influence of 0.40. There are many students who benefit from being in classes in which they regularly gain > 0.40 from a program implemented by a high-impact teacher. The central question should be the debate about allocating resources to sustain and support those who have this $d > 0.40$ influence, and to ask seriously what to change where there is evidence of lower effects. While bus routes, utility bills, and lengthy administrative meetings may be needed to make schools run, the true debate is about the nature, quality, and effects of the influences that we have on students – and in this book it is argued that we should attain at minimum gains of at least or above the average for all students. This is accomplished already in so many classrooms, and great schools can be known for the choice of their debates – about 'knowing thy impact'.

Perhaps the most important thing to remember when using these adjectives to describe effect sizes is that *Visible Learning* has summed up what has happened – the imperative here is the past tense. For example, consider the homework example. The general message from the overall $d = 0.29$ is that the effects of homework are small, and even smaller (near to zero) in elementary schools. On the one hand, this is not a big issue, as the cost of adding homework to the school costs is negligible. On the other hand, the finding should be an invitation to *change* how we do homework in elementary schools, because *homework as it has traditionally been done* (and thus reported in the 161 studies) has not been very effective in elementary schools. What a wonderful opportunity for schools to try something different . . .

Indeed, many New Zealand schools did exactly this: they did not abandon homework (because too many parents judge the quality of a school by the mere presence of homework and get upset if there is none), but they tried different approaches. One school worked with students and parents to create a website of various 'home challenges' and evaluated the effects of this new policy on student motivation, achievement, and parent involvement with their children's learning. When teachers and schools evaluate the effect of what they do on student learning (and this was the major message in *Visible Learning*), we have 'visible learning inside'. The term refers not to the specific presence or otherwise of an initiative, *but to the evaluation of its effect*. Such an evaluation must, of necessity, take into account local conditions, local moderators, and local interpretations. And *that* is the main message in this current book: become evaluators of your effect. I want you to aim for a $d > 0.40$ effect, which, on average, is most definitely attainable.

The barometer and the hinge-point

One of the tensions in writing *Visible Learning* was to present the evidence without overwhelming the reader with data. I wanted a visual image to summarize the oodles of data. My partner devised the illustration shown in Figure 2.1 as a 'barometer of influences'.

The arrow in Figure 2.1 points to the average effect of the various meta-analyses on the particular topic (in Figure 2.1, it is $d = 0.29$ for the five homework meta-analyses). The variability (or standard error) of the average effect sizes from each meta-analysis is not always easy to determine. Across all 800+ meta-analyses, the typical standard error of the mean is about $d = 0.07$. To provide a broad sense of variance, any influence for which the average 'spread of effects' was less than $d = 0.04$ was considered low, between $d = 0.041$ and $d = 0.079$ was deemed medium, and greater than $d = 0.08$ was deemed large. While these are crude estimates, rather than focus on them, it is more important *to read the discussion about each influence to ascertain whether important sources of variance can be identified*

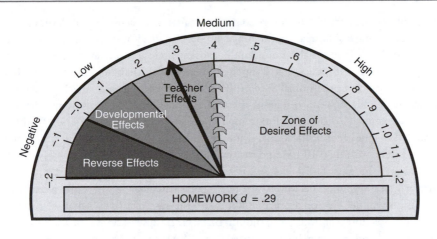

KEY

Standard error	.027 (Low)
Rank	88th
Number of meta-analyses	5
Number of studies	161
Number of effects	295
Number of people (4)	105,282

FIGURE 2.1 The barometer for the influence of homework

to explain differential effects within that influence. The information under the barometer provides more detail on how confident we can be about the summary information: the number of meta-analyses on each category (five in Figure 2.1, based on 161 studies, and 295 effect sizes). There were 105,282 students in the four meta-analyses that provided information about sample size (one did not provide sample size information). The average effect is d = 0.29, with a standard error of 0.027 (considered 'low' relative to all meta-analyses). The effects of homework ranked 88th out of all 138 influences.

Like all summaries of literature, caution should be the byword when interpreting overall effects. The nuances and details of each influence are important, and these are discussed in more detail in *Visible Learning*. The overall hinge-point of 0.40 is suggested as a starting point for discussion – clearly, there are many hinge-points (for example, one for each influence), but the variability, the moderators, the quality of the studies (and meta-analyses), and the costs of implementation need to be considered.

There is also, as noted in Chapter 1, the finding that most changed my way of thinking: when you look at the distribution of all 50,000-plus effect sizes, *almost everything works.* All that is needed to enhance achievement is a pulse. This indicates that it is not enough merely to provide evidence that you have a positive effect on achievement; we need also to identify a level of evidence that might be considered the minimum level for claiming a worthwhile positive effect. When I looked at the distribution of effects (see Figure 1.1), it seemed to follow an approximate normal distribution, so I used the average effect of 0.4 as the 'hinge-point' for identifying actions that could be considered to be 'working' in terms of making a visible difference to student learning. Because it is the 'average' point, it becomes an achievable, 'real-world' hinge-point, not an idealistic or aspirational target.

The 0.40 hinge-point is also important because it is close to the average effect that we can expect from a year's schooling. I searched longitudinal databases, interrogated the US National Education Longitudinal Study (NELS), Trends in International Mathematics and Science Study (TIMSS), the Program for International Student Assessment (PISA), the Australian National Assessment Program in Literacy and Numeracy (NAPLAN), the National Assessment of Educational Progress (NAEP), and Progress in International Reading Literacy Study (PIRLS), and my own longitudinal data based on nearly 1 million New Zealand students. The average yearly gain was 0.4, although it was slightly higher for lower-grade students and lower for upper-grade students. So $d = 0.4$ is what we can expect as growth per year on average, and it is also the case that 0.4 is what we can expect from all possible interventions. Hill, Bloom, Black, and Lipsey (2008) analysed the norms for 13 major standardized achievement tests (in USA), and found an average growth in maths and reading of about 0.40 – and, like in the NZ sample, the effects for each year were greater in the younger and lower in the older grades. So while $d = 0.40$ is a worthwhile average, we may need to expect more from the younger grades ($d > 0.60$) than for the older grades ($d > 0.30$). I choose this average (0.4) as the benchmark for assessing the influence that teachers have on achievement. In my work in schools since the publication of *Visible Learning*, we have used this hinge-point as the basis for discussions. (Please note that I did *not* say that we use this hinge-point for *making* decisions, but rather that we use it to *start discussions* about the effect of teachers on students.)

The story

The simple principle underlying most of the syntheses discussed in this book is 'visible teaching and learning'. Visible teaching and learning occurs when learning is the explicit and transparent goal, when it is appropriately challenging, and when the teacher and the student both (in their various ways) seek to ascertain whether and to what degree the challenging goal is attained. Visible teaching and learning occurs when there is deliberate practice aimed at attaining mastery of the goal, when there is feedback given and sought, and when there are active, passionate, and engaging people (teacher, students, peers) participating in the act of learning. It is teachers seeing learning through the eyes of students, and students seeing teaching as the key to their ongoing learning. The remarkable feature of the evidence is that the greatest effects on student learning occur when teachers become learners of their own teaching, and when students become their own teachers. When students become their own teachers, they exhibit the self-regulatory attributes that seem most desirable for learners (self-monitoring, self-evaluation, self-assessment, self-teaching). Thus, it is visible teaching and learning by teachers and students that makes the difference.

A key premise is that the teacher's view of his or her role is critical. It is the specific mind frames that teachers have about their role – and most critically a mind frame within which they ask themselves about the effect that they are having on student learning. Fundamentally, the most powerful way of thinking about a teacher's role is for teachers to see themselves as *evaluators* of their effects on students. Teachers need to use evidence-based methods to inform, change, and sustain these evaluation beliefs about their effect. These beliefs relate to claims about what each student can do as a consequence of the teacher's

FIGURE 2.2 What teachers see

actions, and how every resource (especially peers) can be used to play a part in moving students from what they can do now to where the teacher considers they should be – and to do so in the most efficient, as well as effective, manner. It matters what teachers do – but what matters *most* is having an appropriate mind frame relating to the impact of what they do. An appropriate mind frame combined with appropriate actions work together to achieve a positive learning effect.

What I am *not* saying is that 'teachers matter': this cliché is the most unsupported claim from the evidence in *Visible Learning*. It is a cliché that masks the fact that the greatest source of variance in our system relates to teachers (both between teachers, and even in that a single teacher can vary in his or her impact across students, across days, and across lessons). What *does* matter is teachers having a mind frame in which they see it as their role to evaluate their effect on learning.

As I argued in *Visible Learning* (Hattie, 2009: 22–4), when teachers see learning occurring or not occurring, they intervene in calculated and meaningful ways to alter the direction of learning to attain various shared, specific, and challenging goals. In particular, they provide students with multiple opportunities and alternatives for developing learning strategies based on the surface and deep levels of learning some content or domain matter, leading to students building conceptual understanding of this learning, which the students and teachers then use in future learning. Learners can be so different, making it difficult for a teacher to achieve such teaching acts: students can be in different learning places at various times, using a multiplicity of unique learning strategies, meeting different and appropriately challenging goals. Learning is a very personal journey for the teacher and the student, although there are remarkable commonalities in this journey for many teachers and students. It requires much skill for teachers to demonstrate to all of their students that they can see the students' 'perspective, communicate it back to them so that they have valuable feedback to self-assess, feel safe, and learn to understand others and the content with the same interest and concern' (Cornelius-White, 2007: 23).

The act of teaching requires deliberate interventions to ensure that there is cognitive change in the student; thus the key ingredients are being aware of the learning intentions, knowing when a student is successful in attaining those intentions, having sufficient understanding of the student's prior understanding as he or she comes to the task, and knowing enough about the content to provide meaningful and challenging experiences so that there is some sort of progressive development. It involves a teacher who knows a range of learning strategies with which to supply the student when they seem not to understand, who can provide direction and redirection in terms of the content being understood and thus maximize the power of feedback, and who has the skill to 'get out the way' when learning is progressing towards the success criteria.

Of course, it helps if these learning intentions and success criteria are shared with, committed to, and understood by the learner – because in the right caring and idea-rich environment, the learner can then experiment (be right and wrong) with the content and the thinking about the content, and make connections across ideas. A safe environment for the learner (and for the teacher) is an environment in which error is welcomed and fostered – because we learn so much from errors and from the feedback that then accrues from going in the wrong direction or not going sufficiently fluently in the right direction. In the same way, teachers themselves need to be in a safe environment to learn about the success or otherwise of their teaching from others.

To create such an environment, to command a range of learning strategies, and to be cognitively aware of the pedagogical means that enable the student to learn requires dedicated, passionate people. Such teachers need to be aware of which of their teaching strategies are working or not, need to be prepared to understand and adapt to the learner(s) and their situations, contexts, and prior learning, and need to share the experience of learning in this manner in an open, forthright, and enjoyable way with their students and their colleagues.

As I noted in *Visible Learning*, we rarely talk about passion in education, as if doing so makes the work of teachers seem less serious, more emotional than cognitive, somewhat biased or of lesser import. When we do consider passion, we typically constrain such expressions of joy and involvement to secluded settings not in the public space of being a teacher (Neumann, 2006). The key components of passion for the teacher and for the learner appear to be the sheer thrill of being a learner or teacher, the absorption that accompanies the process of teaching and learning, the sensations of being involved in the activity of teaching and learning, and the willingness to be involved in deliberate practice to attain understanding. Passion reflects the thrill, as well as the frustrations, of learning; it can be infectious, it can be taught, it can be modelled, and it can be learnt. It is among the most prized outcomes of schooling and, while rarely covered in any of the studies reviewed in this book, it infuses many of the influences that make the difference to the outcomes. It requires more than content knowledge, acts of skilled teaching, or engaged students to make the difference (although these help). It requires a love of the content, an ethical, caring stance deriving from the desire to instil in others a liking, or even love, of the discipline being taught, and a demonstration that the teacher is not only teaching, but also learning (typically about the students' processes and outcomes of learning). In the current economic climate of many countries, property values have plummeted, leading to fewer resources available for the education budget. As Doug Reeves pointed out to me, passion may be the only natural renewable resource that we have.

Learning is not always pleasurable and easy; it requires over-learning at certain points, spiralling up and down the knowledge continuum, building a working relationship with others in grappling with challenging tasks. Students appreciate that learning is not always pleasurable and easy, and indeed can engage with and enjoy the challenges that learning entails. This is the power of deliberate practice and concentration. It also requires a commitment to seeking further challenges – and herein lies a major link between challenge and feedback, two of the essential ingredients of learning. The greater the challenge, the higher the probability that one seeks and needs feedback, but the more important it is that there is a teacher to provide feedback and to ensure that the learner is on the right path to successfully meet the challenges.

The key to many of the influences above the $d = 0.40$ hinge-point is that they are deliberate interventions aimed at enhancing teaching and learning. It is critical that teachers learn about the success or otherwise of their interventions: those teachers who are students of their own impact are the teachers who are the most influential in raising students' achievement. Seeking positive effects on student learning (say, $d > 0.40$) should be a constant theme and challenge for teachers and school leaders. Because this does not happen by serendipity or accident, the excellent teacher must be vigilant to what is working and what is *not* working in the classroom – that is, teachers must be vigilant as to the consequences for learning based on their classroom climate, their teaching, and their students' co-teaching and co-learning. They must also assess the merits of any gains in terms of the 'worthwhileness' of the learning aims.

It is critical that the teaching and the learning are visible. There is no deep secret called 'teaching and learning': teaching and learning are visible in the classrooms of successful teachers and students; teaching and learning are visible in the passion displayed by the teacher and learner when successful learning and teaching occurs; and teaching and learning requires much skill and knowledge by both teacher and student (initially by the teacher and later more by the student). The teacher must know when learning is occurring or not, know when to experiment and when learn from the experience, learn to monitor, seek and give feedback, and learn when to provide alternative learning strategies when other strategies are not working. What is most important is that teaching is visible to the student, and that the learning is visible to the teacher. The more the student becomes the teacher and the more the teacher becomes the learner, then the more successful are the outcomes (see Hattie, 2009: 25–6).

This explanation of visible teaching relates to teachers as activators, as deliberate change agents, and as directors of learning (Hattie & Clinton, 2011). This does not mean that they are didactic, spend 80 per cent or more of the day talking, and aim to get through the curriculum or lesson come what may. The model of visible teaching and learning combines, rather than contrasts, teacher-centred teaching and student-centred learning and knowing.

As well as surface and deep learning, we also want efficiency or fluency as a valued outcome. We know what 'fluency' is when we talk of being fluent in a language; the same concept can apply to any learning. 'Over-learning' can be a factor in helping us to achieve fluency. Over-learning is what happens when we reach a stage of knowing what to do without thinking about it; its critical feature is that it reduces the load on our thinking and cognition, allowing us to attend to new ideas. To reach a state of over-learning requires much deliberate practice – that is, extensive engagement in relevant practice activities for improving performance (as when swimmers swim lap after lap aiming to over-learn the key aspects of their strokes, turns, and breathing). It is not deliberate practice for the sake of repetitive training, but deliberate practice focused on improving particular aspects of performance, to better understand how to monitor, self-regulate, and evaluate one's performance, and to reduce errors.

Conclusions

The major argument presented in this book is that when teaching and learning are visible, there is a greater likelihood of students reaching higher levels of achievement. To make teaching and learning visible requires an accomplished 'teacher as evaluator and activator', who knows a range of learning strategies to build the students' surface knowledge, deep knowledge and understanding, and conceptual understanding. The teacher needs to provide direction and redirection in terms of the content being understood, and thus make the most of the power of feedback. The teacher also needs to have the skill to get out of the way when learning is taking place and the student is making progress towards meeting the criteria against which successful learning will be judged. Visible teaching and learning also requires a commitment to seeking further challenges (for the teacher and for the student) – and herein lies a major link between challenge and feedback, two of the essential ingredients of learning. The greater the challenge, the higher the probability that one seeks and needs feedback, and the more important it is that there is a teacher to ensure that the learner is on the right path to successfully meet the challenge.

It is some teachers with certain mind frames that make the difference. That teachers are the greatest source of variance is often disputed, but how many more studies do we need to show their impact? There are production studies that relate specific attributes of teachers (such as education, experience); there are variance studies that evaluate teacher effects across different classrooms; there are association studies that relate teaching practices to student achievement. All of these methods control differing effects of students (for example, prior achievement, socio-economic status). These various value-added studies typically show high levels of variability due to teacher effects (hence the claim that it is 'not all teachers that make the difference'), but the variance is the largest source over which we have any control (Alton-Lee, 2003).

The conclusions in *Visible Learning* were cast as six signposts towards excellence in education, as follows.

1. Teachers are among the most powerful influences in learning.
2. Teachers need to be directive, influential, caring, and actively and passionately engaged in the process of teaching and learning.
3. Teachers need to be aware of what each and every student in their class is thinking and what they know, be able to construct meaning and meaningful experiences in light

of this knowledge of the students, and have proficient knowledge and understanding of their subject content so that they can provide meaningful and appropriate feedback such that each student moves progressively through the curriculum levels.

4. Teachers and students need to *know the learning intentions* and the criteria for student success for their lessons, know *how well they are attaining* these criteria for all students, and know *where to go next* in light of the gap between students' current knowledge and understanding and the success criteria of 'Where are you going?', 'How are you going?', and 'Where to next?'

5. Teachers need to move from the single idea to multiple ideas, and to relate and then extend these ideas such that learners construct, and reconstruct, knowledge and ideas. It is not the knowledge or ideas, but the learner's construction of this knowledge and ideas that is critical.

6. School leaders and teachers need to create schools, staffrooms, and classroom environments in which error is welcomed as a learning opportunity, in which discarding incorrect knowledge and understandings is welcomed, and in which teachers can feel safe to learn, re-learn, and explore knowledge and understanding.

In these six signposts, the word 'teachers' is deliberate, because a major theme is when teachers meet to discuss, evaluate, and plan their teaching in light of the feedback evidence about the success or otherwise of their teaching strategies and their conceptions about progress and appropriate challenge. This is not critical reflection, but *critical reflection in light of evidence* about their teaching.

The messages in *Visible Learning* are not another recipe for success, another quest for certainty, another unmasking of truth. There is no recipe, no professional development set of worksheets, no new teaching method, and no band-aid remedy. It is a way of thinking: 'My role, as teacher, is to evaluate the effect I have on my students.' It is to 'know thy impact', it is to understand this impact, and it is to act on this knowing and understanding. This requires that teachers gather defensible and dependable evidence from many sources, and hold collaborative discussions with colleagues and students about this evidence, thus making the effect of their teaching visible to themselves and to others.

Powerful, passionate, accomplished teachers are those who:

■ focus on students' cognitive engagement with the content of what it is that is being taught;

■ focus on developing a way of thinking and reasoning that emphasizes problem-solving and teaching strategies relating to the content that they wish students to learn;

■ focus on imparting new knowledge and understanding, and then monitor how students gain fluency and appreciation in this new knowledge;

■ focus on providing feedback in an appropriate and timely manner to help students to attain the worthwhile goals of the lesson;

■ seek feedback about their effect on the progress and proficiency of *all* of their students;

■ have deep understanding about how we learn; and

■ focus on seeing learning through the eyes of the students, appreciating their fits and starts in learning, and their often non-linear progressions to the goals, supporting their deliberate practice, providing feedback about their errors and misdirections, and caring that the students get to the goals and that the students share the teacher's passion for the material being learnt.

This focus is sustained, unrelenting, and needs to shared by all in a school. As Reeves (2011) has demonstrated, there is a strong link between a sustained focus across all involved within a school on limited goals and improved student achievement. The above are the 'foci' that can make a sustained improvement.

> Without focus, even the best leadership ideas will fail, the most ideal research-based initiatives will fail, and the most self-sacrificing earnest leaders will fail. Worst of all, without focus by educational leaders, students and teachers will fail.
>
> (Reeves, 2011: 14)

Exercise

Provide the following list to all teachers (and parents) and ask them to decide whether, on average, they have low, medium, or high impacts on student achievement. After completing the task, provide the effects (see Appendix D) and ask what may now need to be changed in this school and in your class. (Hint: there are eleven high, nine medium, and ten low effects.)

INFLUENCE	IMPACT		
Ability grouping/tracking/streaming	High	Medium	Low
Acceleration (for example, skipping a year)	High	Medium	Low
Comprehension programs	High	Medium	Low
Concept mapping	High	Medium	Low
Cooperative vs individualistic learning	High	Medium	Low
Direct instruction	High	Medium	Low
Feedback	High	Medium	Low
Gender (male compared with female achievement)	High	Medium	Low
Home environment	High	Medium	Low
Individualizing instruction	High	Medium	Low
Influence of peers	High	Medium	Low
Matching teaching with student learning styles	High	Medium	Low
Meta-cognitive strategy programs	High	Medium	Low
Phonics instruction	High	Medium	Low
Professional development on student achievement	High	Medium	Low
Providing formative evaluation to teachers	High	Medium	Low
Providing worked examples	High	Medium	Low
Reciprocal teaching	High	Medium	Low
Reducing class size	High	Medium	Low
Retention (holding back a year)	High	Medium	Low
Student control over learning	High	Medium	Low
Student expectations	High	Medium	Low

Teacher credibility in eyes of the students	High	Medium	Low
Teacher expectations	High	Medium	Low
Teacher subject matter knowledge	High	Medium	Low
Teacher–student relationships	High	Medium	Low
Using simulations and gaming	High	Medium	Low
Vocabulary programs	High	Medium	Low
Whole language programs	High	Medium	Low
Within-class grouping	High	Medium	Low

3

Teachers: the major players in the education process

It might have seemed more obvious to start with the students, but that would not be the correct place to start! We so often make claims about students, their learning styles, their attitudes, their love or not of schooling, their families and backgrounds, and their culture. In so many cases, this discussion is about why we can or cannot have an effect on their learning.

We so often worry about who students are. While it is the case that the largest source of variance in learning outcomes is attributable to the students, this should not mean that we stop at what students can and cannot do. We invent so many ways in which to explain why students cannot learn: it is their learning styles; it is right or left brain strengths or deficits; it is lack of attention; it is their refusal to take their medication; it is their lack of motivation; it is their parents not being supportive; it is because they do not do their work, and so on. It is not that these explanations are wrong (although some are – there is no support for learning styles, for example) or right (parental expectations and encouragement are powerful factors), but the underlying premise of most of these claims is the belief that we, as educators, cannot change the student. It is this belief that is at the root of deficit thinking. The belief that background factors have the strongest influence on learning would be an argument for putting more resources into poverty and home programs rather than into schooling. We *must* consider ourselves positive change agents for the students who come to us – for most, it is compulsory that they come to school and sometimes they come reluctantly, but mostly (at least initially) students are eager to be challenged into learning. My point is that teachers' beliefs and commitments are the greatest influence on student achievement *over which we can have some control* – and this book outlines these beliefs and commitments.

We so often worry about what teachers do. It would be easy to say that it is 'teachers who make the difference'. This is, indeed, *not* the case being made in this book. There are just as many teacher influences below $d = 0.40$ as there are above, and in most school systems there is more variance within a school than between schools. This within-school variance highlights the variance provided by teacher effects, and while we may wish to believe that all of our teachers are excellent, this is not always the view of those who have been their students. Rather, there are some teachers doing some things that make the difference. The effect of high-effect teachers compared with low-effect teachers is about $d = 0.25$, which means that a student in a high-impact teacher's classroom has almost a year's advantage over his or her peers in a lower-effect teacher's classroom (Slater, Davies, & Burgess, 2009). A major claim in this chapter is that the differences between high-effect and low-effect teachers are primarily related to the attitudes and expectations that teachers have when they decide on the key issues of teaching – that is, what to teach and at what level of difficulty, and their understandings of progress and of the effects of their teaching. It is some teachers doing some things with a certain attitude or belief system that truly makes the difference. This brings me to the first set of attributes that relate to 'visible learning inside': passionate and inspired teachers.

We start with the teachers' and school leaders' mind frames. For example, Sam Smith (2009) introduced a very powerful target-setting program in a large urban high school, and many of the teachers refused to participate, claiming that they were not responsible for whether students met targets or not: 'If they did not do their homework, failed to complete assignments, did not attend class, then why should teachers be held responsible for students meeting targets?' The teachers argued that teacher targets were related more to ensuring coverage of the curriculum, providing worthwhile resources and activities, and ensuring order and fairness in the classroom.

Russell Bishop (2003) has provided one of the most effective interventions available for minority students in mainstream classrooms and he starts with the beliefs of teachers. He argued that teachers come into classrooms with very strong theories about students and often resist evidence that their students do not conform to these theories. These teachers have theories about race, culture, learning, development, and students' levels of performance and rates of progress. One of the first acts in Bishop's intervention is to survey students' views on these matters. He then shows the teachers the difference between the students' beliefs and the teachers' own. Only then can Bishop start the intervention, which is about teachers' beliefs, first and foremost.

VISIBLE LEARNING – CHECKLIST FOR INSPIRED AND PASSIONATE TEACHING

1. All adults in this school recognize that:
   a. there is variation among teachers in their impact on student learning and achievement;
   b. all (school leaders, teachers, parents, students) place high value on having major positive effects on all students; and
   c. all are vigilant about building expertise to create positive effects on achievement for all students.

The case for the passionate, inspired teacher

VISIBLE LEARNING – CHECKLIST FOR INSPIRED AND PASSIONATE TEACHING

2. This school has convincing evidence that all of its teachers are passionate and inspired – and this should be the major promotion attribute of this school.

One of the more exciting periods of my research work was when I was at the University of North Carolina working with Richard Jaeger, Lloyd Bond, and many others on the technical issues relating to the National Board for Professional Teaching Standards (NBPTS). Laurence Ingvarson and I recently edited a book about this exciting time, and the breakthroughs in performance assessment in education, the development of scoring rubrics, and the psychometrics relating to these issues that have truly changed our way of looking at teachers, classrooms, and identification of excellence (see Ingvarson & Hattie, 2008). The NBPTS is still, in my estimation, the best system for dependably identifying excellent teachers, although there is still much to do to improve it. Using multiple indicators of the effect of teachers on students, moving away from evaluating the correlates as opposed to the actual effects on students, and making sure that the evaluation methods are also excellent professional development is at the heart of the NBPTS model. This chapter, however, is not a review of the NBPTS, because there are other sources and websites that can provide this background. Instead, one study is highlighted that underlines the importance of passionate and inspired teachers.

Richard Jaeger and I started by reviewing the literature (in the more traditional way than that used when undertaking a meta-analysis) on the distinctions between expert and experienced teachers, rather than using the more usual distinction between experienced and novice teachers. We sent our findings to many of the pre-eminent researchers in this field, and to expert teachers, for their comment, changes, and input. We identified five major dimensions of excellent, or 'expert', teachers. Expert teachers have high levels of knowledge and understanding of the subjects that they teach, can guide learning to desirable surface and deep outcomes, can successfully monitor learning and provide feedback that assists students to progress, can attend to the more attitudinal attributes of learning (especially developing self-efficacy and mastery motivation), and can provide defensible evidence of positive impacts of the teaching on student learning. Herein lies the differences between the terms 'expert' and 'experienced'.

VISIBLE LEARNING – CHECKLIST FOR INSPIRED AND PASSIONATE TEACHING

3. This school has a professional development program that:
   a. enhances teachers' deeper understandings of their subject(s);
   b. supports learning through analyses of the teachers' classroom interactions with students;

c. helps teachers to know how to provide effective feedback;

d. attends to students' affective attributes; and

e. develops the teacher's ability to influence students' surface and deep learning.

a. Expert teachers can identify the most important ways in which to represent the subject that they teach

In *Visible Learning*, it was shown that teachers' subject-matter knowledge had little effect on the quality of student outcomes! The distinction, however, is less the 'amount' of knowledge and less the 'pedagogical content knowledge', but more about how teachers see the surface and the deeper understandings of the subjects that they teach, as well as their beliefs about how to teach and understand when students are learning and have learned the subject. Expert teachers and experienced teachers do not differ in the amount of knowledge that they have about curriculum matters or knowledge about teaching strategies – but expert teachers do differ in how they organize and use this content knowledge. Experts possess knowledge that is more integrated, in that they combine the introduction of new subject knowledge with students' prior knowledge; they can relate current lesson content to other subjects in the curriculum; and they make lessons uniquely their own by changing, combining, and adding to the lessons according to their students' needs and their own teaching goals.

As a consequence of the way in which they view and organize their approach, expert teachers can quickly recognize sequences of events occurring in the classroom that in some way affect the learning and teaching of a topic. They can detect and concentrate more on information that has most relevance, they can make better predictions based on their representations about the classroom, and they can identify a greater store of strategies that students might use when solving a particular problem. They are therefore able to predict and determine the types of error that students might make, and thus they can be much more responsive to students. This allows expert teachers to build understandings as to the how and why of student success. They are more able to reorganize their problem-solving in light of ongoing classroom activities, they can readily formulate a more extensive range of likely solutions, and they are more able to check and test out their hypotheses or strategies. They seek negative evidence about their impact (who has not learnt, who is not making progress) in the hurly-burly of the classroom, and use it to make adaptations and to problem-solve.

These teachers maintain a passionate belief that students can learn the content and understandings included in the learning intentions of the lesson(s). This claim about the ability to have a deep understanding of the various relationships also helps to explain why some teachers are often anchored in the details of the classroom, and find it hard to think outside the specifics of their classrooms and students. Generalization is not always their strength.

b. Expert teachers are proficient at creating an optimal classroom climate for learning

An optimal classroom climate for learning is one that generates an atmosphere of trust – a climate in which it is understood that it is okay to make mistakes, because mistakes are the essence of learning. For students, the process of reconceptualizing what they know so that they can take on board new understandings may mean identifying errors and disbanding previous ideas. In so many classrooms, the greatest reason why students do not like to expose their mistakes is because of their peers: peers can be nasty, brutal, and viral! Expert teachers create classroom climates that welcome admission of errors; they achieve this by developing a climate of trust between teacher and student, and between student and student. The climate is one in which 'learning is cool', worth engaging in, and everyone – teacher and students – is involved in the process of learning. It is a climate in which it is okay to acknowledge that the process of learning is rarely linear, requires commitment and investment of effort, and has many ups and downs in knowing, not knowing, and in building confidence that we *can* know. It is a climate in which error is welcomed, in which student questioning is high, in which engagement is the norm, and in which students can gain reputations as effective learners.

c. Expert teachers monitor learning and provide feedback

This ability of expert teachers to problem-solve, to be flexible, and to improvise ways in which students can master the learning intentions means that they need to be excellent seekers and users of feedback information about their teaching – that is, of feedback about the effect that they are having on learning.

A typical lesson never goes as planned. Expert teachers are skilled at monitoring the current status of student understanding and the progress of learning towards the success criteria, and they seek and provide feedback geared to the current understandings of the students (see Chapter 7 for more on the nature of this 'gearing'). Through selective information gathering and responsiveness to students, they can anticipate when the interest is waning, know who is not understanding, and develop and test hypotheses about the effect of their teaching on all of their students.

d. Expert teachers believe that all students can reach the success criteria

Such an expectation requires teachers to believe that intelligence is changeable rather than fixed (even if there is evidence to show it may not be – see Dweck, 2006). It requires teachers to have high respect for their students and to show a passion that all can indeed attain success. The manner used by the teacher to treat and interact with students, to respect them as learners and people, and to demonstrate care and commitment for them also needs to be transparent to students.

This notion of passion is the essence of so much, and while we may find it difficult to measure, we certainly know it when we see it:

Passionately committed teachers are those who absolutely love what they do. They are constantly searching for more effective ways to reach their children, to master the content and methods of their craft. They feel a personal mission . . . to learning as much as they can about the world, about others, about themselves – and helping others to do the same.

(Zehm & Kotler, 1993: 118)

To be passionate about teaching is not only to express enthusiasm but also to enact it in a principled, values-led, intelligent way. All effective teachers have a passion for their subject, a passion for their pupils and a passionate belief that who they are and how the teacher can make a difference in their pupils' lives, both in the moment of teaching and in the days, weeks, months and even years afterwards.

(Day, 2004: 12)

Students can see it. The Measures of Effective Teaching Project (Gates Foundation, 2010) has estimated the value-added component of 3,000 teachers and at the same time asked students of these teachers to complete surveys of their experiences in these classes. The set of seven factors (the '7 Cs') listed in Table 3.1 show dramatic differences in how students see the classes of those teachers (called 'high added-value teachers') who have added higher-than-expected achievement gains (taking into account students' prior achievement, at the 75th percentile) compared with students in classes in which the gains are much lower (at the 25th percentile). For example, teachers whose students claim that they 'really try to understand how students feel about things' are more likely to be at the 75th percentile than at the 25th in terms of the value-added learning that occurs in classes.

The picture of expert teachers, then, is one of involvement and respect for the students, of a willingness to be receptive to what the students need, of teachers who demonstrate a sense of responsibility in the learning process, and of teachers who are passionate about ensuring that their students are learning.

e. Expert teachers influence surface and deep student outcomes

The fundamental quality of an expert teacher is the ability to have a positive influence on student outcomes – and, as noted in Chapter 1, such outcomes are not confined to test scores, but cover a wide range: students staying on at school and making an investment in their learning; students developing surface, deep, and conceptual understandings; students developing multiple learning strategies and a desire to master learning; students being willing to take risks and enjoying the challenge of learning; students having respect for self and others; and students developing into citizens who have challenging minds and the disposition to become active, competent, and thoughtfully critical participants in our complex world. For students to achieve these outcomes, teachers must set challenging goals, rather than 'do your best' goals, and invite students to engage in these challenges and commit to achieving the goals.

TABLE 3.1 Differences in students' views of high-value and low-value teachers on seven factors of classroom climate (the '7 Cs')

DIMENSIONS	EXAMPLE ITEMS	AT THE 25TH PERCENTILE	AT THE 75TH PERCENTILE
Care	My teacher in this class makes me feel that s/he really cares about me My teacher really tries to understand how students feel about things	40% 35%	73% 68%
Control	Students in this class treat the teacher with respect Our class stays busy and doesn't waste time	33% 36%	79% 69%
Clarify	My teacher has several good ways of explaining each topic that we cover in this class My teacher explains difficult things clearly	53% 50%	82% 79%
Challenge	In this class, we learn a lot almost every day In this class, we learn to correct our mistakes	52% 56%	81% 83%
Captivate	My teacher makes lessons interesting I like the ways in which we learn in this class	33% 47%	70% 81%
Confer	Students speak up and share their ideas about class work My teacher respects my ideas and suggestions	40% 46%	68% 75%
Consolidate	My teacher checks to make sure that we understand when s/he is teaching us The comments that I get on my work in this class help me to understand how to improve	58% 46%	86% 74%

How do expert teachers differ from experienced teachers in these five dimensions?

These five dimensions of expert teachers were identified from a literature review and they set the scene for a study in which we compared National Board certified teachers (NBCs) ('expert teachers') with teachers who had applied for, but did not become, NBCs ('experienced teachers'). While we sampled more than 300 teachers, the final study concentrated on those close to the 'pass' mark. We choose 65 middle childhood/generalists or early adolescence/English language arts teachers; half scored just above and half scored just below the cut-off score. For each of the five dimensions of expert teachers, we devised a series of student tasks, class observation schedules, interviews with the teacher and students, and surveys, and we collected artefacts of the instruction that we observed (see Smith, Baker, Hattie, & Bond, 2008, for details). There were major differences in the means of the two groups across all dimensions.

The magnitude, or importance, of the differences in these means is best demonstrated by graphing the effect size of each of the dimensions (see Figure 3.1). The more accomplished teachers set tasks that had a greater degree of challenge; they were more sensitive to context and they had a deeper understanding of the content being taught. More importantly, there was little difference between the classrooms of expert and experienced teachers in surface-level achievement outcomes, but there were major differences in the proportions of surface and deep understandings: 74 per cent of the work samples of students in the classes of NBCs were judged to reflect a deep level of understanding, compared

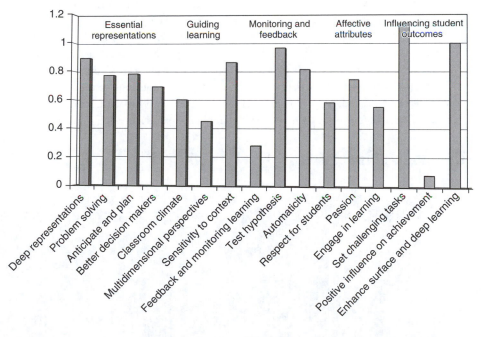

FIGURE 3.1 Effect sizes of differences between expert and experienced teachers

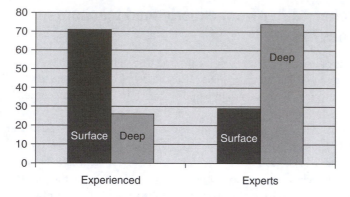

FIGURE 3.2 Percentage of student work classified as surface or deep learning

with 29 per cent of the work samples of non-NBC teachers (see Figure 3.2). Students of expert teachers are much more adept at deep, as well as surface, understanding, whereas experienced non-experts are as adept at surface, but not deep, learning.

Although there have been many claims of what makes an effective teacher, too few have been based on evidence from classrooms. Too often the lists have been based on simple analyses of individual parts of teaching, on small numbers of teachers, and on teachers that have not already been identified as expert based on rigorous and extensive assessment processes. The study reported above started with an extensive review of literature and a synthesis of many thousands of studies. It then led to a very detailed specification of information that was gathered in classrooms over many days. This information was then independently coded, using some exciting new developments in classroom observation methodology. The results are clear: expert teachers *do* differ from experienced teachers – particularly in the degree of challenge that they present to students, and, most critically, in the depth to which students learn to process information. Students who are taught by expert teachers exhibit an understanding of the concepts targeted in the instruction that is more integrated, more coherent, and at a higher level of abstraction than the understanding achieved by students in classes taught by experienced, but not expert, teachers.

The inspired teacher

VISIBLE LEARNING – CHECKLIST FOR INSPIRED AND PASSIONATE TEACHING

4. This school's professional development also aims to help teachers to seek pathways towards:
   a. solving instructional problems;
   b. interpreting events in progress;
   c. being sensitive to context;
   d. monitoring learning;
   e. testing hypotheses;

> f. demonstrating respect for all in the school;
> g. showing passion for teaching and learning; and
> h. helping students to understand complexity.

Steele (2009) has used our studies to develop a model of 'inspired teaching'. She made distinctions between the 'unaware', 'aware', 'capable', and 'inspired' teacher; that inspiration comes both from teachers being evaluators of their own effect and from teachers taking inspiration from the students – their reactions, learning, and challenges. She traces the pathways for each of the dimensions: the path to solving instructional problems; the path to interpreting events in progress; the path of being sensitive to context; the path to monitoring learning; the path to testing hypotheses; the path to demonstrating respect; the path to showing passion for teaching and learning; and the path to helping students to understand complexity.

Take, for example, showing passion for teaching and learning. Steele notes that passion is not mysterious: it relates to the level of enthusiasm that the teacher shows, the extent of commitment to each student, to learning, and to teaching itself, and it can be seen when listening to teachers talking about student learning.

> These teachers are firmly convinced that they are responsible for student learning and consistently bend their efforts toward doing a better job every day.
>
> (Steele, 2009: 185)

These teachers see better ways in which to teach their students; they believe that how they talk about the specific topic and the ways in which they lead students to experience it can make each lesson more engaging; and they believe that they are personally responsible for student learning. Most of us recall our favourite teachers because they cared deeply that we shared their passion and interest in their subject, they seemed to take extra effort to make sure that we understood, they tolerated and learned from our mistakes, and they celebrated when we attained the success criteria. These passionate teachers had the same time, same curriculum, same exam constraints, same physical settings, and the same class sizes as other teachers, but they certainly communicated the excitement of the challenge, and their commitment and caring for learning.

Steele notes that nearly all enter the teaching profession with a sense of idealism and purpose. As we confront the realities and challenges of schools and classrooms, we can then choose four roads: quit (as do about 50 per cent within the first five years); become disconnected and simply perform the role of teaching; work to become competent and seek promotion out of the classroom; or learn to experience the joy of inspired teaching. The difference between the inspired teacher and the capable teacher is large. I do acknowledge that some commentators prefer to talk about inspired *teaching* (rather than *teachers*), arguing that individual teachers can be inspired on some days, but not necessarily on all days – and maybe not for all students all of the time. This is indeed the case. We know, for example, that Roger Federer is not a brilliant tennis player with every shot – but this should not mean that we can speak only of inspired tennis playing, and not of inspired tennis players.

Federer is inspiring and most of us would claim that he is an expert tennis player. Similarly, inspired teachers do not always have inspired teaching, but overall the probabilities are such that we can talk about inspired teachers. Yes, in my own tennis playing, I too can play an occasional shot like Roger Federer and, in these moments, could be considered an inspired player (at least in my own mind), but overall I am not an expert tennis player.

There are certainly many things that inspired teachers do *not* do: they do *not* use grading as punishment; they do *not* conflate behavioural and academic performance; they do *not* elevate quiet compliance over academic work; they do *not* excessively use worksheets; they do *not* have low expectations and keep defending low-quality learning as 'doing your best'; they do *not* evaluate their impact by compliance, covering the curriculum, or conceiving explanations as to why they have little or no impact on their students; and they do *not* prefer perfection in homework over risk-taking that involves mistakes.

We can have high expectations of teachers and schools to have major impacts on students' growth in learning. We expect this of our sports coaches – not to win all of the time, but to teach and improve the quality of each player's skills, to play the game in the spirit of the rules, to develop individual as well as team work, to value commitment and loyalty to improvement, and to be fair to all players about the dual success criteria of most child sport (participation and aim to win). Our expectations of those in our schools need be no different.

The major theme underlying the five dimensions of expert teachers discussed in this chapter is that they are about the impact that teachers have – and not about teachers' personal or personality attributes (Kennedy, 2010). If only teacher education programs were more concerned about how budding teachers can know about the effect that they have, and less about knowing who they are and how to go about teaching, then we may get a better outcome. The ultimate requirement is for teachers to develop the skill of evaluating the effect that they have on their students. It is not so much a concern, for example, that beginning teachers *know* about diversity; it is more a concern that they know about the effects that they have on the diverse student cohort that they are likely to be teaching. They need to be able to react to the situation, the particular students, and the moment. Teachers work in remarkably varied situations, have interactions with many different students, and work in schools with much variance in conditions (planning times, interruptions, collaborative opportunities). To expect sustained effect on a regular basis is too big an ask – but the ask in this book is that teachers constantly attend to the nature and quality of the effect that they are having on every student.

Conclusions

VISIBLE LEARNING – CHECKLIST FOR INSPIRED AND PASSIONATE TEACHING

5. Professionalism in this school is achieved by teachers and school leaders working collaboratively to achieve 'visible learning inside'.

There is so often a rush to solve the problem of 'the teachers', but this is a mistaken direction. The messages in this book should not take us into the territory of measuring teachers, paying better teachers more, changing the training, and fixing entry into the profession – albeit that these are important and fascinating questions. Instead, the message of this book is to enable each teacher to better understand his or her effect on his or her students, and to assist teachers to develop a mind frame of evaluation to help them to move into the group of highly effective teachers (that is, those who regularly have impacts $d <$ 0.40) that we all should be inspired to join.

This is how a profession works: it aims to help to identify the goal posts of excellence (and they are rarely simple, uni-dimensional, and assessed by a test alone, as the outcomes of education outlined above should clearly show); it aims to encourage collaboration with all in the profession to drive the profession upwards; and it aims to esteem those who show the competence. Too often, we see the essential nature of our profession as autonomy – autonomy to teach how we know best, autonomy to choose resources and methods that we think are best, and autonomy to go back tomorrow and have another chance of doing what we have already done many times. As I noted in *Visible Learning*, we have good evidence that most, if not all, of our methods, resources, and teaching do have a positive effect on achievement – and many attain greater-than-average effects. The profession needs to be embracing the notions of what it is to be successful in teaching, helping all in a collaborative manner to attain this excellence, and recognizing major effects when they are evident. We have no right, however, to regularly teach in a way that leads to students gaining less than $d = 0.40$ within a year.

Clearly, this approach of evaluating the effects of teaching places more emphasis on student learning; often, we have been much more concerned with teaching rather than learning. At best, for some, learning occurs if the students complete the task, show interest and engagement, and 'pass' tests. Moving towards understanding learning, however, means starting with the private world of each student and the semi-private world of peer interactions, as well as the more public teacher-managed effect on students. Nuthall (2007) noted that 25 per cent of the specific concepts and principles that students learn are critically dependent on private peer talk or the choice of resources with which students can engage. The key is what is going on in each student's mind – because influencing these minds is the point of the lesson!

When students are interviewed as to what they want from teachers, the same theme of understanding their learning comes through. McIntyre, Pedder, and Rudduck (2005) summarized an extensive series of research on student voice and concluded that students want a constructive focus on learning. Students do not digress to complaining about perceived injustices, or describing personal teacher characteristics; they wanted to talk about their learning and how to improve. As Chapter 7 will show, our studies underline the importance that students place on 'moving forward'. The students preferred concise explanations, recognition that students can learn at different rates, tasks that connected new with the familiar, and a greater independence and autonomy in their classroom learning than that to which they were often accustomed. As McIntyre et al. noted, it is as easy as it is legitimate for teachers to claim that students' suggestions rarely take adequate account of the complexity of the teacher's task, but it is only those teachers who have the mind frame that students' perceptions are important who make the sustained efforts needed to engage students more in learning.

Exercises

1. Using a six-point Likert scale (from 'Strongly disagree' to 'Strongly agree') administer the '7 Cs' 'measure of effective progress' discussed above. Use the results as the basis for a discussion about how you could change what you do as a teacher to have more students rate all of the items either '5' or '6'.

2. Consider forms of evidence from the NBPTS (http://www.nbpts.org) about teacher quality. Discuss how you might use this evidence to enhance your teaching, or collect the evidence and then discuss with colleagues how you might modify your teaching to increase your impact on *all* students

3. Invite all teachers to write a description of 'yourself as a teacher'. Pool all responses (with no names) and then meet to decide if this description is consistent with the inspired and passionate teacher.

4. Monitor the topics of debate in staff meetings, coffee sessions, and professional development meetings, then classify them according to domains of discussion (for example, structural, teaching, curricular, assessment, student). If they are not about the impact of our teaching, discuss what would be required in this school to shift the debates to the impact of teaching on students – and then engage in those debates.

5. Ask your teachers (or student teachers) to interview students (preferably students from another teacher's class to reduce bias and perceived pressure), asking: 'What does it mean to be a "good learner" in this classroom?' Share the interview results (minus student names) with your fellow teachers.

6. With other teachers, learn how to use the SOLO surface and deep categories (see Hattie & Brown, 2004) to develop learning intentions, success criteria, questions for assignments, and teacher and student in-class questions, and to provide feedback on student work. Ensure that there are high levels of agreement across teachers as to which categories are surface and which are deep.

7. Ask each teacher to think about the last time that they showed passion in their teaching. Ask students the same question (about their teachers). Compare these examples of passionate teaching.

2

The lessons

The aim of the next five chapters is not to suggest that there is a linear route through from planning to impact, but to frame the findings from *Visible Learning* into the key stages of decision making through which teachers work when they are engaged in the staccato of teaching and learning. Decisions are so often made to engage students in interesting activities, to excite them to participate in learning, and to ensure that, when the bell rings, they have completed the assigned tasks and at least enjoyed the activity. Such dull aspirations for students may entice the willing, the bright, and those with high levels of 'inhibitory control', but will not continue to challenge students to reinvest in the game of schooling. Lingard (2007) and his team observed 1,000 classroom lessons and noted the low levels of intellectual demand, and there are many observational studies that highlight the overpowering presence of teachers talking and students sitting passively waiting. The claim is that these behaviours are not the case in all classrooms. Instead, the claim is that teachers must have the mind frame to foster intellectual demand, challenge, and learning, because these are the more powerful predictors of interest, engagement, and higher level and conceptual thinking that make students want to reinvest in learning.

There is an emphasis on planning, being clear about the purposes and outcomes of lessons (both by the teachers and students), having expectations or targets of what the impact should be, and then continually evaluating the impact of the teacher on the learner. It is important, however, to note that while the emphasis in this book is very much on the teacher, this does not mean that students cannot learn via other sources (such as the Internet, peers, family) or that they cannot become their own teachers. Such self-learning is surely a goal of our teaching efforts.

The methods and processes outlined in these next chapters often cite the importance of teachers critiquing each other, planning together, evaluating together, and finding many other ways in which to work together. I acknowledge that this is a resource–intensive claim. The plea is to find ways in which to resource this learning together within schools, because this would be a much more effective and efficient use of educational funding than that typically spent on the peripheries and structural issues of schooling – which so often have less effect, such as offering summer school ($d = .23$), reducing class size ($d = .21$), ability grouping ($d = .12$), open learning communities ($d = .01$), extra-curricular programs ($d = .17$), or retention (-.16). Accomplishing the maximum impact on student learning depends on teams of teachers working together, with excellent leaders or coaches, agreeing on worthwhile outcomes, setting high expectations, knowing the students' starting and desired success in learning, seeking evidence continually about their impact on all students, modifying their teaching in light of this evaluation, and joining in the success of truly making a difference to student outcomes.

4

Preparing the lesson

Planning can be done in many ways, but the most powerful is when teachers work together to develop plans, develop common understandings of what is worth teaching, collaborate on understanding their beliefs of challenge and progress, and work together to evaluate the impact of their planning on student outcomes.

There are four critical parts in planning that we need to consider up front: the *levels of performance* of the students at the start (prior achievement), the *desired levels* at the end of a series of lessons (or term, or year) (targeted learning), and the *rate of progress* from the start to the end of the series of lessons (progression). The fourth component is *teacher collaboration and critique in planning*.

VISIBLE LEARNING – CHECKLIST FOR PLANNING

6. The school has, and teachers use, defensible methods for:
   a. monitoring, recording, and making available, on a 'just in time' basis, interpretations about prior, present, and targeted student achievement;
   b. monitoring the progress of students regularly throughout and across years, and this information is used in planning and evaluating lessons;
   c. creating targets relating to the effects that teachers are expected to have on all students' learning.

Prior achievement

David Ausubel claimed:

> . . . if I had to reduce all of educational psychology to just one principle, I would say this: 'The most important single factor influencing learning is what the learner already knows. Ascertain this and teach him accordingly.'
>
> (Ausubel, 1968: vi)

It is the case that prior achievement is a powerful predictor of the outcomes of lessons ($d = 0.67$).

What a student brings to the classroom each year is very much related to his or her achievement in previous years: brighter students tend to achieve more and not-so-bright students achieve less. Our job as teachers is to mess this up, by planning ways in which to accelerate the growth of those who start behind, so that they can most efficiently attain the curriculum and learning objectives of the lessons alongside the brightest students. This means knowing their trajectories of learning, the current learning strategies used, and how willing and ready the student is to invest in learning. So, before the lesson is planned, the teacher must know what a student already knows and can do. This allows the teacher to tailor the lesson, so that the student can bridge the gap between his or her current knowledge and understanding, and the target knowledge and understanding. Thus it is also critical to have a clear understanding of the student's current position and the target position.

Any lesson planning must therefore begin with a deep understanding of what each student already knows and can do, and how the instruction is aimed at increasing the progress and levels of achievement for each of the students. The primary concern is to add value to all students, wherever they start from, and to get *all* students to attain the targeted outcomes.

One of the important understandings that teachers need to have about each student is his or her ways of thinking. By this, it is not intended to delve into learning styles (visual, kinaesthetic, etc.), for the effectiveness of which there is zero supporting evidence, but to understand a student's strategies for thinking, so that he or she can be helped to advance his or her thinking. One of the more well-known theories of learning – Piaget's – is still among the most powerful that we know. While there have been many advances on how we think since Piaget produced his influential research, it is worth going back to his work to make at least one key point: before teachers can help students to 'construct' knowledge and understanding, they need to know the different ways in which students think.

Piaget (1970) argued that children develop their thinking through a succession of stages.

1. The first is the 'sensorimotor' stage, which occurs between birth and the age of 2. Children rely on seeing, touching, and sucking objects, and they are learning the relationship between their bodies and the environment. They learn object permanence – that is, that an object exists independent of them, even when it cannot be seen.

2. The second is the 'preoperational' stage (2–7 years), during which the child believes that everyone thinks as he or she does, and has difficulty viewing life from any other perspective than his or her own. During this stage, children learn to form concepts and use symbols, and thence acquire language skills. Thinking is concrete and irreversible; hence it is difficult for them to think in abstract terms or reverse events in their minds.

3. It is in the next, the 'concrete operational' stage (7–12 years) that logical thinking emerges, reversibility begins to occur, and children can begin to explore concepts.

4. At the formal operational stage (from the age of 12 to adulthood), children can think in abstract or hypothetical terms, are able to form hypotheses, and can reason through analogy and metaphors.

Of course, there have been many critiques, modifications, and enhancements of this work. The greatest criticism relates to the notion of fixed stages tied to ages: it is argued that students can be in multiple stages (which Piaget also argued), that the stages are not necessarily tied to these ages (Piaget suggested that these were guides), and that there is no strict sequence. Case (1987, 1999) showed that the achievement of staged milestones in cognitive development did not proceed at a uniform pace across all content domains of knowledge. He showed that enhancing a child's information-processing and working memory capacities could lead to better overall understanding.

The key issue is that children may think differently from adults/teachers, which means that attention needs to be given to *how* and not only to *what* the child is learning. Based on Piaget's notions, Shayer (2003) developed a program of 'cognitive acceleration' based on three main drivers: the mind develops in response to challenge or disequilibrium, so any intervention must provide some *cognitive conflict*; the mind grows as we learn to become conscious of, and so take control of, its own processes; and cognitive development is a social process promoted by high-quality dialogue among peers supported by teachers. The program attained effect sizes of 0.60+.

Shayer (2003) suggests two basic principles for teachers. First, teachers need to think of their role as one of creating interventions that will increase the proportion of children attaining a higher thinking level, such that the students can use and practise these thinking skills during the course of a typical lesson – that is, teachers must attend first to *how* the students are thinking.

> If you cannot assess the range of mental levels of the children in your class, and simultaneously what is the level of cognitive demand of each of the lesson activity, how can you plan and then execute – in response to the minute by minute responses of the pupils – tactics which result in all engaging fruitfully?
>
> (Shayer, 2003: 481)

Second, learning is collaborative and requires dialogue, and this requires teachers to be attentive to all aspects of peer-to-peer construction and mediation (particularly in whole-class discussion, by encouraging and creating spaces for all views, comments, and critique). This allows teachers to be more aware of both the processing levels of different aspects of the activity and how each student's response indicates the level at which they are processing – that is, teachers need to listen as well as to talk.

One disturbing trend is that the average age at which students move into Piaget's formal operational stage in the UK seems to be increasing (Shayer, 2003). Shayer suggests that the reason may be the amount of attention paid to tests that measure the accumulation of knowledge. (If this is an outcome that is valued by the authorities, then teachers and students learn to work out successful ways in which to deliver on what the authorities ask from schools, to the detriment of higher levels of thinking!) Further, the levels of processing of the average 11-year-old and 12-year-old about to enter high school spans about 12 development years (on average, from the ages of 6 to 18) and fewer than 50 per cent of (school) year 11 and 12 students are formal operational thinkers.

The message is that we must know what students already know, know how they think, and then aim to then progress all students towards the success criteria of the lesson.

The self-attributes that students bring to the lesson

VISIBLE LEARNING – CHECKLIST FOR PLANNING

7. Teachers understand the attitudes and dispositions that students bring to the lesson, and aim to enhance these so that they are a positive part of learning.

As well as bringing their prior achievement, students bring many other dispositions to the classroom. These include motivation to learn, strategies to learn, and confidence to learn. In my earlier years in academia, I spent many years studying the notion of self-concept and its measurement (Hattie, 1992): how do students see themselves; what do they see as most important; and how does this relate to their learning and outcomes? There were two major directions in this research literature: research about the structure of self-concept (what are the various ways in which we see ourselves and how do they work together to form an overall self-concept?); and research about the processes of self-concept (how do we process information about ourselves?). I proposed a model to bring these two directions together – called the 'rope model' of self-concept (Hattie, 2008).

The metaphor of the rope aimed to emphasize that there is no single strand underlying our self-concept, but that there were many overlapping concepts of self, and the strength in the rope 'lies not in one fibre running throughout its length, but in the overlapping of many fibres' (Wittgenstein, 1958: section 67). These many fibres relate to the processes of self-concept – such as self-efficacy, anxiety, performance or mastery goal orientations – that we use to select and interpret the information that we receive, and which we use to present ourselves to others. Teachers need to know how students process self-information so that the teacher can develop and enhance the students' confidence in tackling challenging tasks, resilience in the face of error and failure, openness and willingness to share when interacting with peers, and pride in investing energy in actions that will lead to successful outcomes.

A major claim of the rope model is that students are 'choosers' and aim to impose some sense of order, coherence, and predictability in their world; we make choices about how to interpret events, about alternative courses of action, and about the value of making these decisions or not (which is why some naughty kids seek evidence to confirm their view of themselves as naughty kids). These choices aim to *protect*, *present*, *preserve*, and *promote* our sense of self such that we can 'back ourselves' – that is, maintain a sense of self-esteem. A major purpose of schooling is to enable students to 'back themselves' as learners of what we consider worth knowing.

We have spent many years working with adolescents in prisons; they, too, back themselves and use similar self-strategies to acquire a depth of knowledge and understanding – about socially undesirable tasks and outcomes (Carroll, Houghton, Durkin, & Hattie 2009). We have argued that they, too, esteem challenge, commitment, and passion, and build many well-developed strategies of learning to attain success in those areas in which they 'back themselves' as learners. Teachers and schools need to make schools inviting places in which to learn the knowledge that we value, but teachers and schools should never presume that all students will come to school wanting to share these values. Those in schools need to extend an invitation to students to engage in learning that is considered valuable – and this requires appropriate challenge and helping students to see the value of investing in the deliberate practice of learning school-based subjects (Purkey, 1992).

Some of the self-processes to which teachers need to pay attention, and that they must modify where necessary, include self-efficacy, self-handicapping, self-motivation, self-goals, self-dependence, self-discounting and distortion, self-perfectionism, and social comparison.

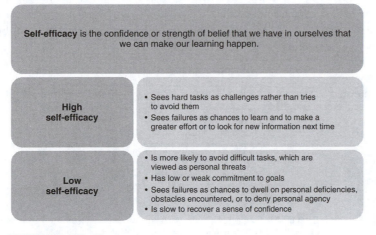

FIGURE 4.1 Self-efficacy

Self-efficacy This is the confidence or strength of belief that we have in ourselves that we can make our learning happen. Those with high self-efficacy are more likely to see hard tasks as challenges rather than try to avoid them, and when they have failures, they see them as a chance to learn and to make a greater effort or to look for new information next time. Those with low self-efficacy are more likely to avoid difficult tasks, which they view as personal threats; they are likely to have low or weak commitment to goals, and are more likely, in 'failure' situations, to dwell on personal deficiencies, obstacles encountered, or to deny personal agency, and they are slow to recover their confidence.

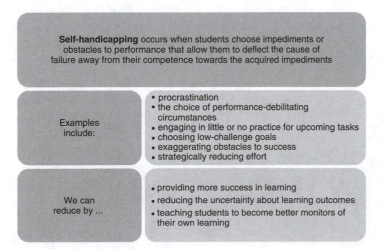

FIGURE 4.2 Self-handicapping

Self-handicapping This occurs when students choose impediments or obstacles to performance that enable them to deflect the cause of failure away from their competence towards the acquired impediments. Examples include procrastination, the choice of performance–debilitating circumstances (for example, 'the dog ate my homework'), engaging in little or no practice for upcoming tasks, having low–challenge goals, exaggerating obstacles to success, and strategically reducing effort. In the event of failure, the person has an immediate excuse. We can reduce self-handicapping by providing more success in learning, reducing the uncertainty about learning outcomes, and teaching students to become better monitors of their own learning.

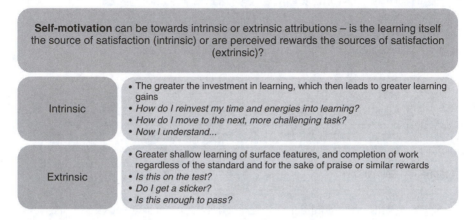

FIGURE 4.3 Self-motivation

Self-motivation This can be towards intrinsic or extrinsic attributions: is the learning itself the source of satisfaction, or are perceived rewards the sources of satisfaction? 'How do I reinvest in learning more?', 'How do I move to the next, more challenging task?', and 'Now I understand . . .' are examples of the former. 'Is this on the test?', 'Do I get a sticker?', and 'Is this enough to pass?' are examples of the latter. A combination of both is probably needed, but the more the balance moves towards intrinsic motivation, the greater the investment in learning, which then leads to greater learning gains. Too much external motivation can lead to shallow learning of the surface features, completion of work regardless of the standard, and completing work for the sake of praise or similar rewards.

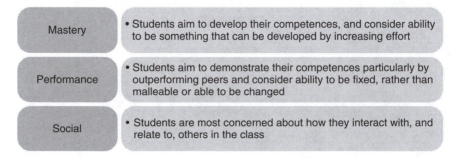

FIGURE 4.4 Self-goals

Self-goals There is a rich literature on the goals that students can have. There are three major types of goal, as follows.

- *Mastery goals* arise when students aim to develop their competence and they consider ability to be something that can be developed by increasing effort.

- *Performance goals* arise when students aim to demonstrate their competence particularly by outperforming peers, and they consider ability to be fixed, and not malleable or able to be changed.

- *Social goals* arise when students are most concerned about how they interact with, and relate to, others in the class.

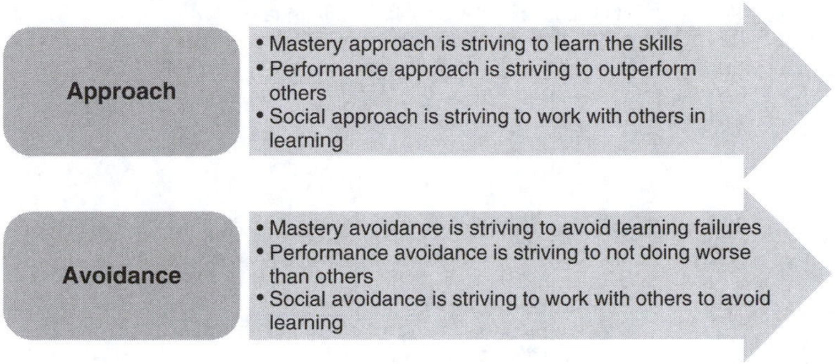

Approach
- Mastery approach is striving to learn the skills
- Performance approach is striving to outperform others
- Social approach is striving to work with others in learning

Avoidance
- Mastery avoidance is striving to avoid learning failures
- Performance avoidance is striving to not doing worse than others
- Social avoidance is striving to work with others to avoid learning

FIGURE 4.5 Approach and avoidance

These goals can be either 'approach' goals (when the student is striving to learn or master the lesson intention), or 'avoidance' (when the student is striving not to do worse than before or than others). The relation to achievement is higher for approach goals than it is for avoidance.

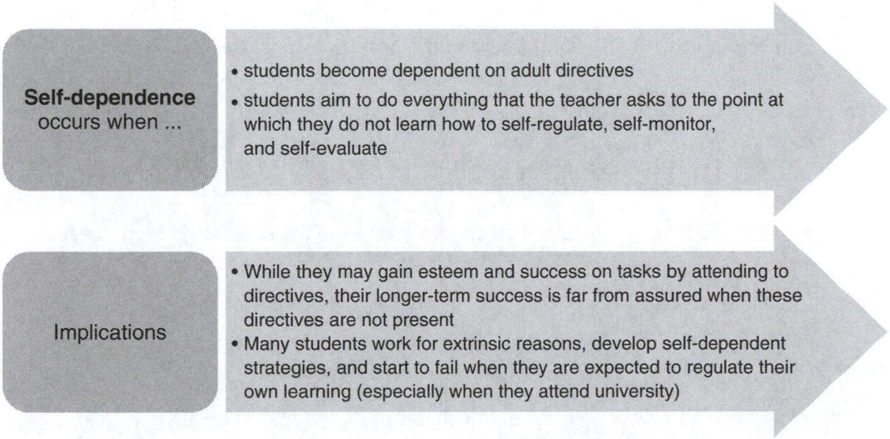

Self-dependence occurs when ...
- students become dependent on adult directives
- students aim to do everything that the teacher asks to the point at which they do not learn how to self-regulate, self-monitor, and self-evaluate

Implications
- While they may gain esteem and success on tasks by attending to directives, their longer-term success is far from assured when these directives are not present
- Many students work for extrinsic reasons, develop self-dependent strategies, and start to fail when they are expected to regulate their own learning (especially when they attend university)

FIGURE 4.6 Self-dependence

Self-dependence This can occur when students become dependent on adult directives. In many gifted classes, especially, students can aim to do everything that the teacher asks of them to the point that they do not learn how to self-regulate, self-monitor, and self-evaluate. While they may gain esteem and success in tasks by attending to these directives, their longer-term success is far from assured when these directives are not present. I have met so many bright students who work for extrinsic reasons, develop self-dependent strategies, and start to fail when they are expected to regulate their own learning (especially when they attend university).

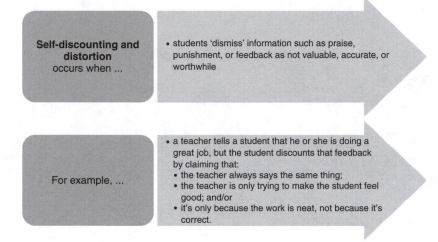

Self-discounting and distortion
occurs when ...
- students 'dismiss' information such as praise, punishment, or feedback as not valuable, accurate, or worthwhile

For example, ...
- a teacher tells a student that he or she is doing a great job, but the student discounts that feedback by claiming that:
- the teacher always says the same thing;
- the teacher is only trying to make the student feel good; and/or
- it's only because the work is neat, not because it's correct.

FIGURE 4.7 Self-discounting and distortion

Self-discounting and distortion This can be invoked by students 'dismissing' information such as praise, punishment, or feedback as neither valuable, accurate, nor worthwhile. For example, when a teacher tells a student that he or she is doing a great job, the student's reaction may be to discount this by claiming 'She always says that,' 'She's only trying to make me feel good,' or 'It's only because it's neat, not because it's correct'.

Self-perfectionism

We can set standards for ourselves that are so demanding that, when we do not meet them, we see it as failure.

We can demand that the resources be perfect and blame the absence of resources (e.g. time) when we do not succeed.

We can procrastinate because conditions are not perfect for success.

We can attend to irrelevant details and overzealously invest time in tasks that may not be worth that increased investment.

We demand an 'all or nothing' approach, believing the task to be not at all, or very much, worth completing.

FIGURE 4.8 Self-perfectionism

Self-perfectionism This comes in many forms: we can set such demanding standards for ourselves that, when they are not met, we see it as failure; we can demand that resources be perfect and blame their absence (for example, a lack of time) when we do not succeed; we can procrastinate because conditions are not perfect for success; we can attend to irrelevant details and overzealously invest time in tasks that may not be worth the increased investment; or we may have an 'all or nothing' approach, believing that the task is not at all or very much worth completing. While there can be a sense of pleasure derived from taking painstaking effort, there are more likely to be negative consequences.

Hopelessness

Refers to ...
- the student expecting that achievement gains will not occur for him or her and that he or she is helpless to change the situation

Occurs when ...
- the student avoids and does not engage in achievement tasks
- the student protects his or her sense of self by gaining reputation or success from other activities (e.g. naughty behaviour)
- the student does not see that achievement gains are due to his or her actions or in his or her control
- the student considers beliefs not to be readily changeable
- the student learns to devalue school learning
- contexts are harsh, overly demanding, or punitive

FIGURE 4.9 Hopelessness

Hopelessness This refers to the student expecting that achievement gains will not occur for him or her and that he or she is helpless to change the situation. In such a situation, the student avoids and does not engage with achievement tasks, protects their sense of self by gaining reputation or success from other activities (such as naughty behaviour), and does not see that achievement gains are due to his or her actions or in his or her control. Such hopelessness is likely to come from prior academic failures, holding beliefs that achievement is not readily changeable, but is more likely to be fixed, low levels of self-efficacy, not valuing school learning, not having appropriate learning strategies for the task, and from being in a context that is harsh, overly demanding, or punitive (Au, Watkins, Hattie, & Alexander 2009).

Social comparison This is ever-present in classrooms. Students often monitor others' behaviour for cues and attributions to explain or enhance their own conceptions of self. For example, very successful mathematics students might have a high maths self-concept in an average maths class, but after being sent to a gifted maths class, their self-concept could plummet as they compare themselves with this new cohort. Marsh et al. (2008) has termed this the 'big fish, little pond' effect. It is essential to teach such students that they can have

Social comparison	• Students often monitor others' behaviour for cues and attributions to explain or enhance their own conceptions of self.
'Big pond, little fish'	• Successful students have a high maths self-concept in an average class • After being sent to a gifted class, this self-concept might plummet because they now compare themselves with this new cohort • We need to teach such students that they can have multiple sources of comparison
Public boasting	• Students compare with those less fortunate than themselves, and present themselves as more confident to impress others and maybe even themselves • Can create an impression of competence and engender peers' dislike of the student, particularly when they become aware of that student's poor performance

FIGURE 4.10 Social comparison

multiple sources of comparison, so as to reduce any negative effect (Neiderer, 2011). Low self-esteem individuals often use social comparison – particularly comparing to those less fortunate than themselves – and they often attempt to present themselves as more confident to impress others and maybe even themselves. Public boasting, however, can create an impression of competence and engender dislike of the student among peers – particularly when they become aware of that student's actual poor performance.

When students invoke learning rather than performance strategies, accept rather than discount feedback, set benchmarks for difficult rather than easy goals, compare their achievement to subject criteria rather than with that of other students, develop high rather than low efficacy to learning, and effect self-regulation and personal control rather than learned hopelessness in the academic situation, then they are much more likely to realize achievement gains and invest in learning. These dispositions can be taught; they can be learned.

The more transparent the teacher makes the learning goals, the more likely the student is to engage in the work needed to meet the goal. Also, the more the student is aware of the criteria of success, the more the student can see and appreciate the specific actions that are needed to attain these criteria. Of course, he or she could choose to not engage, to be actively unengaged, or simply to wait and see. If the teacher does not clearly set out the learning intentions, then often the only goal for a student is to compare himself or herself to other students – and how easy it is to choose someone who is not quite as good as you, meaning that success is almost guaranteed! Schunk (1996) showed that when goals are made transparent at the start of the lesson, students have higher confidence that they can attain them. Their confidence grows as they make progress in skill acquisitions, and their confidence thus helps to sustain motivation and skilful performance. Rapid formative assessments (see Chapter 7) used throughout lessons also helps students to 'see' their progress, and thus monitor their investment and confidence in learning.

Targeted learning

VISIBLE LEARNING – CHECKLIST FOR PLANNING

8. Teachers within the school jointly plan series of lessons, with learning intentions and success criteria related to worthwhile curricular specifications.

There are two parts in targeted learning: the first is being clear about what is to be learned from the lesson(s) (the learning intention); the second is having a way of knowing that the desired learning has been achieved (the success criteria). Targeted learning involves the teacher knowing where he or she is going with the lesson and ensuring that the students know where they are going. *These pathways must be transparent for the student.* Such teacher clarity is essential, and by this I mean clarity by the teachers as seen by the students. Teachers need to know how to keep all in the class on track for the learning goal and then evaluate their success in moving all to the goal. Transparent learning intentions can also lead to greater trust between student and teacher, such that both parties become more engaged in the challenge provided and invested in moving towards the target. It does not mean knowing if and when the students complete the activities, but knowing whether they gain the concepts and understandings relative to the intentions of the lesson(s).

Learning intentions

The goals (that is, the learning intentions) of any lesson need to be a combination of surface, deep, or conceptual, with the exact combination depending on the decision of the teacher, which in turn is based on how the lesson fits into the curriculum. Goals may be short-term (for a lesson or part of a lesson), or longer-term (over a series of lessons), and thus may be tracked in terms of importance and effectiveness relative to the complexity of desired learning and duration of the lesson or lessons. Good learning intentions are those that make clear to the students the type or level of performance that they need to attain, so that they understand where and when to invest energies, strategies, and thinking, and where they are positioned along the trajectory towards successful learning. In this way, they know when they have achieved the intended learning. Effective teachers plan effectively by deciding on appropriately challenging goals and then structuring situations so that students can reach these goals. If teachers can encourage students to commit to achieving these challenging goals and if they provide feedback to the students on how to be successful in learning as they work to achieve the goals, then the goals are more likely to be attained.

Learning intentions describe what it is that we want students to learn and their clarity is at the heart of formative assessment. Unless teachers are clear about what they want students to learn (and what the outcome of this learning looks like), they are hardly likely to develop good assessment of that learning.

Clarke, Timperley, and Hattie (2003) noted some important features of learning intentions and planning, as follows.

■ Share the learning intentions with students, so that they understand them and what success looks like. This is more than students chanting the learning intentions at the start of the lesson, but a deeper understanding of what is desired, what success will look like, and how the tasks relate to the intention.

- Not all students in the class will be working at the same rate or starting from the same place, so it is important to adapt the plan relating to the intentions to make it inclusive of all students.

- The cascade from curriculum aim, through achievement objective, to learning intention is sometimes complex because the curriculum documents do not all follow the same format and learning does not happen in neat, linear sequences.

- Learning intentions and activities can be grouped, because one activity can contribute to more than one learning intention, or one learning intention may need several activities for the students to understand it fully.

- Learning intentions are what we intend students to learn. They may also learn other things not planned for (which can be positive or negative), and teachers need to be aware of unintended consequences.

- Finish each unit or lesson by referring to the learning intention and help students to understand how much closer they are to the success criteria.

A key issue is that students often need to be explicitly taught the learning intentions and the success criteria. Sandra Hastie (2011) asked about the nature of goals that students set for themselves in the middle school years. She found that, at best, students set performance goals such as: 'I aim to complete the work faster, better, or make the work longer.' She then carried out a series of studies to teach the students to set mastery goals ('I aim to understand the concepts'), but these were not as successful as teaching the teachers how to help students to set mastery goals. The teachers were provided with strategies to show students how to set and write personal best goals, the value of SMART goals (that is, those that are specific, measurable, ambitious, results-oriented, and timely), how students can break goals down into micro-goals, what challenge meant in a goal, what success looked like relative to the goals, and how students could fill in a self-review questionnaire diary. The diary invited students, assisted by their teachers, to write down three goals for themselves based on the unit that they were about to study. They were then provided examples of what success in relation to the goal looked like and rated themselves after each lesson.

Pre-lesson questions included the following.

- 'What are today's goals?'
- 'How much do I already know about today's goal?' ('Nothing' to 'a great deal')
- 'I think today's goal will be . . .' ('Very hard' to 'very easy')
- 'How much effort will I put into today's goal?' ('Nothing' to 'a great deal')

Post-lesson questions included the following.

- 'What was today's goal?'
- 'Did I achieve this goal?' ('Not at all' to 'fully')
- 'How much effort did I put in?' ('Not much' to 'a great deal')

The students were then provided with some reasons to tick explaining why they thought that they achieved the goal, such as:

- 'I wanted to learn about today's lesson';
- 'I wanted to achieve today's goal';
- 'I paid attention';
- 'I checked my answers';
- 'I worked out why I got it wrong';
- 'I looked at examples in my text book', etc.

Similarly, they responded to reasons for not achieving the day's goal, such as:

- 'I was distracted';
- 'I gave up';
- 'It was too hard';
- 'It was too easy';
- 'I didn't understand what I was supposed to be doing';
- 'I rushed my work because I wanted to finish quickly';
- 'The teacher was too busy with others', etc.

Across the 339 students, the effect size for the students' maths scores between the goal and control groups over an eight-week period was 0.22 – a reasonable return for a small investment. As importantly, there were much larger gains for attention and motivation, an enhanced commitment to reach goals, and specific information for teachers as to why students did or did not reach the goals. When teachers show students how to set mastery goals and show them what success on these goals looks like, there is an increased attention and motivation to succeed, and there is greater success. These are taught skills, with important consequences.

Another worthwhile way of setting goals is through personal bests. Andrew Martin (2006) has shown the usefulness of this method, and how personal bests can improve enjoyment of learning, participation in class, and persistence on the task. He distinguished two dimensions of personal bests (PBs): specificity and challenge. Personal bests can reduce the ambiguity about what is to be achieved, and the level of challenge prescribed by a PB must be at least higher than that of a previous best level of performance. Most importantly, PBs relate to the attainment of a *personalized* standard and this is what distinguishes them from many other goals. They are competitive (relative to previous bests) and self-improving (success leads to enhanced performance).

Martin noted that PBs help to sustain motivation, and help in identifying awareness, accessibility, adjustments, and that use of various strategies to attain them. As importantly, striving for PBs may be worthwhile for successful learning, even if the goals are performance or mastery goals.

> [Personal best]-oriented interventions might seek to develop students' skills in setting personalized academic goals that are specific and optimally more challenging than what they have previous achieved and also help students develop strategies to achieve these goals.
>
> (Martin, 2006: 269)

Goals are important for teachers. Butler (2007) found that teachers have different orientations with respect to their thinking about their goals of teaching. First, she asked

TABLE 4.1 Four major factors involved in teachers' orientation to their teaching goals

FOUR MAJOR FACTORS	EXAMPLE	TEACHER MOTIVATIONS OR STRIVINGS
Mastery approach	'I learned something new about myself; students' questions made me think'	To demonstrate superior teaching ability
Ability approach	'My class scored higher than other classes; my lesson plan was the best'	To learn and acquire professional understanding and skills
Work avoidance approach	'My students didn't ask hard questions; my class did not do worse on exam; my class is not furthest behind'	To avoid the demonstration of inferior ability
Ability avoidance approach	'I didn't need to prepare lessons; I got by without working hard; I didn't have any work to mark'	To get through the day with little effort

teachers to comment on what they considered a 'successful day'; she found four major factors that then led to four different forms of motivation, as summarized in Table 4.1.

A key correlate of these motivations was student help-seeking: only the mastery approach was associated with seeing student help-seeking as useful for promoting learning. These teachers communicated to students that asking questions is a good way in which to learn, they provided opportunities for these questions, they invited students to acknowledge and work through their errors, they promoted the message that help-seeking is not a sign of inadequate ability but a desire to learn, and they were more likely to respond to this help-seeking. These teachers felt successful when they were learning something new, when something in their class made them think, when they overcame difficulties, and when they saw that they were teaching better than they had done in the past. They were more likely to agree that they taught in ways that supported students' mastery goal orientations, and which provided students with challenging and stimulating tasks that promote critical and independent thinking (Retelsdorf, Butler, Streblow, & Schiefele, 2010).

The last two motivations (work avoidance and ability avoidance), in particular, were associated with avoidance of – and even undermining – help-seeking. The students in these teachers' classes reported that they were more involved in cheating, would be less likely to turn to these teachers for help, were more likely to be presented with easy tasks that were graded highly, and considered that students who asked questions or sought help were considered to be less intelligent by these teachers.

We need more teachers with mastery approaches.

Success criteria

Success criteria relate to knowledge of end points – that is, how do we know when we arrive? A learning intention of '*To learn to use effective adjectives*', for example, does not give the students the success criteria or how they will be judged. Imagine if I were simply to ask to get in your car and drive; at some unspecified time, I will let you know when you have successfully arrived (if you arrive at all). For too many students, this is what learning feels like. At best, they know that when they get there, they will be asked for more (to 'drive' more), and it should be no wonder that many students get turned off school learning. In the case of the '*effective adjectives*', three success criteria might be: '*What you're looking for is that you have used at least five effective adjectives*', or '*What you're looking for is that you have used an adjective just before a noun on at least four occasions that will help to paint a detailed picture, so that the reader can understand the feel of the jungle and the light of the jungle*'. Students can be actively involved in devising success criteria with the teacher.

We must not make the mistake of making success criteria relate merely to completing the activity or a lesson having been engaging and enjoyable; instead, the major role is to get the students engaged in and enjoying the challenge of learning. It is challenge that keeps us investing in pursuing goals and committed to achieving goals.

Five components of learning intentions and success criteria

VISIBLE LEARNING – CHECKLIST FOR PLANNING

9. There is evidence that these planned lessons:
   a. invoke appropriate challenges that engage the students' commitment to invest in learning;
   b. capitalize on and build students' confidence to attain the learning intentions;
   c. are based on appropriately high expectations of outcomes for students;
   d. lead to students having goals to master and wishing to reinvest in their learning; and
   e. have learning intentions and success criteria that are explicitly known by the student.

There are five essential components of the learning equation as it relates to learning intentions and success criteria: challenge; commitment; confidence; high expectations; and conceptual understanding.

1. Challenge

Challenge is a relative term – relative to a student's current performance and understanding, and relative to the success criteria deriving from the learning intention. The challenge should not be so difficult that the goal is seen as unattainable, given the student's level of prior achievement, self-efficacy, or confidence; rather, teachers and students must be able to see a pathway to attaining the challenging goal – a pathway that can include strategies for understanding the goal or intention, implementation plans to attain it, and (preferably) a commitment to attaining the goal.

One of the fascinating notions is how challenge is related to what we know: in most schools tasks, we need to already know about 90 per cent of what we are aiming to master in order to enjoy and make the most of the challenge (Burns, 2002). In reading, this target is somewhat higher: we need to know more like 95–99 per cent of the words on a page before we enjoy the challenge of reading a particular text (Gickling, 1984). Anything less than 50 per cent virtually assures that students are likely to be not engaged and their success will be limited.

Teachers more often see challenge in the activity itself – that is, that the task is challenging – whereas students see challenge in the difficulty of completing the task –

that is, 'my head hurts' (Inoue, 2007). Tasks may be inherently challenging, but unless the student invests and engages in the task, it may not be challenging for them. While challenge is one of the core ingredients of effective learning, the art is in making the challenge appropriate to the student. This is why relating a task to prior learning is so important.

There is also a reciprocal relation between the challenge of the goals and the power of feedback. If the goals are more challenging, then feedback is more powerful. If the goals are easy, then feedback has a lesser effect. If you already know something, then providing feedback is of low value.

The problem with the notion of challenge is that it is individual: what is well beyond the grasp of one student may be easy for the next. Carol Tomlinson (2005: 163–4) summed this up very well:

> Ensuring challenge is calibrated to the particular needs of a learner at a particular time is one of the most essential roles of the teacher and appears non-negotiable for student growth. Our best understanding suggests that a student only learns when work is moderately challenging that student, and where there is assistance to help the student master at what initially seems out of reach.

When we experience challenge, we often encounter dissonance, disequilibrium, and doubt. Most of us need safety nets if we are going to take the risk of the challenge, and this is particularly so when it is some of our underlying conceptual understandings that may be at risk.

Many teachers find encouraging dissonance, disequilibrium, and doubt to be demoralizing for the students. It certainly is not the intention to make the students struggle, become disheartened, and begin to disengage. This positive creation of tension underlines the importance of teachers in encouraging and welcoming error, and then helping the students to see the value of this error to move forward; this is the essence of great teaching. Shifting the focus from the self to the task, to the nature of the error, and to the strategies to use the error are the skills of teaching. Succeeding at something that you thought was difficult is the surest way in which to enhance self-efficacy and self-concept as a learner.

2. Commitment

Creating lessons in which students are committed to learning is less critical than ensuring that the task is challenging – that is, commitment comes second. 'Commitment' refers to a student's (or teacher's) attachment or determination to reach a goal: the greater the commitment, the better the performance.

Commitment is more powerful when it relates to investing in challenging tasks. We need to be careful that, in making activities interesting, relevant, authentic, and engaging, this does not lead to busy work rather than learning and challenge. Engagement is higher in classrooms in which students perceive instruction as challenging and in which there are peers who are also similarly challenged (Shernoff and Czsikzenhmilayi, 2009). This is not to underestimate the agency of commitment in the learning equation: overall, the effects of adding commitment to challenge are among the powerful ingredients in planning and learning.

As students move through elementary school, a major source of this commitment to school learning comes from peers – through pressure, modelling, and competition (Carroll et al., 2009). The teacher's aim, therefore, is to help students to gain a reputation among their peers as good learners.

3. Confidence

The ability to be confident that one can attain the learning goals is critical. Such confidence can come from the student (from having had past success in learning), from the teacher (in providing the quality of teaching and feedback along the way to ensure success), from the tasks (in ensuring appropriate scaffolding along the ladder of success), and from peers (in terms of feedback, sharing, and lack of distraction). Together, the mantra is 'I think I can . . . I think I can . . . I *know* I can . . .' followed by 'I thought I could . . . I thought I could . . . I *knew* I could . . .'. Such confidence can lead to resilience – particularly in the face of failure. Resilience is the ability to react to adversity, challenge, tension, or failure in an adaptive and productive manner. The proficiency to adapt to these situations is somewhat akin to when we are inoculated with the disease-causing pathogen such that we will build resistance and thus overcome the disease.

4. Student expectations

The influence that was highest of all in *Visible Learning* was self-reported grades. Overall, students have reasonably accurate understandings of their levels of achievement. Across the six meta-analyses (about 80,000 students), the effect was $d = 1.44$, or a correlation of about 0.80 between students' estimates and their subsequent performance in school tasks.

> On the one hand, this shows a remarkably high level of predictability about achievement in the classroom (and should question the necessity of so many tests when students appear to already have much of the information the tests supposedly provide), but on the other hand, these expectations of success (which are sometimes set lower than students could attain) may become a barrier for some students as they may only perform to whatever expectations they already have of their ability.
>
> (Hattie, 2009: 44)

There are at least two groups that are not as good at predicting their performance and who do not always predict in the right direction: minority students and lower-achieving students. These students are less accurate in their self-estimates or self-understanding of achievement. They tend to underestimate their achievement and, over time, they come to believe their lower estimates and lose the confidence to take on more challenging tasks. There have been many studies trying to improve the calibration and to entice students to have higher confidence or efficacy to take on challenging tasks. Changing these students' predictions of their performance has proved to be very difficult, often because this lower confidence and learned helplessness has developed and been reinforced over a long time. As they move into adolescence, these students often consider another alternative: opting out of the place called 'school'.

Student reflection of their performance alone makes no difference. Emphasizing accurate calibration is more effective than rewarding improved performance. The message is that teachers need to provide opportunities for students to be involved in predicting their performance; clearly, making the learning intentions and success criteria transparent, having high, but appropriate, expectations, and providing feedback at the appropriate levels (see

Chapter 7) is critical to building confidence in successfully taking on challenging tasks. Educating students to have high, challenging, appropriate expectations is among the most powerful influence in enhancing student achievement.

5. Conceptual understanding

The nature of success raises questions about the nature of the outcomes. There are at least three levels of understanding: surface, deep, and conceptual (Hattie, 2009: 26–9). The most powerful model for understanding these three levels and integrating them into learning intentions and success criteria is the SOLO (structure of observed learning outcomes) model developed by Biggs and Collis (1982).

In this model, there are four levels, termed 'uni-structural', 'multi-structural', 'relational', and 'extended abstract' – which simply mean 'an idea', 'many ideas', 'relating ideas', and 'extending ideas', respectively. The first two levels are about surface learning and the last two are about deeper processing (see Figure 4.11 for an example). Together, surface and deep understanding lead to the student developing conceptual understanding.

We have used the SOLO model in the development of our assessment system (see Hattie & Brown, 2004; Hattie & Purdie, 1998), and we found that most tests (both teacher-made and standardized state-wide tests) are dominated by surface items. Indeed, most teacher questions in class are surface (and often closed, as well). At minimum, the aim is to balance the surface and deep (in our asTTle assessment engine, we found that at least 30 per cent of items in a test should be surface and 30 per cent deep to create optimal tests). We also use the surface and deep distinction in scoring open-ended items, such as essays, performances, experiments (cf. Glasswell, Parr, & Aikman, 2001; Coogan, Hoben, & Parr, 2003), in classifying study skills programs (Hattie, Biggs, & Purdie, 1996), in identifying expert teachers (Smith et al., 2008), and in evaluating gifted programs (Maguire, 1988).

Steve Martin is a science teacher at Howick College (in Auckland, New Zealand), and he uses learning intentions, success criteria, and complexity (via the SOLO taxonomy) in his preparation of all units of work. Consider, for example, a series of lessons on light and sound. Martin starts with pre-tests – sometimes through class discussion; sometimes with a written test; sometimes by interviewing three students (of differing abilities). He then works through the learning intentions sheets illustrated in Table 4.2 with the students. He now has an excellent system such that he can monitor the progress of students from the point of learning at which they came into the lesson through the various learning intentions, knowing (as do the students) what success looks like – at differing levels of complexity. He also accompanies each learning intentions sheet with resources, key words, and so on.

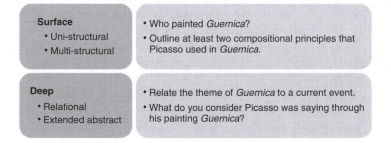

Surface
- Uni-structural
- Multi-structural

- Who painted *Guernica*?
- Outline at least two compositional principles that Picasso used in *Guernica*.

Deep
- Relational
- Extended abstract

- Relate the theme of *Guernica* to a current event.
- What do you consider Picasso was saying through his painting *Guernica*?

FIGURE 4.11 An example of four questions related to the SOLO taxonomy

TABLE 4.2 An example of learning intentions and success criteria categorized by SOLO complexity category

LEARNING INTENTIONS		SUCCESS CRITERIA	
SOLO 1: RECOGNIZE THAT LIGHT AND SOUND ARE TYPES OF ENERGY THAT ARE DETECTED BY EARS AND EYES			
Uni-/multi-structural	Recognize that light/sound are forms of energy and have properties	I can name one/or more properties of light and sound	☐
Relational	Know that sound/light can be transformed into other forms of energy	I can explain how light/sound is transformed into other types of energy	☐
Extended abstract	Understand how light/sound allows us to communicate	I can discuss how light/sound enables us to communicate	☐
SOLO 2: BE ABLE TO DRAW A NORMAL, MEASURE ANGLES, AND DEFINE THE LAW OF REFLECTION			
Uni-/multi-structural	Be able to draw ray diagrams, including the normal, with correctly drawn angles	I can draw a ray diagram with correctly measured angles	☐
Relational	Be able to define the Law of Reflection, linking the terms 'incidence' and 'reflected ray'	I can define the Law of Reflection, linking the terms 'incidence' and 'reflected ray', 'normal' and 'smooth surface'	☐
Extended abstract	Recognize that the Law of Reflection is true for all plane surfaces and can predict what will happen if the surface is rough	I can predict what will happen if light is reflected off a rough surface and explain why it happens	☐
SOLO 3: BE ABLE TO USE RAY BOXES TO UNDERSTAND HOW CONCAVE AND CONVEX MIRRORS BEHAVE			
Uni-/multi-structural	Know that changing the distance of an object from a concave mirror changes the appearance of the image	I can recognize that an image in a concave mirror changes as an object is moved closer or farther away from the mirror	☐
Relational	Be able to explain why concave mirrors are known as 'converging mirrors' and convex mirrors as 'diverging mirrors'	I can explain (using diagrams) why concave and convex mirrors are referred to as 'convergent' and 'divergent' mirrors, respectively	☐
Extended abstract	Recognize patterns in reflected rays from concave and convex mirrors, and be able to make a generalization	I can write a generalization about the patterns of reflected rays in concave and convex mirrors	☐

The curriculum: what should be taught, choice of resources, and progress

VISIBLE LEARNING – CHECKLIST FOR PLANNING

10. All teachers are thoroughly familiar with the curriculum – in terms of content, levels of difficulty, expected progressions – and share common interpretations about these with each other.

Now that the key ingredients of the planning have been outlined, we turn to a critical evaluative question that teachers must address: what knowledge and understanding should be taught? This immediately leads to two sub-questions: what knowledge and understanding is important; and what knowledge and understanding is going to lead to the greatest cognitive understandings and gains?

The starting point when determining what is to be taught, the appropriate complexity, and the desirable goals should be the curriculum – which is usually a hotly contested territory. There can be local, state, national, or international curricula (for example, the International Baccalaureate), and they are all different. They differ, however, more in the emphasis of topics and higher-order themes rather than fundamentally – at least as regards reading and mathematics. The greatest difference is often not at the lowest, more surface levels of curricula, but at the higher-order levels. For example, in our assessment work, we identified 140 specific objectives in reading for New Zealand; when we translated our assessment engine to fit into New York City schools, the same 140 objectives were present, but were grouped into higher-order notions in quite a different manner. Similarly, when New Zealand undertook a major review of its reading curriculum, the higher notions changed from inference, finding information, understanding, connections, knowledge, and surface features (grammar, punctuation, and spelling), to language, inference, purposes, processes, and surface features – but the same 140 objectives were merely re-sorted.

One difference across different curricula can be in order or progressions: some objectives fall before or after others. There is too little evidence as to what is the best order and even, in some domains, whether there is indeed an order. For example, in high-school mathematics, there are many topics that students are invited to learn, but the order of this learning is probably not so critical (as the differences in order among jurisdictions indicate). What seems more important is the increasing level of challenge that can be involved in choosing curricula to be taught. It is the notion of 'challenge' that is most importantly closely tied to the choices of activities, lessons, and outcomes of a lesson. Thus the argument here is that while 'curriculum is the most critical component' for choice of subject matter, it is just as critical that we take account of challenge, commitment, confidence, and conceptual understanding.

It seems that, in many jurisdictions, there is currently an obsession with testing and developing more and more finely grained standards – hence curricula are drafted bottom-up from the standards to the 'rich ideas'. The focus seems to be on the alignment of what is assessed with what is taught, what is reported (that is, the results) and what is taught, what the standards should be and therefore what is taught, and what is subjected to value-added or other accountability issues. The development of common curricula, the evidence about appropriate ordering for teaching the curricula, and most importantly the debates about desirable curricula in a democratic society are often presumed to be answered by these more test-outcome-based questions, rather than based on a debate about what is worth preserving in our society, and what is worth knowing in order to live the desired 'good life'.

Choice of resources

Planning is so often more about the resources and activities, even though the *Visible Learning* approach is to not start with these until well into the planning cycle. There are a million resources available on the Internet and creating more seems among the successful wastes of time in which teachers love to engage. So many jurisdictions are now providing banks of resources and, in our own assessment engine, we have had much success mapping resources to a two-way grid – success shown in the way in which teachers continue to link to the site. The 'What Next' site (http://www.tki.org.nz/r/asttle/whatnext/reading_e.php), which is part of our assessment engine, is organized by the levels (difficulty) of the curricula (levels 2–6) and curricular themes ('big ideas').

On the 'What Next' site, if teachers choose the current mean (that is, the bold dot within the square), they will be able to access material that is at the curricular level that the average student in the group is already achieving. We recommend that teachers do not keep teaching at this level, but choose more challenging resources. Hence teachers should choose an appropriate button *above* the current mean for at least half of the group. If one or two individuals are at Level 4P while the majority of the class is at 3B, a teacher can select suitable material for those two individuals from the 4A or 5B materials, while providing

What Next Report for Test : help guide-customis Group : All Test Candidates					Date Tested : 08 December 2006
			Reading		
	Processes and Strategies	Purposes and Audiences	Ideas	Language Features	Structure
6 Advanced		●			
6 Proficient	●	●	●	●	●
6 Basic		●			
5 Advanced	●	●	●	●	●
5 Proficient		●			
5 Basic	●	●	●	●	●
4 Advanced		●			
4 Proficient	●	●	●	●	●
4 Basic		●			
3 Advanced	●	●	●	●	●
3 Proficient		●			
3 Basic	●	●	●	●	●
2 Advanced		▣			
2 Proficient	●	●	●	●	●
2 Basic		●			

http://asttle.org.nz/whatnext/reading

FIGURE 4.12 The *What Next?* report from e-asTTle

material at 3P or 3A for the majority of the class. The achievement objectives can remain the same for the class, if that is the teacher's wish, but the curricular level of the material will be tailored to the individuals or groups (see Figure 4.12).

By clicking on the desired (dark blue) button, the teacher or student will be taken to various websites that have sets of lesson plans, teacher resources, student resources, exemplars of items at this level of challenge, web links, more open-ended items, and links to teaching strategies. The page also describes the skills and strategies expected at each level, and aims to reduce the variability in how teachers make meaning about these levels. While teachers seem to have no difficulty making and finding resources, the skill is tailoring the resources to the next level of challenge for the student – and this is the power of What Next.

Progression

A few years ago, our team analysed the status of achievement in New Zealand schools in reading, writing, and mathematics (Hattie, 2007). New Zealand performs well in these areas in the international comparisons, so the 'levels' of performance are not the major concern; rather, the single greatest issue that we identified was the need for teachers to have common understandings of progress. For too many teachers, it seems a badge of valour to dismiss the evidence of progress from previous teachers and thus every time a student comes into a new class or school, there is a 'hold' on his or her progress while the new teacher reassesses for his or her purposes the levels of this new student. The so-called 'summer effect', whereby students reduce achievement over summer ($d = -0.10$) is probably as much the result of this 'holding' back by new teachers as they reassess to make their own judgements as it is of the students having been on holiday. (For teachers, it is 'starting from scratch' or a 'fresh start'; for students, it is often 'more of the same'.) This leads to an underestimation of what the students can do and suspicions about what deep learning occurred in 'that previous school'; thus the continuity of the curriculum is broken. If there were transfer plans such that teachers valued and used the information from previous teachers, this drop could be reduced (see Galton, Morrison, & Pell, 2000).

Note that a common understanding of progress means that teachers have understanding among themselves within and preferably across schools of what the notions of challenge and difficulty are when implementing the curriculum. This is to ensure that appropriately higher expectations of challenges are provided to students: teachers need to know what progress looks like in terms of the levels of challenge and difficulty for the students such that if they were to interchange teachers across grades and between schools, their notions of challenge would synchronize with the other teachers' understandings of progress. This does not mean that there is a one right trajectory of progress for all students.

The way in which learning progresses is all too often decided by a committee: curricula are full of desired or proscribed orders for teaching content or concepts. There are recommendations about the 'proper sequences for developing numeracy strategies, for learning historical information, for introducing mathematical ideas', and so on. Instead, it is more critical to analyse closely how students actually progress. Steedle and Shavelson (2009) showed that progressions can differ relative to what the students already know (even if this knowledge is incorrect). In a study of the progressions through a unit on force and motion, Steedle and Shavelson showed that there were different progressions for those students whose understanding is (nearly) scientifically accurate compared with those who believe that velocity is linearly related to force.

Indeed, the most exciting developments in research on identifying trajectories are under way in many research teams. Popham (2011) distinguishes between two kinds of learning progression, which he classes 'upper case' and 'lower case' learning progressions. The upper case is primary and can inform the lower-case notions (see Confrey & Maloney, 2010; Clements & Sarama, 2009; Daro, Mosher, & Corcoran, 2011). Confrey and Maloney (2010), for example, have interviewed many students and watched them learn, and from that have developed various learning trajectories in teaching aspects of mathematics. They then created assessments that help teachers to understand which trajectory a student is on, where on that trajectory he or she is, and the errors that he or she is making that stop the student from progressing.

So many state and country assessment systems seem overly zealous about the levels of achievement. Although I am not saying that levels of achievement are unimportant, there is also the question of how to move each student forward from wherever they start through these levels of achievement (progression of learning). Indeed, we need both: attainment of standards of achievement *and* defensible rates of progress. But if there is an overemphasis on levels of attainment, then those schools that start with students above the norm will appear to be most effective and conversely those that start with students well below the norm will appear to be least effective. But we send students to school to make progress beyond what they bring at the start; hence *progress* is among the most critical dimensions for judging the success of schools.

TABLE 4.3 Distinction between two ways of considering learning progressions (Popham, 2011)

	UPPER-CASE LEARNING PROGRESSIONS	LOWER-CASE LEARNING PROGRESSIONS
1	Describe how students' learning of particular things develops over a period of time	Describe how students' learning of something develops – because of instruction – over a relatively short period, such as a few weeks or a semester
2	Focus on students' achievement of extraordinarily significant curricular aims, such as the 'big or rich ideas' in a content field	Deal with students' mastery of meaningful, but not momentous, curricular aims
3	Is research-ratified in the sense that the nature and sequencing of the learning progression's building blocks have been confirmed by rigorous empirical studies	Based on educators' conceptual analyses of a curricula aim's necessary precursors, rather than on the results of research investigations

Teachers talking to each other about teaching

VISIBLE LEARNING – CHECKLIST FOR PLANNING

11. Teachers talk with each other about the impact of their teaching, based on evidence of student progress, and about how to maximize their impact with all students.

One of the major messages from *Visible Learning* is the power of teachers learning from and talking to each other about planning – learning intentions, success criteria, what is valuable learning, progression, what it means to be 'good at' a subject. Black, Harrison, Hodgen, Marshall, and Serret (2010) found that asking teachers 'What does it mean to be good at [English, math, etc.]?' was a powerful way in which to engage in a discussion about validity and curricular matters. They noted that teachers readily engaged in this debate, and 'through such engagement began to see that they had, in their practice, neglected to critique their own work in the light of their beliefs and values concerning the purpose of learning in their subject' (p. 222). Only by having some common understanding of what it means to be 'good at' something can the resulting debates about forms of evidence, quality of teaching, and student outcomes make sense. This can then lead to a more informed discussion about what progression means – which is at the core of effective teaching and learning. Sharing a common understanding of progression is the most critical success factor in any school; without it, individualism, personal opinions, and 'anything goes' dominate (usually in silence in staffrooms, but living and aloud behind each closed classroom door). Miller (2010) refers to the 'smart swarm' that occurs when all begin to move in the right direction based on collaborative critique, distributed problem-solving, and multiple interactions.

Finding ways in which to have this discussion about progression is the starting point, the sustenance of any school. This requires many methods: moderation; sharing indicators of milestone performance (using examples of student work); sharing marking across classes; collaborative pre-planning across, as well as within, year cohorts. The most successful method that I have encountered is the 'data teams' model, in which a small team meets a minimum of every two or three weeks and uses an explicit, data-driven structure to disaggregate data, analyse student performance, set incremental goals, engage in dialogue around explicit and deliberate instruction, and create a plan to monitor student learning and teacher instruction. These teams can work at the grade level, curriculum or department level, building level, and even system level. These teams allow focus and deep implementation. Says Reeves (2010: 36): '. . . half hearted implementation was actually worse than minimal or no implementation.'

McNulty and Besser (2011) argue that data teams be formed on the basis of three criteria:

- all teachers on an instructional data team have a common standard or common area of focus;
- all teachers on an instructional data team administer a common assessment that leads to regular formative interpretations; and

- all teachers on an instructional data team measure learning with a common scoring guide or rubric.

They then see the data team model as a four-step process.

1. The first step involves collecting and charting the data, the aim of which is to make the data visible, to place a name for every number, to develop trust and respect to spark improvement from all, and (most importantly) to work out the fundamental questions to be asked of the data team.
2. Next, the team begins to use the evidence to prioritize and set, review, and revise incremental goals. This involves being explicit about what success looks like, what high expectations need to be set, and what degree of acceleration is needed to enable all students to reach the success criteria.
3. The team now questions the instructional strategies and how they are impacting on each student, what needs to change, what needs to remain, and (most importantly) what results would convince the team to change or remain. Such 'results indicators' allow teams to make mid-course corrections.
4. Finally, the team monitors the impact of these strategies and the impact on student learning.

The cycle then repeats.

> The essence of data-driven decision making is not about perfection and finding the decision that is popular, it's about finding the decision that is most likely to improve student achievement, produce the best results for the most students, and promote the long-term goals of equity and excellence.
>
> (Reeves, 2011: 24)

There are now many sources that illustrate such data teams in action (such as Anderson, 2010, 2011).

There are many other systems, like data teams, which focus on the evidence of student learning and then create debates about impact, effect, and consequences. Darling-Hammond (2010) has elaborated on instructional data teams; DuFour, DuFour, and Eaker (2008) have argued that teams work together to clarify the learning intentions, monitor each student in a timely manner, provide systematic intervention, and check to see that all reach the success criteria.

The 'response to intervention' model, and instructional rounds pioneered by Elmore, Fiarmen, and Teital (2009) involve the student and the teacher in the presence of content. The model is based on seven principles, as follow.

1. Increases in student learning occur only as a consequence of improvements in the level of content, teachers' knowledge and skill, and student engagement.
2. If you change any single element of the instructional core, you have to change the other two.
3. If you can't see it in the core, it's not there.

4. Task predicts performance.

5. The real accountability system is in the tasks that students are asked to do.

6. We learn to do the work by doing the work, not by telling other people to do the work, not by having done the work at some time in the past, and not by hiring experts who can act as proxies for our knowledge about how to do the work.

7. Description before analysis; analysis before prediction; prediction before evaluation.

The message is not about whether we form professional learning communities, use smart tools, or conduct data teams; rather, it is about teachers being open to evidence of their impact on students, critiquing each other's impact in light of evidence of such impact, and forming professional judgements about how they then need to – and indeed can – influence learning of all students in their class. So often, the process becomes a mantra and allows for lovely meetings that have little effect other than providing a forum for the talkative to wax lyrical. The message is, however, about the impact.

One early reviewer (Rick DuFour) of the book identified three 'big ideas' from *Visible Learning*, as follows.

1. The fundamental purpose of schools is to ensure that all students learn and not merely that all students are taught. Student learning must be lens through which educators look when examining all of their practices, policies, and procedures.

2. Schools cannot help all students to learn if educators work in isolation. Schools must create the structures and cultures that foster effective educator collaboration – collaboration that focuses on factors within our sphere of influence to impact student learning in a positive way.

3. Schools will not know whether or not teachers are learning unless they are clear on what students must learn, and unless they continuously gather evidence of that learning, and then use the evidence:

   a. to better meet the needs of students through systematic instruction and enrichment; and

   b. to inform and improve the individual and collective professional practice of educators.

The reviewer then provided parallel arguments for the importance of collective responsibility, for the topics of debate in professional learning communities, and to bring these three 'big ideas' to life through a recursive process that focuses on four critical questions for every unit that they teach.

1. 'What is it that we want our students to know and be able to do as a result of this unit?' (Essential learning)

2. 'How will they demonstrate that they have acquired the essential knowledge and skills? Have we agreed on the criteria that we will use in judging the quality of student work, and can we apply the criteria consistently?' (Success indicators)

3. 'How will we intervene for students who struggle and enrich the learning for students who are proficient?'

4. 'How can we use the evidence of student learning to improve our individual and collective professional practice?'

These questions are the critical topics for professional learning, communities, data teams, or whatever the form of collective responsibility in our schools. These are the value propositions that we need to highlight about the impact of our schools. These are the most promising strategies for developing the capacity of people within our schools to assume collective responsibility for improving student and adult learning.

If there is any inference throughout these pages that it is the teachers who are responsible for all students learning or not learning, then this is not intentional. Given the range of students for whom schools are responsible, the expanding curricular and social expectations continually placed on schools, and the press, which can point laser-like attention on accountability in schools, it is not reasonable to assume that a single teacher knows everything. It is a collective, school-wide responsibility to ensure that all students are making at least a year's growth for a year's input, and to work together to diagnose, recommend interventions, and collectively evaluate the impact of teachers and programs.

It would be powerful not only to attend to within-school differences in teachers' conceptions of progression, but also to between-school methods. In our own work, my colleagues and I have invited teachers to engage in a 'bookmark' standard-setting exercise. We provide teachers with booklets of about 50 items ordered on the basis of student performance ('easiest' to 'hardest'). We asked them first to complete each item individually, and then to place a 'bookmark' (a sticky label) between the item that demarcates the change between the previous set of items and the next set of items at key reference points. (In New Zealand, the reference points are levels, because the national curriculum is based on levels of schooling rather than years – but the reference points could comprise years of schooling or other milestone points.) We then displayed on an overhead projector the item that each teacher chose as the demarcation item, and created a discussion of the nature of the skills and strategies that led them to claim that the items before and after this cut-item differed. This certainly led to a robust discussion, after which the teachers were asked to repeat the task – but this time in groups of between three and five – and then to repeat the discussion. This method is powerful for generating debate (in a reasonably safe environment) about what teachers see as progression, and what they see as the skills and strategies underlying this progression; an added benefit is that this leads to greater consistency in judgements across schools.

For example, we ran a series of workshops ($N = 438$ teachers) aimed at determining the level of performance on a set of reading items. Teachers were asked to answer 100+ items and then place bookmarks between sets of items that best represented their concept of Level 2 of the New Zealand curriculum (usually completed by years 4 and 5 students) and Level 3 (years 6 and 7), up to Level 6 (years 11 and 12). During the first round, they did this independently and their results were then shown to all teachers in the group. After listening to each other's reasoning about the skills and strategies that underpinned their decisions, they completed a second round in groups of four or five teachers.

The mean item at each level hardly changed across the teachers – indicating that, on *average*, teachers in New Zealand have similar conceptions of the *levels* of the curriculum. But the *variability* among the teachers dramatically reduced (by 45 per cent) after they listened to each other. By simply undertaking this exercise, the judgements made by teachers as to what is meant by student work at different levels of the curriculum became much more consistent. No longer would judgements about levels of performance be based on individual teachers' beliefs, but there could now be assurance that there were more common conceptions of proficiency and progress.

Coaching teachers to talk to each other about the impact of their teaching

Talking is one thing; action is the other. To put the ideas in this book, for example, into action requires having an intention to change, having knowledge of what successful change would look like, and having a safe opportunity to trial any new teaching methods. This often requires some specific coaching. Coaches can serve as 'suppliers of candour, providing individual leaders with the objective feedback needed to nourish their growth' (Sherman & Frea, 2004). Thus coaching is specific to working towards student outcomes. It is not counselling for adults; it is not reflection; it is not self-awareness; it is not mentoring or working alongside. Coaching is deliberate actions to help the adults to get the results from the students – often by helping teachers to interpret evidence about the effect of their actions, and providing them with choices to more effectively gain these effects. There are three elements: the coach; the coached; and the agreed explicit goals of the coaching.

Joyce and Showers (1995) showed the powerful impact of coaching in comparison with other methods for raising understanding, skill attainment, and application. Reeves (2009) has used coaching extensively to facilitate school-based change and he starts from the position that not all coaching is effective. He considers that it is more effective when there is agreement that the focus is on improved performance, when there are clear and agreed learning and performance lesson plans, when there is then specific, relevant, and timely feedback, and when there is an agreed exit from the coaching upon specific planned conclusions. Coaching involves empowering people by facilitating self-directed learning, personal growth, and improved performance.

TABLE 4.4 Impact of various methods of training on outcomes

COMPONENT OF TRAINING	UNDERSTANDING	SKILL ATTAINMENT	APPLICATION
Theory understanding	85%	15%	5–10%
Demonstration	85%	18%	5–10%
Practice and feedback	85%	80%	10–15%
Coaching	90%	90%	80–90%

A well-known method to get teachers talking to each other about teaching

One of the more successful methods for maximizing the impact of teaching and enabling teachers to talk to each other about teaching is direct instruction. I know that many teachers find the mention of this phrase anathema to their concepts of desirable methods, but this is because it is so often incorrectly confused with transmission or didactic teaching (which it is not). It is unfortunate that many implementations of direct instruction are based on purchased, pre-scripted lessons, which certainly undermines one of its major advantages – that is, teachers working together to create the lesson planning. The message here is not to prescribe this as 'the way' (although its average effect size of $d = 0.59$ places it among the more successful programs of which we are aware), but to introduce it as one method that demonstrates the power of teachers working together to plan and critique a series of lessons, sharing understanding of progression, articulating intentions and success criteria, and attending to the impact on student and teacher learning.

The method is more fully outlined in many places (including Hattie, 2009: 204–7). First outlined by Adams and Engelmann (1996), direct instruction involves seven major steps.

1. Before the lesson is prepared, the teacher should have a clear idea of what the *learning intentions* are: what, specifically, should the student be able to do/understand/care about as a result of the teaching?

2. The teacher needs to know what *success criteria* of performance are to be expected, and when and what students will be held accountable for from the lesson/activity. As importantly, the students need to be informed about the standards of performance.

3. There is a need to *build commitment and engagement* in the learning task – a 'hook' to grab the student's attention such that the student shares the intention and understands what it means to be successful.

4. There needs to be guides to *how the teacher should present the lesson* – including notions such as input, modelling, and checking for understanding.

5. *Guided practice* involves an opportunity for each student to demonstrate his or her grasp of new learning by working through an activity or exercise – such that the teachers can provide feedback and individual remediation as needed.

6. *Closure* involves those actions or statements that cue students that they have arrived at an important point in the lesson or at the end of a lesson, to help to organize student learning, to help to form a coherent picture, to consolidate, to eliminate confusion and frustration, and to reinforce the major points to be learned.

7. *Independent practice* then follows first mastery of the content, particularly in new contexts. For example, if the lesson is about inference from reading a passage about dinosaurs, the practice should be about inference from reading about another topic, such as whales. The advocates of direct instruction argue that the failure to follow this seventh step is responsible for most student failure to be able to apply something learned.

Direct instruction demonstrates the power of stating the learning intentions and success criteria up front, and then engaging students in moving towards these. The teacher needs to invite the students to learn, needs to provide much deliberate practice and modelling, and needs to provide appropriate feedback and multiple opportunities to learn. Students need opportunities for independent practice, and then there need to be opportunities to learn the skill or knowledge implicit in the learning intention in contexts other than that in which it was directly taught.

There are two big messages from the *Visible Learning* research relating to direct instruction. The first is the power of *teachers working together critiquing their planning*. This raises the question of how to construct schools in which teachers talk to each other about teaching – not about the curriculum, students, assessment, conditions, or kicking footballs, but about what they mean by 'challenge', 'progress', and 'evidence of the effects anticipated and gained from the lessons'. It is the critique that is powerful; purchasing ready-made scripts defeats a major source of the power of this method.

The second message is the power of designing and evaluating *lesson scripts*. Fullan, Hill, and Crévola (2006) term these 'critical learning instructional pathways' (CLIPs). Their CLIPS include day-to-day detailed pathways from particular parts of the progression to others. Different students can start at different starting points and make different progress along these paths. The paths need to be built on the multiple ways in which students can learn, and allow for deviations to go back and try a different pathway to achieve progress. There is a high need for rapid formative interpretations of progress and feedback to the teacher and to the student on the success of how teachers are implementing their teaching, such that there is forward movement along the pathways in terms of student learning. Obviously, CLIPs require a very detailed understanding of learning in the domain, and require collaborative study of student progress in specifying these paths, and so on. The professionalism of teachers resides in their evaluative ability to understand both the effect of their interventions, and the status and progress of all of their students. (See Steve Martin's lesson planning as one example, at pp. 54–5 above.)

There are some exciting syntheses of various intervention programs that are leading to more evidence-based scripts. Brooks (2002) has provided a systematic analysis of the effects of about 50 scripted reading programs in the UK. Snowling and Hulme (2010) show how to connect from the excellent diagnosis of a reading problem to the optimally matched intervention. They indicate how to identify 'poor responders' to the intervention, the value of a tiered approach to intervention as the student changes during the treatment, the importance of the degree of implementation or dosage of the intervention, and how to use the results from the intervention to improve the teacher's theories about reading difficulties. Elliot (see the preface to this book) would be pleased.

Conclusions

The co-planning of lessons is the task that has one of the highest likelihoods of making a marked positive difference on student learning. This chapter has identified a number of factors that together impact on the quality of this planning: having a good system of reporting student prior attainment to help teachers to know the prior achievement and progress made by each student – and 'knowing prior achievement' means not only recognizing the cognitive performance of students, but also their ways and levels of thinking, and their resilience and other self-attributes (such as confidence, reaction to failure and success). Other critical factors include setting targets for what is desired for each student from the lessons, concentrating on evidence of the progress from prior achievement to target, and working with other teachers before delivering the lessons to engage with their critique as to how to optimize the impact of the lessons on the learning of the students. So often, planning involves a solitary teacher looking for resources, activities, and ideas; rarely are these plans shared. By sharing in the planning process, the likelihood of an end-of-lesson sharing of the evidence of impact and the understanding, and the consequences of relating this evidence to the planning, is more likely to occur.

Two powerful ways of increasing impact is to know *and* share both the learning intentions and success criteria of the lesson with students. When students know both, they are more likely to work towards mastering the criteria of success, more likely to know where they are on the trajectory towards this success, and more likely to have a good chance of learning how to monitor and self-regulate their progress.

There are many related notions to learning intentions and success criteria, such as target-setting, having high teacher and student expectations, helping students to set mastery as well as performance goals, setting personal bests, and ensuring that the intentions and criteria are sufficiently challenging for all students — and a major message in this chapter is that these notions apply as much to the teacher as they do to the students. The nature of the intentions can relate to surface or deep learning, and this choice depends on where students are in the cycle, from novice, through capable, to proficient.

Exercises

1. Create a concept map *with your students* about the learning intentions, the relations between these, and the ideas and resources that they are going to experience, and share notions of what success in the lessons would look like.

2. Hold a staff meeting in which teachers bring along their lesson plans. In pairs, choose a learning intention and its related activity, and create a 'child-speak' learning intention and related success criterion. Get each pair of teachers to read out the original learning intention, then the success criterion, and rework these until all agree. Then match the learning intentions with the learning resources (are they matched, efficient, etc.).

3. After about half a term, hold a feedback meeting in which every teacher gives a presentation based on the effects of sharing learning intentions and success criteria, as outlined in Exercise 2, including successes, problems, and strategies to overcome difficulties.

4. Choose three students who do not seem to be 'getting it' in a subject that you are teaching. Develop a profile of their self-processes — that is, their self-efficacy, self-handicapping, self-motivation, self-goals, self-dependence, self-discounting and distortion, self-perfectionism, and social comparison. Choose a student for which any of these processes are not optimal, devise an intervention, then monitor the impact on the students and their learning.

5. Make the presence and value of learning intentions and success criteria high profile in the school by talking about them in assemblies, with the aim that students and teachers see that this is a whole-school approach with a shared language.

6. Interview students about what 'challenge' means to them: what are some examples of lessons that have been challenging and how committed were they when asked to meet these challenges? Interview teachers about the same and see the overlap.

7. For each student, ascertain their progress prior to the series of lessons about to be taught. For each, set a target in terms of the outcome(s) that you wish to reach. Ensure that this is sufficiently above the student's current level of achievement and that the outcome measures (assignment, project, tests) reflect these target levels, and then monitor progress towards the targets.

5

Starting the lesson

There should be a 'flow' to each lesson from the students' perspective. There are some fundamental premises that lead to this flow – starting with good planning, as outlined in the previous chapter. Other aspects that relate to lesson flow are the conditions for optimal learning environments, the proportions of teacher and student talk, teacher knowledge of the students, and choice of teaching methods.

The climate of the classroom

VISIBLE LEARNING – CHECKLIST FOR STARTING THE LESSON

12. The climate of the class, evaluated from the student's perspective, is seen as fair: students feel that it is okay to say 'I do not know' or 'I need help'; there is a high level of trust and students believe that they are listened to; and students know that the purpose of the class is to learn and make progress.

In *Visible Learning*, the importance of the climate of the classroom was noted as among the more critical factors in promoting learning. These positive climate factors included a teacher's proficiency in reducing disruption to each student's flow of learning, and having 'with-it-ness' or being able to identify and quickly act on potential behavioural or learning problems. There is therefore a certain mindfulness by teachers in the classroom about how what is happening and what is likely to happen can affect the flow of learning for each student.

To achieve such positive classroom control, there needs to be close inspection of the teacher–student relationship. Care, trust, cooperation, respect, and team skills are all present, because these are the skills needed to promote classrooms in which error is not only tolerated, but also welcomed. Teachers and students must be clear of the purpose of a lesson, and understand that learning is a staccato process, full of errors, and that there is a need for all in the class to participate in the learning. (Once again) this requires making explicit the intentions and criteria of successful learning, setting the learning intentions at an appropriately challenging level, and providing support to reduce the gaps between what each student knows and can do, and what it is desired that they will know and be able to do at the end of a series of lessons.

When we are asked to name the teachers that had marked positive effects on us, the modal number is usually two to three, and the reasons typically start with comments about caring, or that they 'believed in me'. The major reason is that these teachers cared that you knew their subject and shared their passion – and aimed always to 'turn you on' to their passion. Students know when teachers care and are committed enough, and have sufficient skills, to turn them on to enjoying the challenges and excitement of their subject (whether it be sport, music, history, maths, or technology).

A positive, caring, respectful climate in the classroom is a prior condition to learning. Without students' sense that there is a reasonable degree of 'control', sense of safety to learn, and sense of respect and fairness that learning is going to take place, there is little chance that much positive is going to occur. This does not mean having rows of adoring students, sitting quietly, listening attentively, and then working cooperatively together to resolve the dilemmas and join in interesting activities; it does mean that students feel safe to show what they do not know, and have confidence that the interactions among other students and with the teacher will be fair and in many ways predictable (especially when they ask for help).

Teachers therefore need to have the skills of 'with-it-ness' – that is, the ability to identify and quickly act on potential problems and be aware of what is happening in the class (the proverbial 'eyes in the back of the head', or 'mindfulness'). Students need to know the boundaries of what is acceptable or not (and what to expect when they move outside these boundaries); they need to be taught how to work in groups (and this does not mean merely sitting in groups) and thus how to be involved in working with others in the learning process. Most importantly, students need to know the intentions of the lesson and the criteria for successfully attaining those learning intentions. There is so much evidence that shows that students want to have a sense of fairness, want to understand the rules of engagement, want to be members of a team in the classroom, and, critically, want to have the sense that all (teachers and students) are working towards positive learning gains.

VISIBLE LEARNING – CHECKLIST FOR STARTING THE LESSON

13. The staffroom has a high level of relational trust (respect for each person's role in learning, respect for expertise, personal regard for others, and high levels of integrity) when making policy and teaching decisions.

To attain this climate requires each student to have a sense of challenge, engagement with and commitment to the task, and success; to attain these in turn there needs to be a sense of goal-directedness, positive interpersonal relations, and social support. The stronger the feeling of trust in a school community, the more successful that school will be. Perhaps the most fascinating study of the power of trust has been Bryk and Schneider's (2002) seven-year analysis of 400 elementary schools. They found that the higher the levels of relational trust among the school community (principals, teachers, students, parents), the greater the improvement on standardized tests. They argued that relational trust is an essential element of positive, effective school governance that focuses on school improvement policies. Such trust is the glue that holds the relationships in both classroom and staffroom together when deciding on policies that advance the education and welfare of the students.

Bryk and Schneider's notion of 'relational trust' refers to the interpersonal social exchanges that take place in a school community (in the classroom and staffroom), and is based on four criteria.

- *Respect* involves the recognition of the role that each person plays in the learning.
- *Competence* in the execution of a role relates to the abilities that one has to achieve the desired outcomes.
- *Personal regard* for others is the perception of how one goes beyond what is required in his or her role in caring for another person.
- *Integrity* is the consistency between what people say and what they do.

How would you score on the five items in Bryk and Schneider's 'Teacher Trust Scale'?

1. 'Teachers in this school trust each other.'
2. 'It's okay in this school to discuss feelings, worries, and frustrations with other teachers.'
3. 'Teachers respect other teachers who take the lead in school improvement efforts.'
4. 'Teachers at the school respect those colleagues who are expert at their craft.'
5. 'Teachers feel respected by other teachers.'

Where relationship trust is present, then expertise is recognized and errors are not only tolerated, but even welcomed. Consider the key elements of successful learning throughout this book: a common denominator is feeling comfortable about making errors. By knowing what we do not know, we can learn; if we were to make no errors, we would be less likely to learn (or even to need to learn) – and we probably are not involved in challenge if there is not an element of being wrong and not succeeding. This is not deficit thinking if the teacher and student see errors as opportunities. Climate and trust are therefore the ingredients for gaining the most from making errors, and thus enabling students to be more impacted by our teaching.

One of the hardest parts of this relational trust is the trust between peers (that is, both students as peers and fellow teachers as peers). Students can be cruel on those of their peers who exhibit that 'they do not know'; thus it is incumbent on teachers to structure classrooms in which 'not knowing' is not a negative and does not lead to negative attributions or reactions, and in which students can work together to work out what they do not know so that they can invest in progressing more efficiently and effectively to the success of the lesson. (This is similarly so for school leaders in relation to teachers in the school.)

Teachers talk, talk, and talk

VISIBLE LEARNING – CHECKLIST FOR STARTING THE LESSON

14. The staffrooms and classrooms are dominated more by dialogue than by monologue about learning.

Classrooms are dominated by teacher talk, and one of the themes of *Visible Learning* is that the proportion of talk to listening needs to change to far less talk and much more listening.

Yair (2000) asked 865 Grades 6–12 students to wear digital wristwatches that were programmed to emit signals eight times a day – leading to 28,193 experiences. They were asked to note 'Where were you at the time of the beep?' and 'What was on your mind?'. Students were engaged with their lessons for only half of the time; this engagement hardly varied relative to their ability or across subjects. Most of the instruction was teacher talk, but such talk produced the lowest engagement. Teachers talk between 70 and 80 per cent of class time, on average. Teachers' talking increases as the year level rises and as the class size decreases! Across the grades, when instruction was challenging, relevant, and academically demanding, then all students had higher engagement and teachers talked less – and the greatest beneficiaries were at-risk students.

Teacher talk also follows a typical pattern: teacher *initiation*, student *response*, and teacher *evaluation* – often referred to as 'IRE' (Meehan, 1979). This three-part exchange leads to teacher-dominated talking, supporting the teacher to continue talking and follow the IRE pattern such that it fosters lower-order cognitive learning outcomes (because so often the initiation involves cues to recall facts and confirmation of declarative knowledge), and limits and discourages students' talking together about their learning (Alexander, 2008; Duschl & Osborne, 2002; Mercer & Littleton, 2007). So little (less than 5 per cent) of class time is devoted to group discussions, or to teacher–student interactions involving the meaningful discussion of ideas (Newton, Driver, & Osborne, 1999), and so often the teacher is off on the next part of his or her monologue before students have responded to the first. Teachers can involve all students in IRE, but it is usually through a choral answer, and many students learn to 'play the game' and thus are physically present, passively engaged, but psychologically absent. Teachers love to talk – to clarify, summarize, reflect, share personal experiences, explain, correct, repeat, praise. About 5–10 per cent of teacher talk triggers more conversation or dialogue engaging the student. Please note that this is not how teachers *perceive* what happens in their classrooms, but what *is* happening – as shown by video analysis, class observations, and event sampling.

This dominance of teacher talk leads to particular relationships being developed in classrooms – mainly aimed at facilitating teacher talk and controlling the transmission of knowledge: 'Keep quiet, behave, listen, and then react to my factual closed questions when I ask you.' 'Interaction' means: 'Tell me what I have just said so that I can check that you were listening, and then I can continue talking.' This imbalance needs redressing and teachers may well get independent analyses of their classrooms to check the proportions of the lesson during which they talk to students. Of course, some didactic imparting of information and ideas is necessary – but in too many classrooms there needs to be less teacher-dominated talk, and more student talking and involvement.

Hardman, Smith, and Wall (2003) have contributed much to the resurgence of interest in classroom observation. They developed handheld devices to continuously record classroom interactions and then used sophisticated software to provide real-time analyses. In one of their studies, for example, based on 35 literacy and 37 numeracy classes in the UK, 60 per cent of each lesson was a whole-class session, with mostly closed questions (69 per hour), evaluation (65 per hour), explaining (50 per hour), and direction (39 per hour); 15 per cent of teachers never asked an open question. As regards students, they most commonly answered a teacher question (118 per hour), gave a choral response (13 per hour), or gave a presentation (13 per hour), and only in nine times per hour did they provide a spontaneous contribution. When highly effective and other teachers were compared, the former had more general class talk and less directive talk.

The more important task is for teachers to listen. Parker (2006) considered listening to involve humility (realizing that we may miss something), caution (not giving voice to every thought that comes into our minds), and reciprocity (understanding the student's perspective). Listening needs dialogue – which involves students and teachers joining together in addressing questions or issues of common concern, considering and evaluating differing ways of addressing and learning about these issues, exchanging and appreciating each other's views, and collectively resolving the issues. Listening requires not only showing respect for others' views and evaluating the students' views (because not all are worthwhile or necessarily leading in the best directions), but also allows for sharing genuine depth of thinking and processing in our questioning, and permitting the dialogue so necessary if we are to engage students successfully in learning. The listening can inform teachers (and other students) about what the student brings to the learning, what strategies and prior achievement he or she is using, and the nature and extent of the gap between where he or she is and where he or she needs to be, and provides opportunities to use the student's 'voice' to encourage the most effective ways of teaching him or her new or more effective strategies and knowledge to better attain the intentions of the lesson.

One of the difficulties of so much teacher talk is that it demonstrates to students that teachers are the owners of subject content, and controllers of the pacing and sequencing of learning, and it reduces the opportunities for students to impose their own prior achievement, understanding, sequencing, and questions. Burns and Myhill (2004) analysed 54 lessons from Years 2–6 UK students (after the introduction of national standard assessment tests, or 'SATs') and reported that, 84 per cent of the time, teachers made statements or asked questions. There was far more telling than listening, far more teachers than students in action, and the most prominent engagement was compliance and responsiveness to teacher demands. For most of the classes that were observed, interactions and questions were factual or giving directions. English (2002) reported an average of three student utterances in a literacy hour, and most interactions were like table tennis: back and forth from teacher to student to teacher. Students seem to come to school to watch teachers working!

Note that if we invite teachers to 'shut up', the message is not then about allowing the students to engage in busy work (or worse, to complete worksheets); rather, it is about productive talking about learning.

Bakhtin (1981) made a very useful distinction between 'monologic' and 'dialogic' talk. The monologic teacher is largely concerned with the transmission of knowledge, and remains firmly in charge of his or her goal, uses a recitation/response/response form of discussion with students, and checks that at least some of the students have acquired at least surface knowledge. The aim is to ensure that students, as far as possible, gain the knowledge desired by the teacher. In contrast, dialogic talk aims to promote communication with and between students, to demonstrate the value of the views of the students, and to help participants to share and build meaning collaboratively. In the former, whole-class talking by the teacher dominates and questioning usually invokes no more than three words – or less than 5 seconds' response by students 70 per cent of the time (Hardman et al., 2003). Students learn that the teacher's voice and views dominate, and this is the model of knowing that is communicated and realized by those who succeed in this model. Mercer and Littleton (2007) have documented these classrooms, which are dominated by recapitulations (reviewing what has gone before), elicitation (asking question to stimulate recall), repetition (repeating student answers), reformulation (paraphrasing a student's response to improve it for the rest of the class), and exhortation (encouraging students to think or remember what has been said earlier).

Consider what we do (as do children) in regular conversation: we have conversations with others that are negotiated, participatory, and meaning-making – both one-on-one and with peers – and there is often as much listening as there is talking. But in the class, talk is typically controlled by the teacher, who provides explanations, corrections, and directives; the student responses are brief, reactionary, and certainly rarely conversational. Mistakes are so often seen as embarrassing, and teachers strive to minimize public errors to avoid the child 'losing face'. Teachers therefore lose major opportunities for exploring these errors and misconceptions collectively.

Alexander (2008) has documented the dialogic classroom, which has a powerful effect on student involvement and learning, noting how teachers begin to probe children's thinking and understanding, in which students ask questions (more than teachers ask them), and in which students comment on ideas. The essential features are defined as: collective (doing learning tasks together); reciprocal (listening to each other, sharing ideas, considering alternatives); supportive (exploring ideas with no fear of negative repercussion from making errors); cumulative (building on own and others' ideas); and purposeful (teachers plan with clear learning intentions and success criteria in mind). Dialogue is seen as an essential tool for learning, student involvement is what happens during and not 'at the end' of an exchange, and teachers can learn so much about their effect on student learning by listening to students thinking aloud. This involves the effective use of talk for learning, in contrast to the ineffective talk for teaching that features in many classrooms.

Questions

VISIBLE LEARNING – CHECKLIST FOR STARTING THE LESSON

15. The classrooms are dominated more by student than teacher questions.

Teachers ask so many questions. Brualdi (1998) counted 200–300 per day, and the majority of these were low-level cognitive questions: 60 per cent recall facts; 20 per cent are procedural. For teachers, questions are often the glue to the flow of the lesson, and they see questions as enabling, keeping students active in the lesson, arousing interest, modelling enquiry, and confirming for the teacher that 'most' of the students are keeping up. But the majority of questions are about 'the facts, just give me the facts', and the students all know that the teacher knows the answer. Teachers are most able to choose students who do or do not know the answers and use this decision about whom to ask to maintain their flow of the lesson. Students are given, on average, one second or less to think, consider their ideas, and respond (Cazden, 2001); the brighter students are given longer to respond than the less able, and thus those students who most need the wait time are least likely to get it. No wonder there are a lot of students in every class hoping not to be asked these questions! More effort needs to be given to framing questions that are worth asking – ones that open the dialogue in the classroom so that teachers can 'hear' students' suggested strategies.

Rich Mayer and colleagues (Mayer, 2004, 2009; Mayer et al., 2009) have an interest in using questioning in classes to promote active learning such that students attend to relevant material, mentally organize the selected material, and integrate the material with prior knowledge so that they advance in their knowing and understanding. Mayer et al. noted the positive effects from asking students to answer adjunct questions while reading a text, asking questions at the end rather than beginning of the learning, teaching students how to ask questions during learning, asking students to take a practice test, and encouraging students to explain aloud to themselves as they read a text. They conducted a series of studies on the effect of immediate response to feedback – in their case, in large lecture halls. A personal response, or 'clicker', involves teachers asking questions and asking students to vote using handheld clickers; in a matter of seconds, a graph is shown indicating the correct answer and the percentage of students voting for each alternative. The effect size from adjunct questions was 0.40, which shows that there can be important gains from only a small change to the typical lecture. Mayer argued that this gain (from immediate feedback) was likely to be due to students paying more attention to the lecture in anticipation of having to answer questions, and mentally organizing and interpreting learning knowledge in order to answer questions. He also argued that students were developing meta-cognitive skills for gauging how well they understood the lecture material and for how to answer exam-like questions in the future. He suggested that it helped students to adjust their study habits to be in tune with the teachers' likely exam questions, and increased their attendance and thus exposure to ideas. It may be that another important reason is involved: the teacher teaches differently, because he or she needs to think before the class about the optimal questions for the intentions of the lesson, think about common mistakes that students are likely to make, and thus become more responsive to gaining feedback about his or her own teaching.

Teachers need to talk, listen, and do – as do students

VISIBLE LEARNING – CHECKLIST FOR STARTING THE LESSON

16. There is a balance between teachers talking, listening, and doing; there is a similar balance between students talking, listening, and doing.

It may be that monologue and dialogue forms of discourse are not opposites; the art lies in knowing when to engage in monologue and when in dialogue. What are the optimal proportions? It is difficult to find evidence to defend the optimal balance and the best example is probably the Paideia research.

The Paideia program is one of the more successful programs with which I have been involved (as both user and evaluator). Paideia aims to move the attention of teachers more towards process and skills than only content, and involves a balance of three modes of teaching and learning: didactic classes in which students learn concepts and curriculum content; coaching labs in which students practise and master skills introduced in the didactic classes; and seminars in which Socratic-type questioning leads students to question, listen, and think critically, and coherently communicate their ideas along with other group members (Hattie et al., 1998; Roberts & Billings, 1999).

The program was introduced into 91 schools in one US school district. Schools that had most implemented Paideia had a more positive school and class climate (for example, $d = 0.94$ for satisfaction and 0.70 for lack of friction between those schools that fully implemented the program or had a high level of implementation compared to those with no or little implementation); students in these schools believed that they were more independent ($d = 0.81$) and task-oriented ($d = 0.67$), and there were enhancements in rule consistency ($d = 0.36$) and rule clarity ($d = 0.36$). Students in Paideia classes had lower levels of self-handicapping and lower use of social comparisons, and they had greater respect for others' ideas even if they disagreed. They were more likely to work as a team, to listen to the ideas and opinions of others, and to take responsibility for their own actions. Most importantly, there were positive effects on reading and maths outcomes over the five years of implementation, as show in Figure 5.1.

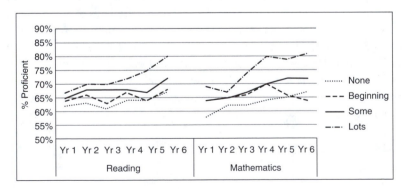

FIGURE 5.1 Percentage proficiency in reading and maths in relation to the degree of implementing Paideia across five years

Proportions of surface, deep, and conceptual understanding

VISIBLE LEARNING – CHECKLIST FOR STARTING THE LESSON

17. Teachers and students are aware of the balance of surface, deep, and conceptual understanding involved in the lesson intentions.

There are three major levels of achievement outcome that teachers need to consider when they prepare, teach, and evaluate their lessons: the surface knowledge needed to understand the concepts; the deeper understandings of how ideas relate to each other and extend to other understandings; and the conceptual thinking that allows surface and deep knowledge to turn into conjectures and concepts upon which to build new surface and deep understandings. These distinctions are often not clear-cut: such knowledge-building includes thinking of alternatives, thinking of criticisms, proposing experimental tests, deriving one object from another, proposing a problem, proposing a solution, and criticizing the solution (Bereiter, 2002).

So much of classroom instruction relates to the surface and the query here is whether this is the desired emphasis. It is more likely that there needs to be a major shift from an over-reliance on surface information and a reduced emphasis that the goal of education is deep understanding or development of thinking skills, towards a balance of surface and deep learning, leading to students more successfully constructing defensible theories of knowing and reality (the conceptual level). There is no place for cramming mills, for test-driven surface instruction, for enquiry schools pushing thinking skill training – for Dickens' Mr Gradgrind, the tyrant teacher in *Hard Times* described as 'a cannon loaded to the muzzle with facts'. Instead, what is needed is a balance between surface knowledge and deeper processes, leading to conceptual understanding. The choice of the classroom instruction and learning activities to maximize these outcomes are hallmarks of quality teaching (Kennedy, 2010).

Students, however, are quite insightful of what teachers really value as they listen to their questions in class, and check their assignments and exams (both the nature of them and the comments on them), and they know from many encounters that the real value in too many classrooms is surface level: 'Just give me the facts, ma'am.' Hence, cramming, knowing lots, and adopting a surface approach to understanding both how and what they should learn is strategic, and thus successful. My recommendation is for teachers to spend more time working through their notions of what success looks like in terms of the balance of surface and deep *before* they teach the lesson; they must make these proportions clear to the students, use a great deal of formative evaluation to understand how the students are learning at both surface and deep levels, and ensure that the assessments and the questions asked by students (and teachers) in the class are appropriate to the desired balance of surface, deep, and conceptual learning.

Other goals of learning can be fluency, efficiency, and reinvestment in learning. Often, to attain deep and conceptual knowledge, we need to over-learn some of the surface information. This then allows us to use our cognitive resources to attend to the relationships between ideas and other deeper understandings. As we become more fluent, we are less likely to engage in mere trial and error in learning, and more likely to build more strategic understanding to apply in these situations of 'not knowing'. The novice aims to produce data, whereas the expert is more interested in data interpretations; the data gathering precedes the data interpretation. These claims are the case for both the learner and for the teacher. With fluency and thus enhanced efficiency, we are more likely to reinvest in learning more about the surface and deeper understandings.

The role of peers and social support

VISIBLE LEARNING – CHECKLIST FOR STARTING THE LESSON

18. Teachers and students use the power of peers positively to progress learning.

While much of learning and testing in our schools has been aimed at the individual, more often we learn and live with each other. The effects of peers on learning is high ($d = 0.52$) and can be much higher indeed if some of the negative influences of peers is mitigated. Peers can influence learning by helping, tutoring, providing friendship, giving feedback, and making class and school a place to which students want to come each day (Wilkinson, Parr, Fung, Hattie, & Townsend 2002). Peers can assist in providing social comparisons, emotional support, social facilitation, cognitive restructuring, and rehearsal or deliberate practice. They can provide caring, support, and help, and can ease conflict resolution, and this can all lead to more learning opportunities, enhancing academic achievement (Anderman & Anderman, 1999). Students, particularly during early adolescence, tend to want to have a reputation among their peers and one aim should be to make this reputation about success in learning academic topics (see Carroll et al., 2009).

For many students, school can be a lonely place, and low classroom acceptance by peers can be linked with subsequent disengagement and lowered achievement. There needs to be a sense of belonging and this can come from peers. Certainly, when a student has friends at school, it is a different and better place. In the studies looking at what happens to students when they move schools, the single greatest predictor of subsequent success is whether the students makes a friend in the first month (Galton et al., 2000; Pratt and George, 2005). It is incumbent therefore upon schools to attend to student friendships, to ensure that the class makes newcomers welcomed, and, at minimum, to ensure that all students have a sense of belonging.

Cooperative learning is certainly a powerful intervention. It exceeds its alternatives: for cooperative learning versus heterogeneous classes, $d = 0.41$; for cooperative versus individualistic learning, $d = 0.59$; for cooperative versus competitive learning, $d = 0.54$; and for competitive versus individualistic learning, $d = 0.24$. Both cooperative and competitive (particularly when the competitive element relates to attaining personal bests and personal levels of attainment rather than competition between students for a higher ranking) are more effective than individualistic methods – pointing again to the power of peers in the learning equation. Cooperative learning is most powerful after the students have acquired sufficient surface knowledge to then be involved in discussion and learning with their peers – usually in some structured manner. It is then most useful for learning concepts, verbal problem-solving, categorizing, spatial problem-solving, retention and memory, and guessing–judging–predicting. As Roseth, Fang, Johnson, & Johnson (2006: 7) concluded: '. . . if you want to increase student academic achievement, give each student a friend.'

Another form of peer learning is through tutoring ($d = 0.54$) and the effects are as great on the tutor as on the person being tutored. This should not be surprising given the adage of this book – that is, that students learn much when they become their own teachers (and teachers of others). If the aim is to teach students self-regulation and control over their own learning, then they must move from being students to being teachers of themselves. And most of us appreciate that we learn a tremendous amount when we are asked to then teach something, rather than sitting being talked at by others. While peer tutoring is useful for getting older or more able students to tutor younger or less able students, there are still major effects from peer tutoring in a cooperative learning situation, particularly when it involves teachers helping student tutors to set mastery goals, monitor performance, evaluate effect, and provide feedback. Thus when students become teachers of others, they learn as much as those they are teaching.

Know the kids and let go of the labels

VISIBLE LEARNING – CHECKLIST FOR STARTING THE LESSON

19. In each class and across the school, labelling of students is rare.

We seem to love labels – labels such as 'mentally disabled', 'struggling', 'dyslexic', 'ADHD' (attention deficit hyperactivity disorder), 'autistic', 'learning styles' (for example, kinesthetic learning), 'OCD' (obsessive–compulsive disorder), and so on. The point of the argument is not to claim that these are not real (they are), but to note how quick we are to medicalize or label (sometimes then to accrue funding) and then explain why we cannot teach or the labelled cannot learn (Hattie et al., 1996). Every time a parent or colleague says that he (they usually are boys) has x or y, then this is the starting point for teaching, not the barrier or reason not to teach.

One of the more fruitless pursuits is labelling students with 'learning styles'. This modern fad for learning styles, not to be confused with the more worthwhile notion of multiple learning strategies, assumes that different students have differing preferences for particular ways of learning (Pashler, McDaniel, Rohrer, & Bjork, 2009; Riener & Willingham, 2010). Often, the claim is that when teaching is aligned with the preferred or dominant learning style (for example, auditory, visual, tactile, or kinesthetic), then achievement is enhanced. While there can be many advantages by teaching content using many different methods (visual, spoken, movement), this must not be confused with thinking that students have differential strengths in thinking in these styles.

There is much evidence that students are assigned quite different styles by different teachers (Holt, Denny, Capps, & DeVore, 2005), and the common measures are notoriously unreliable and not predictive of much at all. The most extensive review, by Coffield, Moseley, Ecclestone, and Hall (2004) found few studies that met their minimum acceptability criteria, and the authors provided many criticisms of the field, such as too much overstatement, poor items and assessments, low validity and negligible effect on practice, and too much of the advocacy being aimed at commercial ends. Learning strategies? Yes. Enjoying learning? Yes. Learning styles? No. More importantly, teachers who speak of 'learning styles' are labelling students in terms of how they (the teachers) think the students think, and thus overlooking the fact that students can change, can learn new ways of thinking, and can meet challenges in learning.

Perhaps the most simplistic labelling is to assume that there are but two ways of learning: a male way and a female way! The difference in effect sizes between boys and girls is small ($d = 0.15$, and this favours boys) – more specifically, for language, $d = 0.03$, for maths, 0.04, for science, 0.07, for affective outcomes, 0.04, for motivation −0.03, but there are much greater differences in motor activities, in which $d = 0.42$. Janet Hyde (2005) has completed the largest study, summarizing 124 meta-analyses and many millions of students on this topic; she speaks about the *gender similarity* hypothesis. Across her four major outcomes, the differences slightly favoured girls in communication ($d = −0.17$), and boys in achievement ($d = 0.03$), and social and personality ($d = 0.20$) outcomes. In relation to the last of these, boys are more aggressive ($d = 0.40$), are more likely to be involved in helping others ($d = 0.30$) and in negotiating ($d = 0.09$), but the greatest differences relate to sexuality (for arousal, $d = 0.30$; for masturbation, $d = 0.95$). Girls were much higher on attention ($d = −0.23$), effortful control ($d = −1.10$), and inhibitory control ($d = −0.42$) – that is, girls display a greater ability to manage and regulate their attention and inhibit their impulses: skills that are most useful in classrooms.

We need to be careful about generalization across countries, because these studies are mainly Western or more developed countries (in which research studies are more plenti-

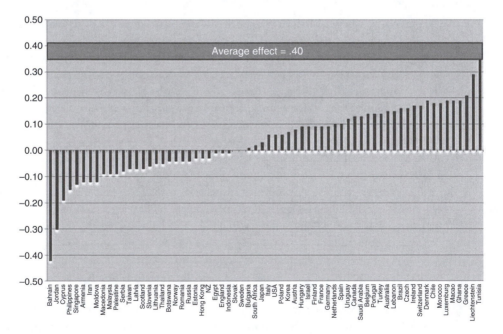

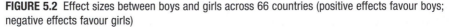

FIGURE 5.2 Effect sizes between boys and girls across 66 countries (positive effects favour boys; negative effects favour girls)

ful). When I calculate the effect sizes from the various international studies (TIMSS, PISA) across 66 countries, then there is marked variability – with major differences favouring girls in Bahrain and Jordan, and favouring boys in Tunisia and Liechtenstein.

I could not find gender differences when students enter school (in relation to the School Entry Assessment Kit: for 'Concepts about print', $d = -0.03$; for 'Tell me', $d = -0.12$; and for 'Number', $d = -0.00$), in the New Zealand National Monitoring study (for Year 4, $d = -0.05$; for Year 8, $d = -0.10$), and in national assessment data (in relation to asTTle: for reading, $d = -0.16$; for maths, $d = 0.02$; for writing, a much larger $d = -0.44$ favouring girls) (Hattie, 2010a). Nor was there a difference in the pass rates relating to the nature of the high-school exams: for teacher internal exams, $d = -0.07$; for external assessment exams, $d = -0.05$.

It is simple: the variability among boys and among girls is very large – and much, much greater than the average difference between boys and girls. The differences in how students learn is not related to their boy or girl attributes, and while the labelling of 'boy' and 'girl' learning may appease some, it is not based on actual differences.

Similarly, the pursuit of multiple intelligences has limited return. Realizing that students have different abilities, talents, and interests is obviously critical, but there is no need for a rhetoric of multiple intelligences that goes beyond this well-argued, well-known, and almost simplistic (but powerful) message. Further, in our society there is, in general, a hierarchy among Gardner's multiple intelligences: we favour verbal and numeracy abilities over those that are kinesthetic, musical, sporting, etc. I say 'in general', because there are obvious cases in which there are exceptions (sports people, musicians), but 'in general' to be successful in these endeavours is much harder given the low probability of success. Instead, there are many daily needs and vocations that involve verbal or numerical abilities. More and more, we need competencies in evaluating and synthesizing, and high levels of people intelligence – which involves respect for self and respect for others. It is not merely high skills and knowledge that is needed, but also the skills to think about, evaluate, and communicate our thinking (see Fletcher & Hattie, 2011) – and all students need these 'intelligences'. Gardner (2009) has cautioned about misleading implications, claiming there were two main implications from his arguments: pay attention to individual differences, and decide on what is really important in your discipline; and teach it and convey it in several different ways. This reiterates the claims above that it is desirable to have *multiple ways of teaching* and that there is no need to classify students into different 'intelligences'.

VISIBLE LEARNING – CHECKLIST FOR STARTING THE LESSON

20. Teachers have high expectations for all students, and constantly seek evidence to check and enhance these expectations. The aim of the school is to help all students to exceed their potential.

Another form of labelling comes from *teacher expectations*. We have known for a long time about the effects that expectations play in classrooms ($d = 0.43$). The question, however, is not 'Do teachers have expectations?', but: 'Do they have false and misleading expectations that lead to decrements in learning or learning gains – and for which students?' Better still: 'Do teachers have high expectations based on what students know and can do?'

There has been a long search to identify which particular students are differentially affected by teacher expectations – by their gender, prior conduct, social class, physical attractiveness, previously taught siblings, name stereotypes, the track in which they are placed, and ethnicity. These differential expectations, however, are not the major issue. Instead, if teachers have high expectations, they tend to have them for all students; similarly, if they have low expectations, they tend to have them for all students. Rubie-Davis (2007; Rubie-Davies, Hattie, & Hamilton, 2006) asked teachers (after about a month of working with the students) to predict where the students would end up at the end of the year in maths, reading, and physical education – and when the students were tested at the end of the year, the teachers proved to have been reasonably accurate. The problem is that even though some teachers set targets below where the students began the year, some set targets with little improvement, and some set targets reasonably randomly – the students met whatever expectations the teachers had.

The role of expectations is a good example of how the mind frames of the teachers are important. There are differences in achievement gains relating to whether teachers *believe* that achievement is difficult to change because it is fixed and innate, compared to teachers who believe that achievement is changeable (the latter leading to higher gains). Teachers need to stop overemphasizing ability, and start to emphasize increased effort and progress (steep learning curves are the right of all students regardless of where they start); they need to stop seeking evidence to confirm their prior expectations, but rather seek evidence to surprise them and find ways in which to raise the achievement of all. School leaders need to stop creating schools that attempt to lock in prior achievement and experiences (such as by using tracking), and instead be evidence-informed about the talents and growth of all students by welcoming diversity and being accountable for all (regardless of the teachers' and schools' expectations). 'Be prepared to be surprised' seems to be an important mantra to use to avoid negative expectation effects. If teachers and schools are going to have expectations (and indeed we *do* have them), then they must make the expectations challenging, appropriate, and checkable, such that all students are achieving what is deemed valuable.

Weinstein (2002) has shown that students know that they are treated in different ways in the classroom due to expectations held by teachers, and are reasonably accurate in informing on when teachers favour some students over others with higher expectations. She also demonstrated that many institutional practices (such as tracking or streaming) can lead to beliefs that preclude many opportunities to learn:

> Expectancy processes do not reside solely 'in the minds of teachers' but instead are built into the very fabric of our institutions and our society.
>
> (Weinstein, 2002: 290)

VISIBLE LEARNING – CHECKLIST FOR STARTING THE LESSON

21. Students have high expectations relative to their current learning for themselves.

An additional 'label' relates to the potentially negative effects of *students' setting their own expectations* too low or too high, and then not having sufficiently high levels of confidence that they can exceed these expectations. Students have reasonably accurate understandings of their levels of achievement, but less about their rate of progress. On the one hand, this shows a remarkably high level of predictability about achievement in the classroom; on the other hand, these expectations may be set at a 'safe' level that they know they can reach without too much effort, and thus that they are failing to challenge themselves to reach higher.

In *Visible Learning*, the top-ranked effect relating to student expectations was self-reported grades ($d = 1.44$). Imagine that I tell my class that they are about to have a test relating to the learning intentions of the past lessons – but before the students sit the test, I ask them to predict their score or grade. They are very good at making such predictions. This should make us pause and ask why we ever set tests; indeed, the best answer to this question is 'so that we, as teachers, know who we taught well, what they mastered or failed to master, who made larger and smaller gains, and what we may need to re-teach'. Tests are primarily to help teachers to gather formative information about their impact. With this mind frame, the students reap the dividends.

The problem with the students being so accurate in their predictions is that their expectations are so often based on the 'doing just enough', or *minimax*, principle – that is, maximum grade return for minimal extra effort. Students so often set 'safe' predictions and our role as educators is to raise these student expectations. Our role is not to enable students to reach their potential, or to meet their needs; our role is to find out what students can do, and make them exceed their potential and needs. Our role is to create new horizons of success and then to help the students to attain them. We can set our aspirations low or, at best, make them about where we think we can reach now; the aim of schooling is to dependably identify talents and then create opportunities to assist in realizing these talents. Many of these talents are not necessarily within the current expectations of students.

Choosing the method

VISIBLE LEARNING – CHECKLIST FOR STARTING THE LESSON

22. Teachers choose the teaching methods as a final step in the lesson planning process and evaluate this choice in terms of their impact on students.

We spend far too much time talking about particular methods of teaching. The debate seems so often to centre on this or that method: we have had battles about direct instruction, constructivism, cooperative versus individualistic teaching, and so on. Our attention, instead, should be on the effect that we have on student learning – and sometimes we need multiple strategies and, more often, some students need different teaching strategies from those that they have been getting. A strong message from the findings in *Visible Learning* is that, more often than not, when students do not learn, they do not need 'more'; rather, they need 'different'.

Various successful methods of teaching were identified in *Visible Learning*, but the book also identified the importance of not rushing to implement only the top strategies; rather, it is important to understand the underlying reasons for the success of the strategies and use this as the basis for making decisions about teaching methods. The programs that had the most success were acceleration ($d = 0.88$), reciprocal teaching ($d = 0.72$), problem-solving teaching ($d = 0.61$), and self-verbalization/self-questioning ($d = 0.64$). These top methods rely on the influence of peers, feedback, transparent learning intentions and success criteria, teaching multiple strategies or teaching using various strategies, and attending to both surface and deep knowing. The least effective methods seem not to involve peers, to focus too much on deep to the detriment of first attending to surface knowledge or skill development, to overemphasize technologies, and to fail to take into account similarities, instead overemphasizing differences.

The message is not to choose a top method, but to choose a method and then evaluate its impact on student learning. So often the evaluation is in terms such as 'It worked for me', 'The students seem to enjoy it', 'The students appeared engaged', or 'It allowed me to get through the curriculum'. The only game in town is the impact of the choice of teaching method on all students learning. Recently, I visited a group of committed educators wishing to make a major difference to minority students in a remote rural area. They had decided to implement direct instruction – which certainly increased the probability of successful impacting on student learning. The measure of success, however, is not the dosage of direct instruction, but evidence of its impact on student gains. I encouraged them first to consider the evidence that the teachers and schools were providing their Board on learning gains (and to be assured by the quality of this evidence, as well as the information provided as to what the school intends as consequences of this evidence), and only then to talk about the dosage and effects of direct instruction. We spend a lot of time in our work devising dashboards of evidence of impact (and never use only test scores, but also value teacher judgement, classroom evidence, student reports, etc.) and then ask what is needed to enhance or, where necessary, change the methods to get the impact for which we are looking (for example, $d = >0.40$ within a year's work).

One of the more difficult tasks is to convince teachers to change their methods of teaching, because so many adopt one method and vary it throughout their career. Because of this long history of use, they often have a corpus of anecdotal evidence suggesting why it has worked for them – so why take a risk and change what seems to work? Teachers do not mind change; they are not so happy about being changed. But *does* it work for all of the students? Perhaps many of the various methods work reasonably well for above-average students (they are going to learn despite our efforts), but the quality of instruction is most paramount for those below average (and whatever method works for these students often also works best for above-average students). As will be discussed in Chapter 6, when we learn something new to us (struggling or bright), we need more skill development and content; as we progress, we need more connections, relationships, and schemas to organize these skills and content; we then need more regulation or self-control over how we continue to learn the content and ideas. The methods with the greatest effects are particularly powerful for students in the earlier stages of learning. The major message, however, is that rather than recommending a particular teaching method, teachers need to be evaluators of the effect of the methods that they choose. When students do not learn via one method, it is more likely that it then needs to be re-taught using a different method; it will not be

TABLE 5.1 Effect sizes from various programs

PROGRAMS	NO. OF METAS	NO. OF STUDIES	NO. OF PEOPLE	NO. OF EFFECTS	ES	SE	RANK
Reciprocal teaching	2	38	677	53	0.74	0.108	9
Vocabulary programs	10	442		1,109	0.67	0.080	15
Repeated reading programs	2	54		156	0.67	0.090	16
Study skills programs	19	1,278	135,778	3,450	0.63	0.076	20
Problem-solving teaching	6	221	15,235	719	0.61	0.056	22
Comprehension programs	16	657	38,393	3,146	0.60	0.051	24
Concept mapping	7	325	8,471	378	0.60	0.088	25
Cooperative vs individualistic learning	4	774		284	0.59	0.096	26
Direct instruction	4	304	42,618	597	0.59	0.055	27
Mastery learning	10	420	9,323	374	0.58	0.042	29
Providing worked examples	1	62	3,324	151	0.57	0.103	30
Peer tutoring	14	767	2,676	1,200	0.55	0.112	32
Cooperative vs competitive learning	7	1,024	17,000	933	0.54	0.191	33
Phonics instruction	19	523	21,134	6,453	0.54		34
Keller's Mastery PIS	3	263		162	0.53		38
Interactive video methods	6	441	4,800	3,930	0.52	0.076	44
Play programs	2	70	5,056	70	0.50		47
Second-/third-chance programs	2	52	5,685	1,395	0.50		48
Computer-assisted instruction	100	5,947	4,239,997	10,291	0.37	0.059	76
Simulations	10	426	10,934	550	0.33	0.081	85
Inductive teaching	2	97	3,595	103	0.33	0.035	86
Inquiry-based teaching	4	205	7,437	420	0.31	0.092	90
Teaching test taking and coaching	11	275	15,772	372	0.27	0.024	97
Competitive vs individualistic learning	4	831		203	0.24	0.232	103
Programmed instruction	8	493		391	0.23	0.084	104
Individualized instruction	10	638	9,380	1,185	0.22	0.060	108
Visual/audiovisual methods	6	359	2,760	231	0.22	0.070	109
Extracurricular programs	8	2,161		1,036	0.19	0.055	115
Co-teaching/team teaching	2	136	1,617	47	0.19	0.057	117
Web-based learning	3	45	22,554	136	0.18	0.124	123
Problem-based learning	9	367	38,090	747	0.15	0.085	126
Sentence-combining programs	2	35		40	0.15	0.087	127
Perceptual–motor programs	1	180	13,000	637	0.08	0.011	136
Whole language	4	64	630	197	0.06	0.056	137
Average/sum	**330**	**20,339**	**4,699,961**	**42,054**	**0.41**	**0.080**	**–**

enough merely to repeat the same method again and again. We, as teachers, need to change if the students do not change in their learning.

Teachers as evaluators and activators

VISIBLE LEARNING – CHECKLIST FOR STARTING THE LESSON

23. Teachers see their fundamental role as evaluators and activators of learning.

An 'activator' is any agency bringing about change, or something that 'increases the activity of an enzyme or a protein that increases the production of a gene product in DNA transcription'. This notion has action, agency, and augmentation – and thus is a most appropriate metaphor for describing the major role of the teacher. The other role is 'evaluator', in which the teacher is asked to attend to the worth and merit of the activation. By having a mind frame that the fundamental role is evaluator and activator, teachers then are focused more on their impact on all students, focused more on the quality of the outcomes that they wish to impact, and are placed in the position of seeing their effect more in terms of the consequences for students than in getting through the curriculum, having students passing exams, and running excellent lessons with engaging activities.

The best way in which to choose the best teaching method (and way in which to change teachers so that they begin to use the best method) is to place more attention on the evaluation of the learning effect sizes from the lesson, and use these as the first discussion point for considering whether the optimal teaching methods have been used. This use of such 'evidence-into-action' can then influence teachers' beliefs about learning, planning, motivation, and the regulation of learning. Note, however, that this approach only creates the right question; it does not answer the question of which is the best teaching method, which answer requires judgement, listening, and expertise. It may well be that one method is better for this student than for that student, for this content rather than for that content – but the key is the impact not the method.

Teacher education programs need to attend less to promoting various teaching strategies and overemphasizing diversity, and more to how new teachers can evaluate the impact of their teaching on students, more to how then to use different and multiple strategies, and more to seeing the similarities and allowing for the diversity of their impact on their group of students. This approach to choosing which teaching method based on evidence of the impact on students entails specific steps (see Appendix E for more details).

1. Be clear about the outcomes (success criteria) of the lesson or series of lessons. (This is most likely to include some outcomes relating to achievement, but there are, of course, many other outcomes.)

2. Decide, preferably before you start teaching the lesson(s), the best way in which to measure the outcomes. (When you first use this method, it is recommended that you use some form of standardized assessment, and then later move to teacher-made assessments.)

3. Administer this outcome measure at the start of the lessons. Such 'progress testing', as it is often called, can establish what the students already know and can do, and can help to identify strengths and gaps. (Yes, they may learn something from doing the test at the outset – but why not?)

4. Conduct the teaching.

5. Re-administer the outcome measure at the end of the lesson or lessons.

    a. Calculate the average score and standard deviation (measure of spread) for the scores at the beginning and the end.

    b. Calculate the effect size for the class (see Appendix E for more on how to estimate effect sizes).

       i. If it is greater than 0.40, then reflect on what seemed to be optimal about that lesson series.

      ii. If it is less than 0.40, then reflect on what seemed to be less than optimal about the lesson series, and make any changes needed to the lesson, the teaching method, activities and so on. (Doing 'more' is rarely the answer.)

    c. Using the measure of spread (*SD*) and assuming that it can be used for each student, calculate the effect size for each student.

       i. If it is greater than 0.40, then reflect on what seemed to be optimal about that lesson series for these students.

      ii. If it is less than 0.40, then reflect on what seemed to be less than optimal about the lesson series, and make the changes needed to the lesson, the teaching method, activities and so on for these students.

Conclusions

The notion of teachers (and school leaders) as evaluators and activators implies deliberate change, directing of learning, and visibly making a difference to the experiences and outcomes for the students (and for the teachers) – and the key mechanism for this activation is a mind frame that embraces the role of evaluation. The key questions for the teacher include the following.

- 'How do I know this is working?'
- 'How can I compare this with that?'
- 'What is the merit and worth of this influence on learning?'
- 'What is the magnitude of the effect?'
- 'What evidence would convince me that I am wrong?'
- 'Where is the evidence that shows that this is superior to other programs?'
- 'Where have I seen this practice installed so that it produces effective results?'
- 'Do I share a common conception of progress with other teachers?'

The 'teacher as evaluator' involves more than using the skills and tools developed within evaluation or social science; indeed, it is primarily about deciding which are the critical analyses to be pursued and ensuring that they are indeed pursued in the context of the impact of students' learning. This is not to claim that there is only one evaluation model or method, because these issues are hotly debated; instead, the claim is that the 'teacher as evaluator' needs to consider the 'goodness of fit' notions of asking and deciding the best methods that led to judgements of merit, such that there is sufficient and appropriate rigour to defend the evidence, and interpretations of this evidence that lead to evaluative claims. (For a discussion on leaders as activators, see Hattie and Clinton, 2011.)

The aim is to get the students actively involved in seeking this evidence: their role is not simply to do tasks as decided by teachers, but to actively manage and understand their learning gains. This includes evaluating their own progress, being more responsible for their learning, and being involved with peers in learning together about gains in learning. If students are to become active evaluators of their own progress, teachers must provide the students with appropriate feedback so that they can engage in this task. Van den Bergh, Ros, and Beijaard (2010: 3) describe the task thus:

> Fostering active learning seems a very challenging and demanding task for teachers, requiring knowledge of students' learning processes, skills in providing guidance and feedback and classroom management.

The need is to engage students in this same challenging and demanding task.

The suggestion in this chapter is to start lessons with helping students to understand the intention of the lesson and showing them what success might look like at the end. Many times, teachers look for the interesting beginning to a lesson – for the hook, and the motivating question. Dan Willingham (2009) has provided an excellent argument for not thinking in this way. He advocates starting with what the student is likely to think about. Interesting hooks, demonstrations, fascinating facts, and likewise may seem to be captivating (and often are), but he suggests that there are likely to be other parts of the lesson that are more suitable for the attention-grabber. The place for the attention-grabber is more likely to be at the end of the lesson, because this will help to consolidate what has been learnt. Most importantly, Willingham asks teachers to think long and hard about how to make the connection between the attention-grabber and the point that it is designed to make; preferably, that point will be the main idea from the lesson.

Having too many open-ended activities (discovery learning, searching the Internet, preparing PowerPoint presentations) can make it difficult to direct students' attention to that which matters – because they often love to explore the details, the irrelevancies, and the unimportant while doing these activities. One of Willingham's principles is that any teaching method is most useful when there is plenty of prompt feedback about whether the student is thinking about a problem in the right way. Similarly, he promotes the notion that assignments should be primarily about what the teacher wants the students to think about (not about demonstrating 'what they know'). Students are very good at ignoring what you say ('I value connections, deep ideas, your thoughts') and seeing what you value (corrections to the grammar, comments on referencing, correctness or absence of facts). Thus teachers must develop a scoring rubric for any assignment before they complete the question or prompts, and show the rubric to the students so that they know what the teacher values. Such formative feedback can reinforce the 'big ideas' and the important understandings, and help to make the investment of energy worthwhile. It is more likely to lead to cognitive understanding, and to reduce the false leads and any overemphasis on surface knowledge – and it will be more rewarding for all.

Exercises

1. Administer the five items from Bryk and Schneider's 'Teacher Trust Scale' (see p. 71) to teachers in the school (anonymously) and discuss with fellow teachers how the levels of trust can then be maximized in this school.

2. During observations of classrooms, monitor the amount of talking and questioning by teachers and students. How many students are engaged in asking and answering fellow students' questions? Is there a teacher initiation, response, and evaluation dominance? Are the questions surface or deep?

3. Consider the following two extracts from Charles Dickens' *Hard Times*. How has teaching and teacher education changed since the 1800s?

[Mr Gradgrind:] 'Now, what I want is, Facts. Teach these boys and girls nothing but Facts. Facts alone are wanted in life. Plant nothing else, and root out everything else. You can only form the minds of reasoning animals upon Facts: nothing else will ever be of any service to them. This is the principle on which I bring up my own children, and this is the principle on which I bring up these children. Stick to Facts, sir!'

So, Mr M'Choakumchild began in his best manner. He and some one hundred and forty other schoolmasters had been lately turned at the same time, in the same factory, on the same principles, like so many pianoforte legs. He had been put through an immense variety of paces, and had answered volumes of head-breaking questions. Orthography, etymology, syntax, and prosody, biography, astronomy, geography, and general cosmography, the sciences of compound proportion, algebra, land-surveying and levelling, vocal music, and drawing from models, were all at the ends of his ten chilled fingers. He had worked his stony way into Her Majesty's most Honourable Privy Council's Schedule B, and had taken the bloom off the higher branches of mathematics and physical science, French, German, Latin, and Greek. He knew all about all the Water Sheds of all the world (whatever they are), and all the histories of all the peoples, and all the names of all the rivers and mountains, and all the productions, manners, and customs of all the countries, and all their boundaries and bearings on the two and thirty points of the compass. Ah, rather overdone, M'Choakumchild. If he had only learnt a little less, how infinitely better he might have taught much more!

4. Run a Paideia-type Socratic questioning session. After teaching some content, group about 15 students in a circle (if more than 15, then have the others sit behind the circle and then later give them the opportunity to become the inner and active circle). Start by asking an open question (one that leads to further discussion and debate), and then allow students to ask each other questions, answer these questions, and engage in dialogue. *At no time* can you, as teacher, intervene with prompts, questions, or answers. After 10–20 minutes, debrief from the session. Most importantly, use the student questions and answers as formative evidence about what you, as teacher, do next. If

you need help with developing opening questions, with ways in which to avoid becoming engaged, and with teaching students to be more respectful of each other, see Roberts and Billings (1999) for more details and advice.

5. Observe a class and 'listen' to what the teacher and students are saying. Then reflect back what you heard to the participants in your own words. Such empathic listening requires you to put yourself in a position to understand the other person; by reflecting back, you demonstrate to the other person that you have respect for what they have said. Allow the other to self-correct what you heard, and in this way share their moments of learning, misunderstanding, inactivity, self-discovery, and challenge. Does the other now feel understood?

6. Google 'Productive pedagogy', which is based on the assumption that teachers need to make highly complex decisions about the impact of their teaching often 'on the run' during a lesson. Evaluate your lesson – especially the start of the lesson – using the following questions.

INTELLECTUAL QUALITY QUESTIONS

Higher-order thinking	Are higher-order thinking and critical analysis occurring?
Deep knowledge	Does the lesson cover operational fields in any depth, detail, or level of specificity?
Deep understanding	Do the work and responses of the students provide evidence of understanding of concepts or ideas?
Substantive conversation	Does classroom talk break out of the IRE pattern and lead to sustained dialogue between students, and between teachers and students?
Knowledge problematic	Are students critiquing and second-guessing texts, ideas, and knowledge?
Meta-language	Are aspects of language, grammar, and technical vocabulary being foregrounded?

RELEVANCE QUESTIONS

Knowledge integration	Does the lesson range across diverse fields, disciplines, and paradigms?
Background knowledge	Is there an attempt to connect with students' background knowledge?
Connectedness to the world	Do lessons and the assigned work bear any resemblance or connection to real-life contexts?
Problem-based curriculum	Is there a focus on identifying and solving intellectual and/or real-world problems?

SUPPORTIVE CLASSROOM ENVIRONMENT QUESTIONS

Student control	Do students have any say in the pace, direction, or outcome of the lesson?
Social support	Is the classroom a socially supportive, positive environment?
Engagement	Are students engaged and on-task?
Explicit criteria	Are criteria for student performance made explicit?
Self-regulation	Is the direction of student behaviour implicit and self-regulatory or explicit?

RECOGNITION OF DIFFERENCE QUESTIONS

Cultural knowledge	Are diverse cultural knowledges brought into play?
Inclusivity	Are deliberate attempts made to increase the participation of all students of different backgrounds?
Narrative	Is the teaching principally narrative, or is it expository?
Group identity	Does teaching build a sense of community and identity?
Citizenship	Are attempts made to foster active citizenship?

The flow of the lesson: learning

Learning is often 'in the head' and an aim of the teacher is to help to make this learning visible. There are many phases to learning and there is no one way of learning or set of understandings that unravel the processes of learning; it is more a combination of phases. An often-needed requirement for this learning to occur is some form of tension, some realization of 'not knowing', a commitment to want to know and understand – or, as Piaget called it, some 'state of disequilibrium'. When this occurs, most of us need assistance (from a learned other, from some resources) to then learn new material and accommodate it as part of our new understanding. There are many possible strategies with which to undertake this learning, and we certainly need to have proficiency in choosing and using these strategies, but most importantly we need to appreciate that the use of strategies requires concentration, much practice, and skills. The operative requirement to enhance student learning is for teachers to see this learning through the eyes of the students.

Too often, beginning teachers and professional development offered to more experienced teachers focus on teaching and not on learning. Attention needs to move from how to teach to how to learn – and only after teachers understand how each student learns can they then move on to make decisions about how to teach. It may seem surprising to some that there are many theories of learning, and many recent books about these theories (such as Alexander, 2006). Schunk (2008), for example, elaborates on the following theories: conditioning; social cognitive; cognitive information processing; cognitive learning processes; and constructivist. He also has chapters on development and learning, cognition and instruction, the neuroscience of learning, content-area learning, and motivation.

Observations of classrooms typically show that there is little direct instruction in 'how to learn', or the development and use of various learning strategies. Moseley et al. (2004), for example, observed 69 classrooms for evidence of strategy teaching. Overall, 80 per cent of the classes involved book reading, information-giving or task instruction; 65 per cent of the lessons included requests for answers to questions, and close to a third involved the provision of specific information. Teaching that involved the use or suggestion of strategies was observed infrequently, with 10 per cent of the teachers offering no such teaching. Ornstein, Coffman, McCall, Grammer, and san Souci (2010) reviewed classroom observation of strategy teaching and concluded that there is very little in the way of explicit conversations about the use of specific strategies. Instead, memory dominates: half of the observation intervals contained some form of deliberate memory request. Providing students with learning strategies in the context of learning the content is certainly powerful;

providing them then with opportunities to practise these strategies comes next, followed by ensuring that the chosen strategies are effective. This comes to the heart of learning to learn: it is about *intention* to use, *consistency* in appropriately using the strategies, and knowing when chosen strategies are *effective*. This learning to learn is often called 'self-regulation', which term highlights the decisions required by the student in the process of learning.

This chapter is about learning, how to make it visible, and how to develop it.

Various phases of learning

Learning starts with 'backward design' – rather than starting from the textbooks or favoured lessons and time-honoured activities. Learning starts with the teacher (and preferably also the student) knowing the desired results (expressed as success criteria related to learning intentions) and then working backwards to where the student starts the lesson(s) – both in terms of his or her prior knowledge and where he or she is in the learning process. The purpose is to reduce the gap between where the student starts and the success criteria for the lesson. This requires a deep understanding not only of each student's prior knowledge, but also of how he or she thinks and where he or she is in developing his or her thinking processes. Thus to teach well requires a deep understanding about how we learn.

> **VISIBLE LEARNING – CHECKLIST FOR DURING THE LESSON: LEARNING**
>
> 24. Teachers have rich understandings about how learning involves moving forward through various levels of capabilities, capacities, catalysts, and competencies.

There are four overlapping considerations in learning. Unfortunately, there are no necessary direct links between each of these four ways of considering learning; rather, they all play their part in the learning processes.

TABLE 6.1 Four major overlapping considerations in the learning process

	CAPABILITY	CAPACITY	CATALYST	COMPETENCE
	Piaget levels	SOLO levels	Motivation	Processes
1	Sensorimotor	An idea	See a gap	Novice
2	Pre-operational	Ideas	Goal setting	Capable
3	Concrete operational	Relate the ideas	Strategies development	Proficient
4	Formal operational	Extend the ideas	Close the gap	

a. Capabilities in thinking

Piaget (1970) noticed that children moved from very intuitive to more scientific and socially acceptable responses, especially as they become exposed to other peers and adults who take an interest in talking with them (see also Chapter 4). He proposed four major phases relating to how student thinking develops qualitatively over time.

- *Sensorimotor* Students view the world from their own viewpoint primarily through movement and senses, and cannot perceive the world from others' viewpoints.
- *Preoperational* Via the acquisition of motor skills and language, sutdents become more adept at using symbols, can use an object or role play to represent something else, but cannot yet mentally manipulate information, or adopt the viewpoint of others.
- *Concrete operational* Students begin to think logically, but in very concrete terms.
- *Formal operational* Students develop abstract reasoning and can think more logically.

Being aware of the student's stage and his or her movement through the levels of thinking is among the most critical sources of knowledge. This knowledge not only helps teachers to optimize the point at which the student is starting, but also is key to knowing the next higher level of the thinking processes towards which the student should be moving. Shayer and Adey (1981) termed this assisting as 'cognitive acceleration', based on three of Piaget's main drivers of cognitive development:

1. that the mind develops in response to challenge or to disequilibrium, meaning that the intervention must provide some *cognitive conflict*;
2. that the mind has a growing ability to become conscious of, and so take control of, its own processes, meaning that the intervention must encourage students to be *metacognitive*; and
3. that cognitive development is a social process promoted by high-quality discussion amongst peers and mediated by a teacher or other more mature person, meaning that the intervention must encourage *social construction*.

They were careful to not align these drivers to ages, because there is not a one-to-one relationship between age and Piagetian stages. Further, this is not discovery learning or peer collaboration without intervention:

> remember that every moment of the lesson management involves the teacher being aware both of the processing levels of different aspects of the activity, and also how each pupil's response indicates the level that they are processing at, and hence where they are presently moving up toward.
>
> (Shayer, 2003: 484)

Their intervention programs regularly attained effect sizes of between 0.3 and 1.0 in achievement.

A major message that Shayer draws from this research is the important role played by teachers in structuring learning to ensure that students create their learning for themselves and with other peers, particularly when the lessons have two or three steps of learning of the important concepts at and just above the level of thinking used by the student. This means that a teachers needs to know how each student thinks, and the thinking demands of each step in the lesson both by the student and the peers with whom they are working. This, he claims, stops peer learning or collaborative learning from degenerating into the 'blind leading the blind'. It requires teachers to intervene to keep the learning moving upwards all of the time in relation to the demands of the subject knowledge being taught. This notion of teaching 'at or +1 above' where the students are thinking is a major theme of this chapter.

b. Phases of thinking: surface to deep

VISIBLE LEARNING – CHECKLIST FOR DURING THE LESSON: LEARNING

25. Teachers understand how learning is based on students needing multiple learning strategies to achieve surface and deep understanding.

The four phases of the SOLO taxonomy were introduced in Chapter 4. As students encounter lessons, they acquire an idea or ideas, and then relate and extend that (or those) idea(s). Unlike the models of thinking (such as Piaget), students can begin at any of these levels, but the ability to relate and extend depends on their knowing the ideas that are expected to be related and extended. Too often, students are asked to relate and extend with minimal ideas on which to base this task – leading to impoverished deeper learning. So many schools are naming themselves 'enquiry schools', as if this relating and extending can be accomplished without a firm basis of understanding of the ideas. As has been noted, transfer across subjects is notoriously difficult and merely learning to 'enquire' without embedding that enquiry in a rich basis of ideas is not a defensible strategy. The claim here, instead, is that teachers must know at what phase of learning the student is best invested – in learning more surface ideas, and moving from the surface to a deeper relating and extending of these ideas. The aim is to work at, or +1 beyond, where the student is working now.

c. Phases of motivation

Students do not remain in a constant state of being motivated! This too invokes knowing the phase of motivation and work at this or +1. Winne and Hadwin (2008) outlined a four-stage model of motivation, as follows.

1. *See a gap* The student needs to see a gap between what he or she knows now and the intended learning. In the first stage – task definition – the student processes information about the task.

2. *Goal-setting* When he or she has sufficient (but not necessarily complete) information, he or she moves to phase two; this involves goal-setting and planning, whereby the learner frames a goal and works out a plan to approach the goal (with assistance as needed).

3. *Strategies* When the students have goals and planning, they can search for strategies with which to move closer to the intention. This third stage involves enacting these strategies.

4. *Close the gap* The student critically examines whether he or she has sufficiently closed the gap to claim success and thus be able to move on.

It is often moving from the first to second stages that can be the most difficult (for teachers and for students). Some students never get past the first stage, and Winne and Hadwin noted that some teachers seem reluctant to allow students to get past the first stage. To make the transition involves being aware of the goals of the lesson, the nature of the gap, and then developing cognitive strategies and planning, as well as having the motivation to reduce this gap.

d. Phases of how we learn

A recent major review of how people learn (Bransford, Brown, & Cocking, 2000) identified three major phases moving from novice to capable to proficient, as follows.

1. Students come into class with preconceptions about how the world works, and teachers need to engage with this initial understanding; otherwise, the students may fail to grasp the new concepts and information.

2. For teachers to develop student competence, students must have a deep foundation of factual knowledge, understand the ideas in the context of a conceptual framework, and organize knowledge in ways that facilitate retrieval and application.

3. By building on these competences, a meta-cognitive approach to instruction can then help students to learn to take control of their own learning by defining their learning goals and monitoring their progress in achieving the goals.

Learning is premised on understanding what the students begin with, then acquiring a balance of surface and deep understandings, and finally helping students to take more control over their learning. These three principles mean that learning requires the active involvement of the learner; learning is primarily a social activity; new knowledge is constructed on the basis of what is already understood and believed; and learning develops by employing effective and flexible strategies that help us to understand, reason, memorize, and problem-solve. Learners must be taught know how to plan and monitor their learning, how to set their own learning goals, and how to correct errors.

The 'learning' aim of any set of lessons is to get students to learn the skills of teaching themselves the content and understanding – that is, to *self-regulate* their learning. This requires helping students to develop multiple strategies of learning, and to realize why they need to invest in deliberate practice and concentration on the learning. This requires using learning strategies to progress from surface and deep knowing; it requires assistance in reducing the cognitive load such that attention can be given to developing these strategies of learning; and it requires giving students multiple opportunities to learn the ideas and to engage in deliberate practice, and an environment in which they can concentrate on their learning. All of this depends on expectations and mind frames that students 'can do' this learning, the presence of appropriate challenge, and the use of appropriate feedback taking into consideration the student's current phase of learning.

There are, at least, three overlapping phases of learning: novice, through to capable, then onto proficient. This process can occur at many of the above phases: it can be when learning something for the first time; it can be during learning as we encounter new notions to build onto or replace our current thinking; and it can occur immediately after we become proficient and then need to start again with more challenging ideas that are new to us.

1. In the first, *novice* phase, we try to understand the requirements of the activity and focus on generating ways forward without making major mistakes.

2. Then, as we acquire some *capability*, we are able to minimize more errors, our performance improves, and we no longer need to focus as intently on each aspect of the task or on the component parts of the knowledge.

3. In the final, *proficient* phase, we become more automated in our reactions to newer ideas, need less effort to execute each task, and as we become more automated, then, in some ways, we become less able to control the execution of the skills.

e. Differential instruction

VISIBLE LEARNING – CHECKLIST FOR DURING THE LESSON: LEARNING

26. Teachers provide differentiation to ensure that learning is meaningfully and efficiently directed to all students gaining the intentions of the lesson(s).

All four of the above phases of learning emphasize teachers knowing where students are, and then aiming to move them '+1' beyond this point; thus teaching of the 'whole class' is unlikely to pitch the lesson correctly for all students. This is where the skill of teachers in knowing the similarities across students and allowing for the differences becomes so important. Differentiation relates primarily to structuring classes so that all students are working 'at or +1' from where they start, such that all can have maximal opportunities to attain the success criteria of the lessons.

One of the truisms in most schools is that the year of schooling reflects the spread of capabilities more than anything else. By Year 5, there is likely to be at least five years of spread in the capabilities of students in the class, by Year 10, it is more likely ten years of spread. How to accommodate this spread is of major concern, and there have been many answers such as personalization, differentiation, or catering for individual differences. Many schools (especially high schools) resort to structural methods (for example, tracking/ streaming, pull-out programs), but despite these methods all classes are full of heterogeneity (and this is more often than not advantageous, because students can learn much from each other). Teaching to these differences has become a mantra for some; in some cases, diversity is taken to extremes – it merely means that all students are different. While there is no doubt that every student in the class is likely to be different, an art of teaching is seeing the commonality in diversity, in having peers work together, especially when they bring different talents, errors, interests, and disposition to the situation, and understanding that differentiation relates more to the phases of learning – from novice, through capable, to proficient – rather than merely providing different activities to different (groups of) students.

For differentiation to be effective, teachers need to know, for each student, where that student begins and where he or she is in his or her journey towards meeting the success criteria of the lesson. Is that student a novice, somewhat capable, or proficient? What are his or her strengths and gaps in knowledge and understanding? What learning strategies does he or she have and how can we help him or her to develop other learning strategies that he or she needs? Depending on their phase of learning, their understanding of surface and deep thinking, their phase of motivation, and their strategies of learning, the teacher will have to provide different ways in which students can demonstrate mastery and understanding along the way to meeting the success criteria. It should be obvious why rapid formative feedback can be so powerful for teachers to know the phase of learning, and then help them to achieve more '+1' outcomes.

Tomlinson (1995) demonstrated that there are four characteristics of effective differentiated instruction.

1. The first is that *all* students need to have the opportunity to explore and apply the key concepts of the subject being studied and then to achieve success.

2. Frequent formative interpretation is needed to monitor the students' path to success in the learning intention. This, more than most other activities, will help to generate the highest probability of successful teaching and learning.

3. Flexibly grouping students so that they can work alone, together, or as a whole class, as appropriate, makes it possible to make the most of the opportunities created by difference and commonality.

4. As much as possible, we should engage students in an active manner to explore and reach the success targets.

To these, I would add a fifth: often the differentiation needs to be better related to differential learning gains – those who gain more may need different instruction than those who gain less. In other words, rather than think about differentiation in terms of different for brighter and struggling students, think about it terms of those who have gained or not gained; those who have not gained (irrespective of starting point) are more likely to need different instruction.

These five characteristics help to ensure that the learning intentions and success criteria are transparent to all students. The key is for teachers to have a clear reason for differentiation, and relate what they do *differently* to where the student is located on the progression from novice to capable, relative to the learning intentions and success criteria.

The grouping aspect is often not well understood. The aim is to not necessarily to group students by their phase of learning, etc., but rather to group by a mixture of those at and those +1 above, so that peer mediation can be part of moving all forward. Having students both at or +1 above the phase of learning can help students to move forward as they discuss with, work together with, and see the world through the eyes of the other students.

The mistake is to assume that because students 'sit in groups', there is learning in groups. Galton and Patrick (1990) have shown that merely placing students in groups rarely means that they work in groups in any form of differentiation. Figure 6.1 shows that while most

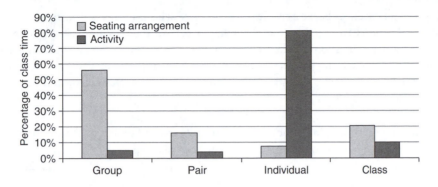

FIGURE 6.1 Proportion of class time and class activity spent in various grouping arrangements

classrooms are structured in groups or pairs, most activity is still individual or whole-class instruction.

One method for structured differentiation is the 'jigsaw' method (Aronson, 2008). This involves groups of students working on a set of tasks, with each student being assigned a particular task (part of the 'jigsaw'). The student from each group might then join with students from other groups who also have that particular task, and all will get specific teaching on the task. After their individual research and learning about the task, they go back to their own groups and present their findings. A group report is then prepared.

f. Comments on the phases of learning

The message in the above sections is that it is critical for teachers to be aware of the various phases of learning and where each student is in his or her learning. Providing instruction at the wrong level for each student is missing the mark; it is inefficient and ineffective. The key is to provide instruction sufficiently above the current student level and aiming to move the student '+1' in their learning progression. This means that the teacher (and student) is best equipped when they know not only the prior achievement knowledge and understanding of the student, but also how each student processes information, know the appropriate balance of surface to deep, know how to best motivate students to see a gap, to goal-set, and to develop strategies, and have a deep understanding of how students are learning.

Adaptive experts

VISIBLE LEARNING – CHECKLIST FOR DURING THE LESSON: LEARNING

27. Teachers are adaptive learning experts who know where students are on the continuum from novice to capable to proficient, when students are and are not learning, and where to go next, and who can create a classroom climate to attain these learning goals.

Thus teachers need to be 'adaptive learning experts' who not only use many of effective strategies, but also have a high level of flexibility that allows them to innovate when routines are not enough (Bransford et al., 2000). Adaptive experts know when students are not learning, know where to go next, can adapt resources and strategies to help students to meet worthwhile learning intentions, and can recreate or alter the classroom climate to attain these learning goals.

> Adaptive experts also know how to continuously expand their expertise, restructuring their knowledge and competencies to meet new challenges.
>
> (Darling-Hammond, 2006: 11)

These teachers have high levels of empathy, and know how 'to see learning through the eyes of the students' and show students that they understand how they are thinking and how then their thinking can be enhanced. This requires that teachers pay special attention to the way in which students define, describe, and interpret phenomena and problem-solving situations, so that they can begin to understand these experiences from the unique perspectives of students (Gage & Berliner, 1998). Indeed, a powerful way in which to see such learning through the eyes of the students is to listen to student questions, and how students then answer their peers' questions. (See Roberts and Billings, 1999, on the Paideia method for more details on how to do this.)

Note that it is not *routine expertise* that we want; rather, it is *adaptive expertise*. Routine expertise by teachers or students aims to identify what is wanted and aims to get there; teachers or students identify what has worked for them before and so use that method again. The approach can be summarized as: 'Let's get the problem solved as efficiently as possible and we can move on.' But the problem is that when these routines do not work, many students are left behind. In contrast, adaptive experts listen for when the learning is occurring so that they can work out the point at which to intervene (or not) to advance the learning. Sometimes, they need to disrupt the equilibrium, to break the habit, or to see error as an opportunity for intervention. Teacher and student adaptive experts see themselves as evaluators fundamentally engaged as thinkers and problem-solvers.

Learning strategies

VISIBLE LEARNING – CHECKLIST FOR DURING THE LESSON: LEARNING

28. Teachers are able to teach multiple ways of knowing and multiple ways of interacting, and provide multiple opportunities for practice.

Recently, a consortium of approximately 35 eminent researchers summarized some of the major empirically grounded processes for learning (Graesset, Halpern, & Hakel, 2008). Their findings, with some added, relate to multiple ways of knowing, multiple ways of interacting, multiple opportunities for practice, and much feedback to know that we are learning.

Multiple ways of knowing The major message is that multiple ways of presenting material need to be provided close to each other with minimal distracting material. We can only process so much at a time, but we need multiple ways of seeing new ideas without overloading our working memory.

- Ideas that need to be associated should be presented near to each other in space and time.
- Materials presented in verbal, visual, and multimedia form provide richer representations than can a single medium.
- Cognitive flexibility improves with multiple viewpoints that link facts, skills, procedures, and deep conceptual principles.
- Materials and multimedia should explicitly link related ideas and minimize distracting irrelevant material.
- The information presented to the learner should not overload working memory.

Multiple ways of interacting We learn best by interacting with the ideas, by deliberately rephrasing the ideas, and by finding 'coat hangers' to link to previous notions (or examples) – particularly when there is tension between what we know and what we are encountering. We need to be explicitly taught how to process such learning.

- Outlining, integrating, and synthesizing information produces better learning than rereading materials or other passive strategies.
- Stories and example cases tend to be remembered better than facts and abstract principles.
- Deep reasoning and learning is stimulated by problems that create cognitive disequilibrium, such as obstacles to goals, contradictions, conflict, and anomalies – and students need to be told that this is a normal part of learning.
- Success at fluent and flexible transfer requires a deep understanding of the rich, 'big ideas' that connect the surface knowledge. We need 'coat hangers' to which to attach our understandings across problems, situations, and content domains.
- Most students need training in how to self-regulate their learning and other cognitive processes.

Multiple opportunities for practising Most of us, struggling or gifted, need multiple opportunities to learn new ideas, preferably over time, and we need to see the purpose of deliberately practising.

- An understanding of an abstract concept improves with multiple and varied examples.
- Spaced schedules of studying produce better long-term retention than a single session.
- To maintain engaged and sustained learning, there is a need to see value and purpose in the practice, and a need to develop a growing sense of confidence when facing challenges in this learning.

Knowing that we are learning When we learn, we can make many errors, go in wrong directions, learn wrong information, and meet many challenges – and thus we are often dependent on 'just in time, just for me' feedback to ensure that we move efficiently and effectively towards the success criteria.

- Feedback is most powerful when the nature of feedback is related to the student's degree of proficiency (from novice to proficient).

- Making errors is often a necessity for learning then to occur; students need safe environments in which they can go beyond their comfort levels, make and learn from errors, and know when they have erred.

- Learning wrong information can be reduced when feedback is immediate.

- Challenges help to make learning easier and thereby have positive effects on long-term retention.

Bransford et al. (2000) on *How People Learn* is a powerful resource that can help teachers to understand many of the current findings and debates about learning. The above findings are elaborated and these are linked to three big ideas: 'understand prior achievement'; 'use this as a link'; and 'think about thinking'.

- *Understand prior achievement* First, we use our existing knowledge to make sense of and learn new information. When people develop new knowledge, they build on and connect it to their previous knowledge or understandings. This highlights the importance of teachers understanding what students already know and can do – because this is the connection for new thinking. Sometimes, this old knowledge may need to be unlearned (if, for example, it is wrong, or misconceived), but it is the foundation for future learning.

- *Linking between old and new* Although we start with existing knowledge, new learning is not simply tacked on, 'brick by brick', to the old knowledge – which is why the relationships between old and new understandings are so important. We come to know ideas, and then we can be asked to relate and extend them. This then leads to conceptual understanding, which can then in turn become a new idea – and so the cycle continues. These conceptual understandings form the 'coat hangers' on which we interpret and assimilate new ideas, and relate and extend them. Sometimes, these 'coat hangers' can be deficient and then new ideas can be rejected or not be understood; thus our prior understanding can become a barrier to learning new knowledge. Teachers therefore need to be aware of each student's surface and deep knowing, and the ways in which students have current conceptions, and constantly check to see if the new ideas are being assimilated and accommodated by each learner.

- *Think about thinking* We need to develop an awareness of what we are doing, where we are going, and how we are going there; we need to know what to do when we do not know what to do. Such self-regulation, or meta-cognitive, skills are one of the ultimate goals of all learning: they are what we often mean by 'lifelong learning' and it is why we want 'students to become their own teachers'. This regulation of our own learning does not happen in a vacuum, and certainly is based on surface and deep understanding. It is not feasible to teach 'self-regulation' outside the content domains.

We completed a meta-analysis on the effects of teaching students various skills of studying and developing self-regulation (Hattie et al., 1996). Of interest was whether these study programs need to be developed near or far from the outcome content domain – that is, could study strategies be taught in the content domain, or could they be generalized across domains? The answer was that simple strategies (such as mnemonics, memory systems) could be taught outside the content, but that most strategies have to be taught within the content domain – once again, transfer across content is not easy. Programs that were provided outside of the context of the subject matter (the more general study skills programs) are effective only when surface knowledge is the outcome; programs run in-context (that is, those associated highly with the subject matter to be learnt) were most effective at surface and deeper levels of knowing and understanding.

It is likely that 'learning-to-learn' programs that are not embedded in the context of the subject to be learnt are of little value. Our recommendations were that thinking and study skills training should:

a. be in context;

b. use tasks within the same domain as the target content; and

c. promote a high degree of learner activity and meta-cognitive awareness.

The student needs to know various strategies that are appropriate to the task at hand – that is, the 'how', 'when', 'where', and 'why' of their use. Strategy training needs to be embedded in the teaching context itself.

Given these arguments, Bransford et al. (2000) argued that classrooms need to be:

- *learner-centered* – because it is all about where the student is on the journey from novice, through competent, to proficient;

- *knowledge-centred* – there needs to be knowledge so that connections and relations can be built;

- *assessment-rich* – to better understand and articulate what we already know and can do, and to know when we are moving towards proficient and understand where to next and

- *community-centered* – because there is no one way from novice to proficient, so we need to share and learn from each other (particularly so that we can see and enjoy the trials and tribulations of how we each progress), and share the relevance in what we are aiming to learn.

VISIBLE LEARNING – CHECKLIST FOR DURING THE LESSON: LEARNING

29. Teachers and students have multiple strategies for learning.

It is easy to become swamped when reviewing the various strategies of learning. Lavery (2008) compared the relative effects of many of these strategies and found overall a 0.46 effect, which is quite high – and the effect would be expected to be even higher if the strategies were more attuned to the phase of each student's learning.

She found the highest effects from strategies that aimed at the 'forethought' phase of learning, such as goal-setting and planning, self-instruction, and self-evaluation (Table 6.2).

- *Goal-setting and target-setting* have been referenced above as powerful methods for learning.

- *Self-instruction* (that is, using self-talking and self-questioning) is an invaluable tool for the learner to focus attention and check the use of various strategies – but such self-instruction skills need to be taught.

- *Self-evaluation* strategies allow the learner to self-reflect on performance in relation to the previously set goals – which is much more important than self-monitoring (such as ticking off completed tasks), because it requires the extra step such that the learner actually evaluates what he or she has monitored.

Many of the top strategies (such as organizing and transforming, summarizing and paraphrasing) promote a more active approach to learning tasks and high levels of engagement with the content. The less active are much lower in the rankings (record-keeping, imagery, time management, and restructuring the learning environment).

Sitzmann and Ely (2011) also reviewed many learning strategies and those with the highest relations to achievement included setting goals, the ability to concentrate and persist on a task, the amount of effort expended on the learning, and the confidence to succeed on the task.

Not only can these strategies be taught, but they may also require the unlearning of less-effective strategies. Thus the effects of teaching may not be seen in the immediate as students drop some and adapt to other strategies. Students who struggle to begin to understand are in most need of being taught these strategies, and for these students it may be worthwhile also to teach some of the more generic strategies first – such as note-taking, mnemonics, highlighting main ideas, and then self-testing, monitoring, and correctly applying the learned information. As was noted when discussing how to teach success criteria, providing worked examples is effective. Kobayashi (2005), for example, found that note-taking effects were higher when students were given instructor's notes from which to work, because these provided exemplars for their own note-taking and a rubric from which to work when learning from the notes. The effects were higher when notes were provided ($d = 0.41$) compared with not provided ($d = 0.19$), and it was the reviewing of the notes that was more effective than the taking of the notes. The length of time reviewing did not matter, and nor did the format of the presentation (video, audio, or live). An important reason for this effectiveness is that note-taking lowers mental effort while increasing mental efficiency (Wetzels, Kester, van Merrienboer, & Broers, 2011).

One way in which learning strategies impact on achievement is via gaining confidence that the student knows what to do when he or she does not know what to do. Such confidence can help students to engage in the process of learning, to restate the problem to identify what they know and do not know, to try different strategies, to look for patterns,

TABLE 6.2 Various meta-cognitive strategies and their effect sizes (Lavery, 2008)

STRATEGY	DEFINITION	EXAMPLE	NO. OF EFFECTS	ES
Organizing and transforming	Overt or covert rearrangement of instructional materials to improve learning	Making an outline before writing a paper	89	0.85
Self-consequences	Student arrangement or imagination of rewards or punishment for success or failure	Putting off pleasurable events until work is completed	75	0.70
Self-instruction	Self-verbalizing the steps to complete a given task	Verbalizing steps in solving a mathematics problem	124	0.62
Self-evaluation	Setting standards and using them for self-judgement	Checking work before handing it in to a teacher	156	0.62
Help-seeking	Efforts to seek help from either a peer, a teacher, or another adult	Using a study partner	62	0.60
Keeping records	Recording of information related to study tasks	Taking class notes	46	0.59
Rehearsing and memorizing	Memorization of material by overt or covert strategies	Writing a maths formula down until it is remembered	99	0.57
Goal-setting/planning	Setting of educational goals or planning sub-goals and planning for sequencing, timing, and completing activities related to those goals	Making lists to accomplish during studying	130	0.49
Reviewing records	Efforts to re-read notes, tests, or textbooks to prepare for class or further testing	Reviewing class textbook before going to lecture	131	0.49

TABLE 6.2 Continued

STRATEGY	DEFINITION	EXAMPLE	NO. OF EFFECTS	ES
Self-monitoring	Observing and tracking one's own performance and outcomes, often recording them	Keeping records study output	154	0.45
Task strategies	Analysing tasks and identifying specific, advantageous methods for learning	Creating mnemonics to remember facts	154	0.45
Imagery	Creating or recalling vivid mental images to assist learning	Imagining the consequences of failing to study	6	0.44
Time management	Estimating and budgeting use of time	Scheduling daily studying and homework time	8	0.44
Environmental restructuring	Efforts to select or arrange the physical setting to make learning easier	Studying in a secluded place	4	0.22

to build resilience to not knowing, and to use success in learning to reinforce their 'ownership' of learning.

Backward design

VISIBLE LEARNING – CHECKLIST FOR DURING THE LESSON: LEARNING

30. Teachers use principles from 'backward design' – moving from the outcomes (success criteria) back to the learning intentions, then to the activities and resources needed to attain the success criteria.

One of the best ways in which to maximize learning is to use the notion of 'backward design' (Wiggins & McTighe, 2005). Knowing our intentions and what success of a lesson should look like before we start to plan is the essence of such backward thinking. Such knowing also allows us to improvise and change during the process of teaching, while remaining reluctant to change the notions of success.

This means that the focus of decision-making is more about developing the strategies of learning to achieve the success targets, and less about implementing a particular teaching method (such as cooperative learning, or reciprocal teaching). During a lesson, the teacher needs to be able to react to where the students are as they progress from what they know (their prior learning) towards their desired learning (successfully achieving the intended learning of the lesson). This facility to change and continually innovate is what adaptive expertise is about – particularly among teachers and more and more among students as they develop their self-regulation skills.

Sometimes, students have to 'un-learn', or 'go backwards', before they can go forward. Especially by the end of elementary school, students have developed some system of study – whether that involves an Internet search, doing the maths and being satisfied when they have any answer and not so concerned by whether it is the right answer or if they have used the best strategy, learning to memorize or use mnemonics when necessary, or just hoping like crazy that the questions will not be too hard. Not all study methods are equally helpful. Those students that engage in worthwhile practice tend to do so in an environment that is unlikely to contain distractions, more often check and monitor their progress, and have a sense of the quality of their work. These methods often need to be taught – especially to those who may struggle to gain the surface knowledge and then various strategies to have this level of regulation when working alone.

Learning requires two major skills

VISIBLE LEARNING – CHECKLIST FOR DURING THE LESSON: LEARNING

31. All students are taught how to practise deliberately and how to concentrate.

Deliberate practice

Sometimes, learning is not fun. Instead, it is just hard work; it is just deliberate practice; it is simply doing some things many times over. There is a long history of this idea: Bryan and Harter (1898) claimed that it took about ten years to become an expert; Simon and Chase (1973) argued that chess masters needed to acquire some 50,000 chunks or patterns to have a chance of becoming experts. Malcolm Gladwell (2008) has made this point in the popular press – that it typically requires 10,000+ hours of practice to lead to expertise. He presents cases of people whose success we often attribute to trading on high ability (Bill Gates, The Beatles, Michael Jordan) as having spent an inordinate number of hours practising and learning before their ability became known to the rest of us. What these people did, he argued, was participate in deliberate practice: 'Practise, practise, and practise.' Yes, it was practice in many different aspects of the task, and this too is important. It is not repetitive skill and drill, but practice that leads to mastery. A major role of schools is to teach students the value of deliberate practice, such that students can see how practice leads to competence.

I have coached cricket for many years and know how many hours it takes to learn a particular batting stroke or bowling skill. To learn the square cut requires working with the bowling machine, or in the nets, for hours, concentrating in some sessions on footwork, in others on head stillness or follow-through, learning the downward motion of the bat with full extension of the arms, watching yourself via video and self-talking through these sessions, and learning when to play it (to the short-pitched ball wide on the off-side off the back foot to a faster bowler). During these sessions, I am not a score-keeper, judge, or test administrator; instead, I constantly monitor the batsman's decisions, movements, and reactions, and reflect back what worked, when it worked, and what to practise next. In this case, the effects of the decisions are obvious to the student and the test of learning is execution of this shot in a match (in which I am but a spectator on the sidelines). It is the choice of practice tasks; it is the variation in developing the skills; it is repeating again and again – plus providing rapid formative feedback to ensure that the student's mind is in charge of the decisions of the body to execute the right stroke on the right occasion.

Consider another example: the way in which many video games work. The intention of the game is transparent and what success means is also clear – although success is defined more in terms of many specific and individual actions during the playing and not only reaching 'the end'. For example, in playing *Super Mario Bros*, many players would not know for some time what the end of the game looked like (it took me a three-week holiday repeatedly playing this game even to work out that there *was* an end to the game). There is constant feedback (about success and failure) and constant challenge; indeed, feedback and challenge are the hallmarks of most video games. The aim for the player is to master the steps in the game, to get past their previous blockage, and to continue to be rewarded by the feedback of success and about the failures. Why do students routinely make different choices when their goal is improved performance rather than when their goal is pleasing the nearest adult?

We can learn so much from this in our classrooms. Students thrive on formative feedback during the lesson; they do not want to be blocked by lack of feedback (this is boredom-inducing, or 'turn off to the lesson' time), and they do not want to wait until the end of the lesson to know that they are on the right track. Both cricket and video games involve students desiring to master the skills, and then being able to perform them in a more controlled manner. Both mastery and performance are involved, and thus it is important to choose tasks that invite students to engage in deliberate practice, being transparent about the end value of the practice, and providing much formative feedback to enhance the impact of the practice. Some students are prepared to invest a lot in mastering process – that is, they like learning, playing the game, and may be less interested in the outcomes. Others are less likely to invest in learning unless they know what the product or outcome is before they start.

Many are more driven by the outcomes and thus can spend much time ensuring that the product or performance is well done – such as producing beautiful booklets, pretty posters, or magnificent models. This is what many motivation theorists refer to as 'performance motivation', and this is different from being motivated by the desire to master the processes leading to the product. Students motivated by the desire to master the processes invest more in strategies to enhance the processes, and students motivated by the performance invest in the strategies to enhance the product. Some just want to finish regardless of how they get there. Take mathematics, for example: some students wish to complete the exercises regardless of whether they are right or not – regardless of whether they have confidence in the processes that lead to their answers. Sometimes, giving these students the answer can make them learn to invest in the processes more. The name of the game is to develop mastery to perform thus, and less to perform hoping to then master.

The key for understanding the processes of learning (or self-regulation) is that it is taught, such that the student learns to monitor, control, or regulate their own learning (that is, to know when and how to execute the cut shot). It involves learning when to apply a strategy, how to apply that strategy, and evaluating how effective the strategy has been for improving learning. It requires self-observation, self-judgement, and self-reaction. It requires teaching how to evaluate the consequences of actions (for example, learning what to do next, learning to know you are correct, and applying efficient and effective strategies), having a degree of control over resources, and becoming more efficient in learning (such as reducing distractions). It requires teachers allowing, as well as developing, students' mastery self-talk, allowing them to make mistakes, and to esteem success in understanding and mastering the learning processes, and giving them some control over their learning. It requires deliberate investment of effort to learn, develop, and practise the skills of knowing how to learn, as well as being aware of the need for deliberate practice. It requires teaching students that certain things are worth learning, and how to discern what is and what is not worth learning. It also, of course, means knowing what the learning intentions are and what success looks like. These are the very proficiencies that we ask of teachers when planning and conducting a lesson, and this is why the notion of self-regulation is similar to 'students becoming their own teachers'.

Self regulation relates to developing *intentions* to make decisions about learning strategies, awareness of how to evaluate the *effectiveness* of these strategies to attain success in learning, and *consistency* in choosing the best learning strategies across tasks and content areas. Early in the learning of a new topic, novices often have limited strategies available; hence the need to teach them various strategies. We may need to teach students at this early phase various learning strategies, such that they have a larger repertoire from which to choose; in too many cases, novices may have some strategies that they continue to apply, but which may lead to a failure to learn (because they have few other strategies on which to fall back).

As teachers, we need to diagnose the nature of the strategies that students are using, and ensure that they are working to inspire confidence in deliberately practising the skills involved in the task, as well as ensuring that they are optimal to attaining the success criteria. It may mean reducing the cognitive load to allow the student the mental space to explore using strategies (for example, giving students the answer so that they can concentrate on the process, or providing worked examples), providing teaching on content and different strategies, ensuring optimal opportunities for deliberate practice, and demanding and valuing effort (Ornstein et al., 2010: 46).

It may be overstating the case, but it is critical to note that deliberate practice is different from mere practice. Deliberate practice requires concentration, and someone (either the student, or a teacher, or a coach) monitoring and providing feedback during the practice. The task or activity is typically outside the realm of current performance, invokes a challenge for the student, and it greatly helps if the student both is aware of the purpose for the practice and has a vision of what success looks like.

Concentration or persistence

To engage in such deliberate practice requires many skills – and one often underestimated is the proficiency to concentrate, or *persistence*. 'Persistence' refers to concentration or sustained attention at a task, even in the presence of internal and external distractions (Andersson & Bergman, 2011). We concentrate in different ways, but for novices it is often imperative that there are minimal distractions. This does not mean quiet rooms, no background ambience, and solitude; it does mean deliberate attempts to focus on the task – which deliberateness is the key, because rarely do most of us (particularly novices to the task) concentrate spontaneously. Learning is not as spontaneous as many would wish.

It is via deliberate practice and concentration that learning is fostered – and it is more the quality than quantity of study time that is critical. Plant, Ericsson, Hill, and Asberg (2005) have shown that students with higher achievement scores can attain the same or better grades with less study time. They note that most practice while 'playing the game' (such as golf, cricket, history), particularly with friends, is far less effective in improving the performance than coached or solitary deliberate practice. More experience in chess, for example, 'does not reliably improve chess performance once the effects of solitary practice are accounted for' (p. 112). It is not the amount of practice, but the amount of deliberate effort to improve performance that matters. The optimal combination of deliberate practice and concentration occurs when learners are given tasks that are initially outside their current realm of dependable performance, but which:

> can be mastered within hours of practice by concentrating on critical aspects and by gradually refining performance through repetitions after feedback. Hence, the requirement for *concentration* sets deliberate practice apart from both mindless, routine performance, and playful engagement.
>
> (Ericsson, 2006: 694; italics in original)

It helps when teachers and students actively seek such challenging tasks:

> Deliberate practice activities need to be set at an appropriate, challenging level of difficulty, and enable successive refinement by allowing for repetition, giving room to

make and correct errors, and providing informative feedback to the learner. . . . Given that deliberate practice requires students to stretch themselves to a higher level of performance, it requires full concentration and is effortful to maintain for extended periods. Students do not engage in deliberate practice because it is inherently enjoyable, but because it helps them improve their performance.

(van Gog, Ericsson, Rikers, & Paas, 2005: 75)

How to see the learning through the eyes of the students

VISIBLE LEARNING – CHECKLIST FOR DURING THE LESSON: LEARNING

32. Processes are in place for teachers to see learning through the eyes of students.

Nuthall (2007) spent many years listening in classrooms. He argued that there are three worlds of the classroom: the *public world* that the teachers see and manage; the *semiprivate world* of ongoing peer relationships; and the *private world* of the student's own mind. About 70 per cent of what happens between students is not seen or known by the teacher. This must surely give us pause for thought about the usefulness of teacher reflection on what they *think* happened, and the value of professional learning circles that retrospectively confirm what teachers saw. Why contemplate only the 30 per cent that was seen? We need to pay much more attention to evidence about the effect that we have on students, and make adjustments to our thinking, teaching, expectations, and actions in light of this evidence. Such evidence, from multiple sources, needs to be the source of our reflection and professional critique.

There is no doubt that classrooms can be complex, seemingly chaotic and confusing, and difficult to monitor. A key skill is the development of 'situation awareness' (called 'with-it-ness' in Chapter 5), because this is a key feature of many experts (Wickens, 2002). Rather than simplify the classroom (quiet rows, teacher talking), teachers need to build competencies in making meaning, seeing patterns, anticipating and making decisions, and monitoring so that they can adjust on the fly. Part of the skill in developing this awareness is learning what not to attend to, and thus developing the skills of scanning, identifying opportunities and barriers to learning, categorizing and evaluating student behaviour, and interpreting the situation relative to the instructional decisions and not to classroom management issues.

Such situation awareness requires listening to student questions, and using assessment to provide teachers with information of what is working with whom and when it is working. It helps to have others in the classroom watching students learning and helping teachers to recognize what they cannot see. It helps to make the students fully aware of the learning intentions and success criteria, of the value of deliberate practice, and of what to do when they do not know what to do.

What becomes obvious when observing classrooms is the number of students who are indifferent about the teaching that is occurring – and who thus spend a large proportion of time in a state of ambivalence. These students are not resistors, or naughty; they simply are not engaged in the learning process. In one sense, learning to be ambivalent is a necessary skill for coping with the buzzing and busy nature of our world – with the dominance of teacher talk and the limited interactions that can occur in too many classrooms; in another sense, too much ambivalence can lead to being 'left behind' and to the student adopting a form of learned helplessness ('Just tell me what to do and I will do it'). These students adopt a position that is likely to gain favour ('at least they are not naughty') with those to whom they are accountable, and thus avoid having to cognitively decide on the pros and cons of analysing alternative avenues of action, interpreting complex patterns of information, or making difficult trade-offs. Instead, these students turn off while *looking* engaged. The spark of learning is beginning to be snuffed.

There are many studies of engagement that indicate the general nature of student behaviour in class. For example, the Pipeline Project surveyed 2,686 students in 230 classes over two years (Angus et al., 2009). There were four main groups:

- students behaving productively (60 per cent);
- students who were disengaged, but not aggressive or non-compliant (20 per cent);
- students who were uncooperative, and often aggressive and non-compliant (12 per cent); and
- students who were low-level disruptive with a mix of disruptive behaviour (8 per cent).

What is fascinating is that the uncooperative had the lowest achievement gains over the year, but their gains were not so different from those of the disengaged. The disengaged were students who, for example, found their schoolwork uninteresting, were inclined to give up on challenging tasks, looked for distractions, failed to prepare for lessons, and opted out of class activities. These ambivalent students should be a focus of teachers' attention – and are perhaps the easiest to win back.

Conclusions

If learning were easy, then schooling would be a walkover. This chapter has shown that understanding how each student learns is not straightforward. There are many facets of learning and the argument is that there are four major ways of thinking about how students learn: their capabilities to think (Paiget's model was used to illustrate these capabilities); their capacity to think at various levels (from learning ideas, to relating and extending ideas); their catalyst for learning (from seeing a gap between where they are currently and some target, and then using strategies to reduce the gap); and their competence as they progress through their learning, from novice, through capable, to proficient. For each aspect of learning, teachers cannot assume that students have appropriate strategies and there is a major need to increase the amount of time spent teaching strategies. At present, strategy teaching is notable by its absence.

Struggling students are in most need for strategy teaching, but even able students can have inefficient strategies or become overly dependent on a few strategies, which can have too much dependence on teacher instructions and feedback. We all need to develop sufficient strategies over which we have some control in terms of when and how to use them. Such self-regulation is a major aim of learning.

Given the multiplicity of strategies of learning, and the importance of knowing when to invoke them during the learning process, then there is much pressure on teachers to understand the similarities and allow for the differences within the class. This leads to the importance of differentiated teaching – but without jumping too quickly to 'grouping' students in homogenous groups. The aim is not to retain the students in the phase of learning, but to move them '+1' beyond this current phase. So often, this can be aided by students seeing the different ways in which their peers engage in learning, sharing understandings and misunderstandings, recognizing that challenge is common to the bright and struggling, and seeing that they can work through their learning together.

A strong theme is the necessity for adaptivity – that is, adapting to the challenge, to the environment, to other students, and knowing what to do when you do not know what to do. It also involves being able to persist, concentrate, engage in multiple ways of knowing, interact, and practise. At all times, however, teachers and students must not lose sight of the goals or success criteria of the lesson. This is why it is valuable to use 'backward design', which involves starting with an understanding of the end and then asks how to move students from where they are at present to this end point.

There are multiple strategies of learning, and there is much known about more and less effective strategies. Goal-setting, self-monitoring, concentration, and deliberate practice are among the most effective strategies. These apply to the teacher as they do to the student – and they can be taught. It may seem old-fashioned to overemphasize providing multiple opportunities to learn, for deliberate practice, and for concentration – but they remain among the most powerful strategies for learning. All students can be taught to practise and concentrate, provided that the notions of success are transparent, that there is much formative feedback to move forward, and that there is modification and re-teaching provided during this practice. It is not practice for the sake of practice, but practice to help teachers and students to know how to refine, re-teach, and rehearse the skills and understandings.

To accomplish these difficult notions of 'how students learn' requires teachers to see learning though the eyes of students. We need more than mere reflection of what we saw, given that most of what happens in a classroom is not seen or heard by teachers. We need many methods of assessment, to listen to student dialogue and questioning, help from others observing how students learn in our class, and to ensure that students also are providing us with evidence of how they are thinking and learning.

Exercises

1. Interview five teachers about what they understand in terms of how 'we learn'. How do we as teachers learn? How do students learn? How do these beliefs line up with the arguments about 'how we learn' outlined in this chapter? If necessary, devise a learning plan with these teachers about how to enhance their knowledge about learning strategies.

2. Consider a lesson that you have planned. How does it allow for students at different levels of thinking (as per Piaget's stages), different levels of proficiency (as per novice, capable, proficient), and different levels of complexity (surface and deep)?

3. If you were to group students in your class, how would you do this so that students can move '+1' in their levels of learning from where they started? What evidence would you collect to allow you to know that they are, indeed, moving forward in these groups?

4. What level of attention and debate is provided in your school (or class, or teacher education program) on the following activities? When you have completed this task, check the impact that each has, on average, according to Appendix D in this book.

INFLUENCE	IMPACT		
Ability grouping/tracking	High	Medium	Low
Computer-assisted instruction	High	Medium	Low
Decreasing disruptive behaviour	High	Medium	Low
Extra-curricular programs	High	Medium	Low
Home-school programs	High	Medium	Low
Homework	High	Medium	Low
How to accelerate learning	High	Medium	Low
How to better teach meta-cognitive strategies	High	Medium	Low
How to develop high expectations for each student	High	Medium	Low
How to develop high expectations for each teacher	High	Medium	Low
How to provide better feedback	High	Medium	Low
Individualized instruction	High	Medium	Low
Influence of home environment	High	Medium	Low
Enquiry-based teaching	High	Medium	Low
Integrated curricular programs	High	Medium	Low
Male and female achievement differences	High	Medium	Low
Open vs traditional learning spaces	High	Medium	Low
Peer influences on achievement	High	Medium	Low
Providing formative evaluation to teachers	High	Medium	Low
Reducing class size	High	Medium	Low
School finances	High	Medium	Low
Student control over learning	High	Medium	Low
Teacher–student relationships	High	Medium	Low
Teaching learning strategies	High	Medium	Low
Teaching study skills	High	Medium	Low
Teaching test-taking and coaching	High	Medium	Low
Ways to stop labelling students	High	Medium	Low

5. Have a colleague observe your class. Have this colleague sit in the room, take a script of everything that you say and do, and, most critically, choose two students and note all that they do, react to, talk about (as far as your colleague can hear). At the end, print out the script and together identify each occasion on which the students responded and reacted – that is, what engaged them, what led them to move forward, and so on. Indicate instances in which you made adaptive decisions in light of evidence about how students were or were not learning (see also Exercise 1 in Chapter 8).

6. Search the Internet for advice on implementing the 'jigsaw' classroom. Plan with a colleague a lesson to trial this method. Before implementing it, address the following questions.

   a. How will I deal with the dominant student/the slower student/the bored student/ the overly competitive student?

   b. What evidence will I accept that the method is or is not having a positive impact on students' efficiency or effectiveness in attaining the success criteria of the lesson?

7

The flow of the lesson: the place of feedback

Feedback is among the most common features of successful teaching and learning. But there is an enigma: while feedback is among the most powerful moderators of learning, its effects are among the most variable. I have spent many years pondering this problem and have been building a model of feedback that helps to explain how to take full benefits from feedback in the classroom.

The best way in which to understand feedback is to consider Sadler's (1989) notion of the 'gap': feedback aims to reduces the gap between where the student 'is' and where he or she is 'meant to be' – that is, between prior or current achievement and the success criteria. To make feedback effective, therefore, teachers must have a good understanding of where the students are, and where they are meant to be – and the more transparent they make this status for the students, the more students can help to get themselves from the points at which they are to the success points, and thus enjoy the fruits of feedback. Feedback serves various purposes in reducing this gap: it can provide cues that capture a person's attention and helps him or her to focus on succeeding with the task; it can direct attention towards the processes needed to accomplish the task; it can provide information about ideas that have been misunderstood; and it can be motivational so that students invest more effort or skill in the task (see Hattie & Timperley, 2006).

Feedback can be provided in many ways: through affective processes, increased effort, motivation, or engagement; by providing students with different cognitive processes, restructuring understandings, confirming to the student that he or she is correct or incorrect, indicating that more information is available or needed, pointing to directions that the students might pursue, and indicating alternative strategies with which to understand particular information. A key consideration is that feedback typically comes second – after instruction – and thus its effectiveness is limited if it is provided in a vacuum.

An important notion is that feedback thrives on error, but error should not be considered the privilege of lower-achieving students. All students (as all teachers) do not always succeed first time, nor do they always know what to do next, and nor do they always attain perfection. This is not a deficit, or deficit thinking, or concentrating on the negative; rather, it is the opposite in that acknowledging errors allows for opportunities. Error is the difference between what we know and can do, and what we aim to know and do – and this applies to all (struggling and talented; students and teachers). Knowing this error is fundamental to moving towards success. This is the purpose of feedback.

Further, the focus in this chapter is on using evidence from students about what they do, say, make, or write to then infer what they understand, know, feel, or think (Griffin, 2007). Working from observables is the basis of the formative evaluation of learning. Too often, teachers work from theories or inferences about what students do that are not always open to change in light of what students *actually* do. Instead, teachers need first to concentrate on what students do, say, make, or write, and modify their theories about students in light of these observations (or this evidence). Feedback from such evaluation is what teachers need to seek so that they can then modify their instruction. This is assessment as feedback for teachers, providing rapid formative feedback, or assessment as teaching.

The evidence about its effectiveness is documented in *Visible Learning*. In brief, the average effect size is 0.79, which is twice the average effect of all other schooling effects. This places feedback in the top ten influences on achievement, although there is considerable variability – but how to account for this variability? My argument is that feedback works at four levels and addresses three questions.

The three feedback questions

VISIBLE LEARNING – CHECKLIST FOR DURING THE LESSON: FEEDBACK

33. Teachers are aware of, and aim to provide feedback relative to, the three important feedback questions: 'Where am I going?'; 'How am I going there?'; and 'Where to next?'

	Levels	Major questions		Three feedback questions
1	Task	How well has the task been performed; is it correct or incorrect?		Where am I going? What are my goals?
2	Process	What are the strategies needed to perform the task; are there alternative strategies that can be used?		How am I going? What progress is being made towards the goal?
3	Self-regulation	What is the conditional knowledge and understanding needed to know what you are doing? Self-monitoring, directing the processes and tasks		Where to next? What activities need to be undertaken next to make better progress?
4	Self	Personal evaluation and affect about the learning		

FIGURE 7.1 The feedback levels and questions

Where am I going?

The first question relates to goals – that is: 'Where am I going?' This means that teachers need to know, and communicate to students, the goals of the lesson – hence the importance of learning intentions and success criteria. What seems surprising is that many students cannot articulate the goals of the lesson: at best, their goals are performance-related:

'finish the task'; 'make it neat'; 'include as many resources as possible'. Rarely are the goals mastery-related: 'understand the content'; 'master the skill'. Part of this is that so many lessons are about 'the facts', teachers talking, and 'covering the curriculum', which begs for performance goals, because students have little notion of what mastery looks likes.

Sandra Hastie (2011) interviewed middle-school students, who certainly knew about setting mastery goals in their sport and social lives (see Chapter 4). But most of their academic goals related more to completion of work, being on time, and trying harder than to the quality of the academic outcomes. She taught the teachers how to set mastery goals and communicate these to the students, and then have students monitor their goals and their progress towards these goals each day – and the teachers were requested to monitor their success in communicating their goals to the students.

Samantha Smith (2009) was the 'dean of success' in her high school. She plotted all 1,000+ students' achievement over the previous five years in reading and maths. She used this achievement data to project the expected number of credits and the grade point average (GPA) for each student at the end of the current year. She then gave these to teachers and asked them to read them, to see if they agreed, and to consider whether they would be willing to set slightly higher targets than projected. About half of the teachers in the school agreed to these tasks and half refused ('I am not responsible for students reaching targets; they need to come to class prepared, do their homework, and take responsibility'). At the end of the year, the teachers in the first group greatly outperformed the resistors. Targets can make a difference.

As was argued in Chapter 4, there are two further elements of goals: challenge and commitment. Challenging goals relate to feedback in three major ways.

1. They inform individuals about the level of performance desired, meaning that these individuals can then track their performance towards these targets.

2. Feedback allows students (and/or their teachers) to set further appropriately challenging goals as the previous ones are attained, thus establishing the conditions for ongoing learning. This requires a reasonable understanding of what progress looks like in a subject and this is probably the most critical source of content knowledge required of teachers.

3. If there is no challenge, the feedback is probably of little or any value: if students already know the material or find it too easy, then seeking or providing feedback will have little effect. Indeed, providing feedback of success not only has little or no effect, but it may also be costly as students wait for the feedback, do not go on to new more challenging tasks, and become dependent on the presence of feedback, or when tasks are too easy and they do not spend more time on more challenging activities (see Hays, Kornell, & Bjork, 2010).

The key components of the first feedback question 'Where am I going?' relates to learning intentions, goals and targets, clarity, challenge, and commitment; the key is not only the teacher creating and knowing these, but also students being fully conversant with them. Students who speak in terms of and understand these notions are students who have made great headway in 'regulation of their own learning', and students who are more likely to seek feedback.

How am I going there?

The second question, 'How am I going there?', highlights the notions of progress feedback, or feedback relative to the starting or finishing point, and is often expressed in relation to some expected standard, to prior performance, or to success or failure on a specific part of the task. This is where it is most valuable to provide rapid formative feedback – particularly relative to the criteria of success rather than comparative to where other students are. Wiliam and colleagues (Wiliam & Thompson, 2008; Wiliam, Lee, Harrison, & Black, 2004; Black, Lee, Marshall, & Wiliam, 2003) argued that there are five broad strategies that teachers can use in this phase to make learning more efficient and effective relative to 'How am I going there?': clarifying and sharing learning intentions and criteria for success; engineering effective classroom discussions, questions, and learning tasks; providing feedback that moves learners forward; encouraging students to see themselves as the owners of their own learning; and activating students as instructional resources for one another.

Where to next?

The third question is more consequential: 'Where to next?' Such feedback can assist in choosing the next most appropriate challenges, and can lead to developing more self-regulation over the learning process, and greater fluency and automaticity, to learning different strategies and processes to work on the tasks, to deeper understanding, and to more information about what is and what is not understood. This is the question of most interest to students and the aim is to not only provide them with the answer to 'Where to next?', but also to teach them to have their own answers to this question.

The four feedback levels

VISIBLE LEARNING – CHECKLIST FOR DURING THE LESSON: FEEDBACK

34. Teachers are aware of, and aim to provide feedback relative to, the three important levels of feedback: task; process; and self-regulation.

The three feedback questions work at four levels of feedback – and the four levels correspond to phases of learning: from novice, through proficient, to competent.

1. Task and product level

Feedback at the task and product level is powerful if it is more information-focused (for example, correct or incorrect), leads to acquiring more or different information, and builds more surface knowledge. This type of feedback is most common in classrooms and most students see feedback in these terms. It is often termed 'corrective feedback', or 'knowledge of results', and is commonly given in classrooms through teacher questions (most of which are at this information level); it is most provided in comments on assignments; it is often specific and not generalizable; it is more often the nature of feedback given to a whole class; and it can be powerful particularly when the learner is a novice (Heubusch & Lloyd, 1998). Examples include indicating correct or incorrect responses, needing more or different responses, providing more or different information relevant to the task, and building more task knowledge. Such task feedback is critical and serves as a pedestal on which processing (level 2) and self-regulation (level 3) can be effectively built.

An example of such feedback might be as follows.

> . . . Your learning goal was to structure your account in such a way that the first thing that you wrote was the first thing that you did. Then, you were to write about the other things that you did in the same order that they happened.
>
> You've written the first thing first, but after that it becomes muddled. You need to go through what you've written, number the order in which things happened, and rewrite them in that order.

2. Process level

The second level is feedback aimed at the processes used to create the product or to complete the task. Such feedback can lead to providing alternative processing, reducing cognitive load, helping to develop learning strategies and error detection, cueing to seek a more effective information search, recognizing relationships between ideas, and employing task strategies. Examples include helping to provide connections between ideas, providing strategies for identifying errors, learning how to explicitly learn from mistakes, and providing cues about different strategies or errors. Feedback at this process level appears to be more effective for enhancing deeper learning than it is at the task level, and there can be a powerful interactive effect between feedback aimed at improving the strategies and processes, and feedback aimed at the more surface task information. The latter can assist in improving task confidence and self-efficacy, which in turn provides resources for more effective and innovative information and strategy searching. Chan (2006) induced a failure situation and then found that feedback was more likely to enhance self-efficacy when it was formative rather than summative, and self-referenced rather than comparative to other peers' feedback.

Examples of feedback at this level might be as follows.

> . . . You're stuck on this word and you've looked at me instead of tried to work it out. Can you work out why you might have got it wrong – and can you then try a different strategy?
>
> . . . You're asked to compare these ideas. For example, you could try to see how they are similar, how they are different . . . How do they relate together?

3. Self-regulation or conditional level

The third level is more focused at the self-regulation level, or on the student's monitoring of their own learning processes. Feedback at this level can enhance students' skills in self-evaluation, provide greater confidence to engage further with the task, assist in the student seeking and accepting feedback, and enhance the willingness to invest effort into seeking and dealing with feedback information. Examples include helping students to identify feedback themselves and how to self-evaluate, providing opportunities and awareness of the importance of deliberate practice and effort, and developing confidence to pursue the learning. When students can monitor and self-regulate their learning, they can use feedback more effectively to reduce discrepancies between where they are in their learning and the desired outcomes or successes of their learning. Such feedback – usually in the form of reflective or probing questions – can guide the learner on 'when', 'where', and 'why' in selecting or employing task and process-level knowledge and strategies.

Examples of such feedback might be as follows.

> . . . I'm impressed by how you went back to the beginning of the sentence when you became stuck on this word – but, in this case, it didn't help. What else could you do? When you decide on what it means, I want you to tell me how confident you are and why.
>
> . . . You checked your answer with the resource book [Self-help] and found that you'd got it wrong. Have you got any idea(s) why you got it wrong? [Error detection] What strategy did you use? Can you think of another strategy to try and how else might you work out if you're right?

4. Self level

> **VISIBLE LEARNING – CHECKLIST FOR DURING THE LESSON: FEEDBACK**
>
> 35. Teachers are aware of the importance of praise, but do not mix praise with feedback information.

The fourth level is feedback directed to the 'self' (for example, 'You're a great student', or 'Well done') and is commonly subsumed under the notion of 'praise'. Praise is often used to comfort and support, is ever-present in many classrooms, and is welcomed and expected by students – but it so often directs attention away from the task, processes, or self-regulation. The major message is to provide praise, but not to give it in such a way that it dilutes the power of feedback: keep *praise* and *feedback* about the learning separate.

Praise usually contains little task-related information and is rarely converted into more engagement, commitment to the learning goals, enhanced self-efficacy, or understanding about the task. By incorporating praise with other forms of feedback, the learning information is diluted; praise includes little information about performance on the task and praise provides little help in answering the three feedback questions. Wilkinson (1980) found a low effect size for praise ($d = 0.12$), as did Kluger and deNisi (1996; 0.09), and providing feedback with no praise compared to feedback with praise has a greater effect on achievement (0.34).

There is now increasing evidence for this dilution effect of praise on learning. Kessels, Warner, Holle, & Hannover (2008) provided students with feedback with and without praise; praise led to lower engagement and effort. Kamins and Dweck (1999) compared the effects of praising a person as a whole (for example, 'You're a clever girl') with the effect of praising a person's efforts ('You're excellent in putting in the effort'). Both led to zero or negative effects on achievement. The effects of praise are particularly negative not when students succeed, but when they begin to fail or not to understand the lesson. Hyland and Hyland (2006) noted that almost half of teachers' feedback was praise, and that premature and gratuitous praise confused students and discouraged revisions. Most often, teachers used praise to mitigate critical comments, which indeed diluted the positive effect of such comments (Hyland & Hyland, 2001). Perhaps the most deleterious effect of praise is that it supports learned helplessness: students come to depend on the presence of praise to be involved in their schoolwork. At best, praising effort has a neutral or no effect when students are successful, but is likely to be negative when students are not successful, because this leads to a more 'helpless or hopeless' reaction (Skipper & Douglas, 2011).

This lack of support for praise does not mean that we should be horrible to the students; this is one of the clearest negative influences. Students need to feel that they 'belong' in learning, that there is a high level of trust both between teacher and student and with their peers, and feel that their work is appropriately esteemed (when earned). Indeed, students see praise as important for their success in school and the presence of praise is related to learning outcomes. The message is that for *feedback* to be effective in the act of learning, praise dissipates the message. Praise the students and make them feel welcomed to your class and worthwhile as learners, but if you wish to make a major difference to learning, leave praise out of feedback about learning.

Overall comment on the four levels

The art of effective teaching is to provide the right form of feedback at, or just above, the level at which the student is working – with one exception: do not mix praise into the feedback prompt, because this dilutes the effect! When feedback draws attention to the self, students try to avoid the risks involved in tackling a challenging assignment – particularly if they have a high fear of failure (and thus aim to minimize the risk to the self). Thus, ideally, teaching and learning need to move from the task towards the processes or understandings necessary to learn the task, and then to regulation about continuing beyond the task to more challenging tasks and goals – that is: from 'What do I know and what can I do?', to 'What do I not know and what can I not do?', to 'What can I teach others (and myself) about what I know and can do?' This process results in higher confidence and greater investment of effort, and the aim of providing feedback is to assist students through this process. This flow typically occurs as the student gains greater fluency, efficiency, and mastery. The first three feedback levels form a progression; the hypothesis is that it is optimal to provide appropriate feedback at or one level above that at which the student is currently functioning, and to clearly distinguish between feedback at the first three and the fourth (self) levels.

Frequency of feedback

VISIBLE LEARNING – CHECKLIST FOR DURING THE LESSON: FEEDBACK

36. Teachers provide feedback appropriate to the point at which students are in their learning, and seek evidence that this feedback is appropriately received.

The aim is to provide feedback that is 'just in time', 'just for me', 'just for where I am in my learning process', and 'just what I need to help me move forward'. There is a need to be aware that such feedback can come from many sources (and that such feedback can be wrong!). It may be misleading merely to increase the amount of feedback, or to concentrate on the giving as opposed to the receiving of feedback.

There has been much evidence about the frequency of feedback and most of it is not that informative – because there are more important factors than merely increasing the amount of feedback, or whether it is immediate or delayed. For example, Carless (2006) has shown that most feedback given by teachers is to the whole class and most of this is not received by any student – because no single student believes that it pertains to him or her! Further, feedback can come from many sources: as will be shown below, most feedback comes from peers, and sometimes this exceeds the amount of feedback received from teachers and other sources (such as books or the Internet). Most critically, wherever the feedback comes from, it is often poorly received and hardly used in revision of work.

Teachers consider their feedback to be far more valuable than do the students, because so often the latter find the former's feedback confusing, non-reasoned, and not understandable. Worse, students often think that they have understood the teacher's feedback when they have not, and even when they do understand, claim to have difficulties in applying it to their learning (Goldstein, 2006; Nuthall, 2007). Higgins, Hartley, and Skelton (2001: 270) argued that 'many students are simply unable to understand feedback comments and interpret them correctly'. Much depends on their understanding of the feedback discourse, on whether the provider is perceived as powerful, fair, and trustworthy, and on the emotions (rejection, acceptance) associated with the context and level of investment.

There have been surprisingly few studies that have investigated the actual amount and nature of feedback given *and* received in classrooms. Teachers see feedback more in terms of how much they *give* than the more important consideration of how much feedback is *received* by students. Carless (2006) found that 70 per cent of teachers claimed that they provided detailed feedback that helped students to improve their next assignments – but only 45 per cent of students agreed with their teachers' claims. Further, Nuthall (2005) found that most feedback that students obtained in any day in classrooms was from other students – and that most of this feedback was incorrect.

In our work, I ask a neutral person to sit at the back of classrooms and type a transcript of everything that is said and done in a 40–60 minute lesson. This person also chooses two students close to where he or she is typing, and notes all that they say and do. Of course, it is not possible to get into these students' 'heads', but at the end of the lesson, the script is printed out, and the teacher and a person experienced in decoding lessons highlights each instance in which one of these students *received* feedback (from whomever, and about whatever).

The analyses of the transcripts so often shows that the typical lesson includes very few instances of feedback received – and that much of this is when the student looks across or checks with a peer. So many classrooms are dominated by teacher talk – giving instructions on what to do, conducting the question-and-answer recitation in which so many students do not engage, but are happy to sit and watch the action. This is not implying that no learning is happening, but the power of feedback is rarely operationalized during these soliloquies. Feedback comes into its own when students 'do not know', 'do not know how to choose the best strategies to tackle the work', 'do not know how to monitor their own learning', or 'do not know where to go next'.

In one recent analysis of 18 classes in a school noted for its major success in achievement, there was a feedback instance *given* for one of the two observed students every 25 minutes. The majority of feedback *given* to all students was task-related, and this pattern can be seen across two other studies that have used this breakdown (Table 7.1). The question is how to get the right proportions of the four levels, and 'right' refers to ensuring that the levels of feedback relate to where the students are in the progression from novice to competent. In these various classes (across the three studies), the feedback would be appropriate provided that the students were mostly at the novice or early learning phase. When we showed our distributions (and highlighted scripts) to the teachers and asked if this was appropriate, the claim was a definite 'no': their students were much more involved in processing and self-regulating. These data then served as baseline to change the nature of how feedback was provided in these schools.

Types of feedback

Disconfirmation can be more powerful than confirmation

Confirmation is related to feedback that confirms a student's preconceptions of hypotheses. *Disconfirmation* is related to feedback that corrects an erroneous idea or assumption, or

TABLE 7.1 Percentage of feedback given at the various feedback levels in three studies

	HATTIE & MASTERS (2011)	VAN DEN BERGH, ROSE, & BEIJAARD (2010)	GAN (2011)
Level	18 HS classes	32 teachers in middle school	235 peers
Task	59%	51%	70%
Process	25%	42%	25%
Regulation	2%	2%	1%
Self	14%	5%	4%

which provides information that goes against current expectations (see Nickerson, 1998). Students (and teachers) often seek confirmation evidence by, for example, seeking feedback that confirms their current beliefs or understandings, and disregard feedback that is contrary to their prior beliefs. When feedback is provided that disconfirms, then there can be greater change – provided that it is accepted.

These notions should not be confused with negative and positive feedback, because disconfirmation can be positive and confirmation negative. Feedback is most powerful when it addresses faulty interpretations and not a total lack of understanding (in which latter case re-teaching is often most effective). In this latter circumstance, feedback may even be threatening to the student:

> If the material studied is unfamiliar or abstruse, providing feedback should have little effect on criterion performance, since there is no way to relate the new information to what is already known.
>
> (Kulhavy, 1977: 220)

Disconfirmation feedback can improve retrieval performance (at the task level) when learners receive feedback on incorrect answers, but not when they receive feedback on correct answers (Kang, McDermott, & Roediger, 2007). In similar research, Peeck, van den Bosch, and Kreupeling (1985) found that feedback improved performance from 20 per cent to 56 per cent correct on initially incorrect answers, but made little difference for correct answers (88 per cent with no feedback and 89 per cent with feedback).

Errors need to be welcomed

Feedback is most effective when students do not have proficiency or mastery – and thus it thrives when there is error or incomplete knowing and understanding. (Often, there is little information value in providing task-level feedback when the student has mastered the content.) Errors invite opportunities. They should not be seen as embarrassments, signs of failure, or something to be avoided. They are exciting, because they indicate a tension between what we *now* know and what we *could* know; they are signs of opportunities to learn and they are to be embraced. William James (1897: 19), my favourite psychologist (after whom one of my dogs is named!), put errors into perspective:

> Our errors are surely not such awfully solemn things. In a world where we are so certain to incur them in spite of all our caution, a certain lightness of heart seems healthier than this excessive nervousness on their behalf.

This means that there needs to be a classroom climate in which there is minimum peer reactivity to not knowing or acknowledgement of errors, and in which there is low personal risk involved in responding publicly and failing (Alton-Lee & Nuthall, 1990). Too often, students respond only when they are fairly sure that they can respond correctly – which often indicates that they have already learned the answer to the question being asked. Heimbeck, Frese, Sonnentag, and Keith (2003) noted the paucity of research on errors, and they recommended that rather than being error-avoidant, error training that increases the exposure to errors in a safe environment can lead to higher performance. Such an environment requires high levels of self-regulation or safety (for example, explicit instruction that emphasizes the positive function of errors) for errors to be valuable, and it is necessary to deal primarily with errors as potentially avoidable deviations from goals. Michael Jordan claimed in a Nike advert that he:

> missed more than nine thousand shots in my career. I've lost almost three hundred games. Twenty-six times I've been trusted to take the game-winning shot and missed. I've failed over and over and over again in my life. And that is why I succeed.

Failure or learning from errors is critical also in the staffroom. A school needs to have a culture of no blame, a willingness to investigate what is not working (or what is not working with which students). Care and analysis is needed to correctly attribute failure to the right reasons; clearly, the one reason that is within our powers to fix is our own teaching and mindsets. It may well be that outside factors (the home, resources, etc.) can be major factors, but the mindset that teachers can positively change student outcomes is a powerful prerequisite to making such changes – and reducing the effects of these other factors (even though it may be well be that these factors are powerful). There are so many teachers who become most aware of what is not working and put in place strategies to redress this situation; these teachers have much more success than those who accept the external constraints. The mental toughness and resilience that underlies that 'you' can make a difference in the face of adversity is a common factor underlying success in sports, business, and in schools. Confidence that we can change is a powerful precursor to change. Similarly, we can fall prey to overconfidence – success can lead to us believing that we are better than we actually are – hence the need for working parties to study and explain success, the need to find ways in which we can get better than we are, how we may need to consider alternatives to make these greater differences, and the need not to become complacent when successful. We need to see how the future can undermine a winning formula. Celebrate success, but examine it. Scrums, working groups, walk-throughs, and checking the impact on all students can be part of evaluating (and esteeming) success, seeing where we can improve, investigating which students are not sharing the success, asking about the five things that are working well and the five that are not working so well, and ensuring that we do not become overconfident and miss opportunities. With failure, we often ask 'why?'; similarly, with success, we must ask 'why?'. Evaluation of processes, products, people, and programs needs to be an inherent part of all schools.

Feedback from assessment to teachers

There have been many recent moves toward assessment *for*, rather than an emphasis on assessment *of*, learning. An alternative is to consider 'assessment as feedback', and I have argued that this is very powerful when such assessment feedback is oriented towards the teacher and about which students are moving towards the success criteria, what they have/have not taught well, and the strengths and gaps of their teaching, and when it provides information about the three feedback questions (Hattie, 2009). As teachers derive feedback information from assessments that they set their students, there can then be important adjustments to how they teach, how they consider what success looks like, how they recognize students' strengths and gaps, and how they regard their own effects on students. The essence of such formative interpretations is providing teachers with feedback from assessments about how they need to modify their teaching, and providing students with feedback so that they can learn how to self-regulate and be motivated to engage in further learning. This is more effective than when assessment is aimed at the students, who typically can estimate their performance before completing the assessments and thus often receive minimal feedback from assessments. Teachers too often see assessment feedback as making statements about students and not about their teaching, and hence the benefits of feedback from such testing are often diluted.

In New Zealand, there has been much uptake by teachers and schools about formative interpretations. Most schools are aware of the distinction between formative and summative interpretations. One of the concerns that arose is to not see 'everything' in school as formative interpretations: there is a place for summative interpretations; some tests have little to no formative interpretations; and it was not necessary to justify some negative practices by calling them 'formative'. A group was asked to move beyond formative interpretations and the recommendation was to promote 'student assessment capabilities' (Absolum, Flockton, Hattie, Hipkins, & Reid, 2009). The fundamental premise is that all students should be educated in ways that develop their capability to assess their own learning. So often, the most important assessment decisions tend to be made by adults on behalf of students. Instead, the claim is that the primary function of assessment is to support learning by generating feedback that students can act upon in terms of where they are going, how they are going there, and where they might go next. Such assessment involves active student–teacher collaboration, and teachers who also demonstrate that they use assessment in their formative interpretations. The claim is that when students participate in the assessment of their own learning, they learn to recognize and understand main ideas, and to apply new learning in different ways and situations. Students who have developed their assessment capabilities are more able and motivated to access, interpret, and use information from quality assessments in ways that affirm or further their learning. This is formative interpretation in action.

> **VISIBLE LEARNING – CHECKLIST FOR DURING THE LESSON: FEEDBACK**
>
> 37. Teachers use multiple assessment methods to provide rapid formative interpretations to students and to make adjustments to their teaching to maximize learning.

Rapid formative assessment

The notion of rapid formative assessment is very powerful as a form of feedback. Yeh (2011) compared the cost-effectiveness of 22 approaches to learning and found rapid formative assessment to be the most cost-effective – compared to comprehensive school reform, cross-age tutoring, computer-assisted instruction, a longer school day, increases in teacher education, teacher experience, or teacher salaries, summer school, more rigorous maths classes, value–added teacher assessment, class size reduction, a 10 per cent increase in per pupil expenditure, full-day kindergarten, Head Start (preschool), high-standards exit exams, National Board for Professional Teaching Standards (NBPTS) certification, higher teacher licensure test scores, high-quality preschool, an additional school year, voucher programs, or charter schools. It emerged out of the work of the Black and Wiliam (1998), 'Inside the black box', and starts from the premise that assessment *for* learning is based on five key factors:

- students are actively involved in their own learning processes;
- effective feedback is provided to students;
- teaching activities are adapted in a response to assessment results;
- students are able to perform self-assessments; and
- the influence of assessment on students' motivation and self-esteem is recognized.

From this, Black and Wiliam (2009) derived five major strategies:

1. clarifying and sharing learning intentions and criteria for success;
2. engineering effective classroom discussions and other learning tasks that elicit evidence of student understanding;
3. providing feedback that moves learners forward;
4. activating students as instructional resources for one another; and
5. activating students as the owners of their own learning.

Dylan Wiliam and colleagues have demonstrated the value of formative assessment – that is, that assessment that can lead to feedback during the process of learning (Wiliam, 2011). This means much more than tests, and includes many forms of evidence:

> Practice in a classroom is formative to the extent that evidence about student achievement is elicited, interpreted, and used by teachers, learners, or their peers, to make decisions about the next steps in instruction that are likely to be better, or better founded, than the decisions they would have taken in the absence of the evidence that was elicited.
>
> (Black & Wiliam, 2009: 9)

The key is the focus on decisions that teachers and students make during the lesson, so most of all the aim is to inform teacher or student judgements about the key decisions: 'Should I relearn . . . Practice again . . . Move forward . . . To what?', and so on. In our own work, we have devised reports that help teachers and learners to appreciate which concepts they have mastered or not mastered, and where their strengths and gaps are, which students need additional input or time, which students are reaching the success criteria, and so on (Hattie and team, 2009).

But what Wiliam is most concerned with is feedback during the lesson – that is, short-cycle formative assessments, or what he terms 'rapid formative assessment' (assessments conducted between two and five times per week). For example, Black et al. (2003) described how they supported a group of 24 teachers to develop their use of 'in-the-moment' formative assessment in mathematics and science. They found that the gains in student achievement were substantial – equivalent to an increase of the rate of student learning of around 70 per cent.

Wiliam makes the important distinction between the 'strategies' and the 'techniques' of formative assessment. Strategies relate to identifying where the learners are in their learning, where they are going, and what steps need to be taken to get there. This closely aligns to our three feedback questions: 'Where am I going?'; 'How am I going there?'; 'Where to next?'

Leahy and Wiliam's (2009: 15) work in schools shows that:

> when formative assessment practices are integrated into the minute-to-minute and day-by-day classroom activities of teachers, substantial increases in student achievement – of the order of a 70 to 80 percent increase in the speed of learning – are possible, even when outcomes are measured with externally-mandated standardized tests.

Their overall messages about putting their ideas into practice also mirror much in this book.

- The criteria for evaluating any learning achievements must be made transparent to students to enable them to have a clear overview of the aims of their work and of what it means to complete it successfully.

- Students should be taught the habits and skills of collaboration in peer assessment, both because these are of intrinsic value and because peer assessment can help to develop the objectivity required for effective self-assessment.

- Students should be encouraged to bear in mind the aims of their work and to assess their own progress to meet these aims as they proceed. They will then be able to guide their own work and so become independent learners (Black et al., 2003: 52–3).

Use of prompts as a precursor to receiving feedback

There are many forms of prompts: organizational prompts (for example, 'How can you best structure the learning contents in a meaningful way?'; 'Which are the main points?'); elaboration prompts (for example, 'What examples can you think of that illustrate, confirm, or conflict with the learning content?'; 'Can you create links between the contents of the lesson and your knowledge from other everyday examples?'); and monitoring progress prompts (for example, 'What main points have I understood well?'; 'What main points have I yet to understand?').

Teachers and students who use prompts can invoke feedback from many sources. The major effect of such prompts is to raise the amount of organization and elaboration strategies during learning. Nuckles, Hubner, and Renkl (2009) showed that prompts not only allowed students to identify comprehension deficits more immediately, but also invited students to invest more effort to plan and realize remedial cognitive strategies in order to improve their comprehension. It is also worthwhile to consider the appropriate use of prompts depending on where the students are in the learning process (see Table 7.2).

TABLE 7.2 Examples of prompts

LEVEL OF PROMPT	EXAMPLES
Task	■ Does his/her answer meet the success criteria? ■ Is his/her answer correct/incorrect? ■ How can he/she elaborate on the answer? ■ What did he/she do well? ■ Where did he/she go wrong? ■ What is the correct answer? ■ What other information is needed to meet the criteria?
Process	■ What is wrong and why? ■ What strategies did he/she use? ■ What is the explanation for the correct answer? ■ What other questions can he/she ask about the task? ■ What are the relationships with other parts of the task? ■ What other information is provided in the handout? ■ What is his/her understanding of the concepts/knowledge related to the task?
Self-regulation	■ How can he/she monitor his/her own work? ■ How can he/she carry out self-checking? ■ How can he/she evaluate the information provided? ■ How can he/she reflect on his/her own learning? ■ What did you do to . . .? ■ What happened when you . . .? ■ How can you account for . . .? ■ What justification can be given for . . .? ■ What further doubts do you have regarding this task? ■ How does this compare to . . .? ■ What does all of this information have in common? ■ What learning goals have you achieved? ■ How have your ideas changed? ■ What can you now teach? ■ Can you now teach another student how to . . .?

The key with all prompts is not only to get the prompt relative to the phase of learning, but also to know when to remove the prompt – that is, when to fade out, or allow the student to take on more responsibility. A related notion is 'scaffolding' – and like scaffolds on buildings, the art is to know when it is needed and when it is time to remove the scaffolding. The purpose of scaffolding is to provide support, knowledge, strategies, modelling, questioning, instructing, restructuring, and other forms of feedback, with the intention that the student comes to 'own' the knowledge, understanding, and concepts. Van de Pol, Volman, and Beishuizen (2010) described five intentions for scaffolding:

■ keeping the student on target and maintaining the student's pursuit of the learning intention;

■ the provision of explanatory and belief structures that organize and justify;

- taking over parts of the task that the student is not yet able to perform and thereby simplifying the task (and reducing the cognitive load) somewhat for the student;

- getting students interested in a task and helping them adhere to the requirements of the task; and

- facilitating student performance via feedback, as well as keeping the student motivated via the prevention of minimization of frustration.

Attributes of students and feedback

The culture of the student

The culture of the student may influence the feedback effects. Luque and Sommer (2000) found that students from collectivist cultures (for example, Confucian-based Asia, South Pacific nations) preferred indirect and implicit feedback, more group-focused feedback, and no self-level feedback. Students from individualist/Socratic cultures (for example, the USA) preferred more direct feedback, particularly related to effort, were more likely to use direct enquiry to seek feedback, and preferred more individual, focused, self-related feedback. Kung (2008) found that while both individualistic and collectivist students sought feedback to reduce uncertainty, collectivist students were more likely to welcome self-criticism 'for the good of the collective' and more likely to seek developmental feedback, whereas individualistic students decreased such feedback to protect their egos. Individualistic students were more likely to engage in self-helping strategies, because they aim to gain status and achieve outcomes (Brutus & Greguras, 2008). Hyland and Hyland (2006) argued that students from cultures in which teachers are highly directive generally welcome feedback, expect teachers to notice and comment on their errors, and feel resentful when they do not.

Asking students about feedback

A search of the literature found no reasonable measure asking students what they thought about feedback. Brown, Irving, and Peterson (2009) had developed an instrument based on their conceptions of assessment model, but it had little predictive value, and they recommended searching further. The instrument that I developed started by reviewing their work, and by asking teachers to interview five fellow teachers and five students, taking scripts from classes, and talking with teachers and students about feedback received. The instrument started with over 160 open and closed questions, but this was reduced to 45 after factor analysis and attention to the value of the interpretations from the instrument.

The first part, 'Feedback sounds like . . .', asked students what feedback sounded or looked like to them. There were three scales: feedback as positive, negative, or providing constructive criticism. The second part related to 'Types of feedback', including feedback as corrective and confirming, feedback as improvement, and frequency of feedback (from teachers and peers). The third part concerned 'Sources of feedback' – the argument being that the most effective feedback is related more to the criteria of the lesson (the learning intentions and success criteria) than individual (compared to prior achievement) and preferably not to social (for example, comparative; cf. Harks, Rokoczy, Hattie, Klieme, & Besser, 2011).

There are marked differences in these scales across teachers and schools: teachers see feedback more in terms of comments, criticism, and correctives; students prefer to see feedback as forward-looking, helping to address 'Where to next?', and related to the success criteria of the lesson. Regardless of their perceptions of achievement level, students see the value and nature of feedback similarly. The items with the highest relationship to achievement are: 'Feedback clarifies my doubts about the task'; 'Feedback indicates the quality of my work'; 'Feedback helps me to elaborate on my ideas'; 'Feedback sounds like constructive criticism'; 'Feedback sounds like very specific comments'; 'I understand the feedback I get from this teacher'; and 'Feedback provides worked examples that help me to think deeper'. The major message seems to be that students – regardless of achievement level – prefer teachers to provide more feedback that is forward-looking, related to the success of the lesson, and 'just in time' and 'just for me', 'about my work' (and not 'about me'). Higgins et al. (2001) found that students perceive feedback negatively if it does not provide enough information to be helpful, if it is too impersonal, if it is too general, and if it is not formative – that is, looking forward. It is not 'sufficient simply to tell a student where they have gone wrong – misconceptions need to be *explained* and improvements for future work suggested' (p. 62; italics in original).

The power of peers

Nuthall (2007) conducted extensive in-class observations and noted that 80 per cent of verbal feedback comes from peers – and most of this feedback information is incorrect! Teachers who do not acknowledge the importance of peer feedback (and whether it is enhancing or not) can be most handicapped in their effects on students. Interventions that aim at fostering correct peer feedback are needed, particularly because many teachers seem reluctant to so involve peers as agents of feedback. There is a high correlation (about 0.70) between students' concerns about the fairness and usefulness of peer assessment (Sluijsmans, Brand-Gruwel, & van Merrienboer, 2002), and high correlations between student and teacher marks on assignments. Receiving feedback from peers can lead to a positive effect relating to reputation as a good learner, success, and reduction of uncertainty, but it can also lead to a negative effect in terms of reputation as a poor learner, shame, dependence, and devaluation of worth. If there are positive relations between peers in the classroom, the feedback (particularly critical feedback) is more likely to be considered constructive and less hurtful (see Falchikov & Goldfinch, 2000; Harelli & Hess, 2008).

Mark Gan (2011) noted the problems about peer feedback being so prevalent, but often so wrong. He set about asking how we can improve the feedback given by peers. By the end of his series of studies, he placed much reliance on the power of prompts by teachers to help peers to provide effective feedback. As noted above, these prompts included guiding questions, sentence openers, or question stems that provide cues, hints, suggestions, and reminders to help students to complete a task. Prompts (for example, 'An example of this . . .', 'Another reason that is good . . .', or 'Provide an explanation for . . .') serve two key functions in students' learning: scaffolding and activation. Prompts act as scaffolding tools to help learners by supporting and informing their learning processes. Prompts can be designed to target procedural, cognitive, and meta-cognitive skills of the learner; they can provide new or corrective information, invoke alternative strategies already known by the student, and provide directions for trying new learning strategies. In this sense, prompts can be conceived as 'strategy activators' (Berthold, Nückles, & Renkl, 2007: 566) or aids for cognitive engagement. Part of the art is to help students to engage in 'self-talk' and thus to begin to develop series of prompts that they or their peers can use when they 'do not know what to do next' (Burnett, 2003).

As they move from task to processing to regulation, students can use prompts to monitor and reflect on their own learning approaches, such as problem-solving strategies, enquiry processes, and self-explanations. Examples of reason justification prompts include: 'What is your plan for solving the problem?'; 'How did you decide that you have enough data to make conclusions?' Such prompts help students to organize, plan, and monitor their actions by making their thinking explicit, to identify specific areas that they did not understand and what they needed to know, and to use domain-specific knowledge to reason about the approach that they adopted to solve the problem. Davis and Linn (2000) used the term 'directed prompts' to describe prompts intended to elicit planning and monitoring (for example, 'When we critique evidence, we need to . . .'; 'In thinking about how these ideas all fit together, we're confused about . . .'; 'What we are thinking about now is . . .') or to check for understanding ('Pieces of evidence we didn't understand very well included . . .'). Such generic prompts provide more 'freedom' for students to reflect on their learning, whereas directed prompts may misguide some students with a 'false sense of comprehension'. Students' level of autonomy was found to interact with their use of generic prompts for reflection, with middle-level autonomy students gaining most from the reflection prompts, as they 'were allowed to direct that reflection themselves' (Davis, 2003: 135).

Gan (2011) used the three-level model of feedback (Figure 7.2) to devise methods to coach students to identify what knowledge was required for each level and how to generate feedback that was targeted at that level of understanding. In his control classes, he found that the unprompted or untrained students seemed to adopt a 'terminal' feedback approach, whereby the solution or right answer was provided and praise was used to reinforce the notion of a correct response. This terminal peer feedback approach assumes that students are capable of drawing inferences or making judgements based on the corrective information, and then decide on the corrective action to move from their current state of understanding to meet the success criteria. While it may seem probable for higher-ability students to come up with their own revision strategy, this is most unlikely for lower-ability students. Conversely, the progressive peer feedback approach provides students with a mental picture that breaks down the feedback into concrete steps, allowing students to focus on a specific area on which to work. This organization of learning and feedback may be seen to be reducing the demand on a student's cognitive resources, enabling him or her to draw connections, identify the learning gaps, and take corrective action. This seems a difficult task, so Gan devised a graphic organizer with hierarchical feedback levels.

He used science classes in Singapore and New Zealand to evaluate the effectiveness of this model. It required planning by the teachers to conceive of the task, processes, and desired self-monitoring by students in the content domain. As importantly, the task had to be sufficiently challenging to prompt the need for peers to give each other feedback. This had the added bonus of helping teachers to articulate their actual learning intentions and success criteria, and this was made easier when teachers then critiqued each other's plans and rubrics prior to teaching. The results of his studies indicated that coaching

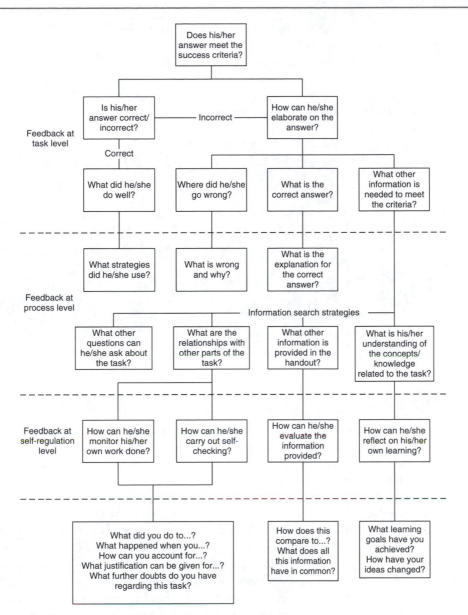

FIGURE 7.2 A rubric to help students to decide on appropriate feedback to peers

students to formulate peer feedback at task, process, and regulation levels had a significant effect on the quality of feedback that students provided in their written laboratory reports.

The students began in their pre-test class by predominantly providing task-level feedback to their peers, with hardly any feedback at the process or regulation level. When students were explicitly coached on how to differentiate the feedback at task, process, regulation, and self levels (using the model), they were able to formulate more feedback at the regulation level (from 0.3 per cent to 9 per cent of all feedback at self-regulation level). The interviews showed that the students and their peers regarded giving and receiving peer feedback to be a potentially enriching experience because it allowed them to identify their learning gaps, collaborate on error detection and correction, develop their ability to self-regulate, including monitoring their own mistakes, and initiate their own corrective measures or strategies. A major message is that the positive value of peer feedback requires deliberate instructional support (such as the use of Gan's model) of the three major feedback levels, and associated prompts for each level.

VISIBLE LEARNING – CHECKLIST FOR DURING THE LESSON: FEEDBACK

38. Teachers:
    a. are more concerned with how students receive and interpret feedback;
    b. know that students prefer to have more progress than corrective feedback;
    c. know that when students have more challenging targets, this leads to greater receptivity to feedback;
    d. deliberately teach students how to ask for, understand, and use the feedback provided; and
    e. recognize the value of peer feedback, and deliberately teach peers to give other students appropriate feedback.

Conclusions

As a father, I was aware of the low levels of feedback that my own boys were likely to receive at school. Each night over dinner, the questions 'What did you learn/do at school today?' or 'What was the best thing that you did today (other than playtime)?' were replaced by 'What feedback did you receive from your teachers today?' At least once a day, the aim was that they attended to at least one piece of feedback if for no other reason than to allow the dinner conversation to move to more interesting matters. It is the critical questions into which students need to be attuned – to learn how to seek or receive feedback about where they are going, how they are going there, and where they should go next.

There is a lot known about feedback, but there is much more to be discovered about how to optimize its power in the classroom. On the one hand, feedback is among the most powerful influences on achievement; on the other hand, it is among the most variable of influences. For feedback to be received and have a positive effect, we need transparent and challenging goals (learning intentions), an understanding of current status relative to these goals (knowledge of prior achievement), transparent and understood criteria of success, and commitment and skills by both teachers and students in investing and implementing strategies and understandings relative to these goals and success criteria. The suggestion is that models of feedback need to consider its multidimensional nature: feedback has dimensions of focus (for example, the three feedback questions), effect (for example, the four feedback levels), propensity (for example, the cultural and personality dispositions of the receiver), and types (see Shute, 2008).

To make feedback more powerful and to ensure that it is received and used, there is a need to know much more about how students set academic mastery goals (more so than performance, social, and certainly avoidance goals), and how teachers and students set targets for learning – because these can then enhance and increase the value of feedback towards these goals and targets. The notion of 'personal bests', and challenge, commitment, progress feedback, and student assessment capabilities (Absolum et al., 2009) are central to the effects of feedback, as are understandings about the various feedback strategies and different types and functions of feedback. Inviting students to have a sense of 'with-it-ness' with respect to feedback should be a major outcome of lessons.

It may also be important to consider the nature and dosage of feedback. It is likely that it is more effective when provided in incremental steps (and this applies to students, teachers, and administrators). So often, feedback is dished out in a long screed, encompassing so many different ideas and prompts, and thus allowing the receiver to be selective or to miss the priorities, and possibly leading him or her to become more confused. Feedback needs to be focused, specific, and clear.

A number of mediators of feedback and achievement have been identified, including the distinction between focusing on giving or receiving feedback, how the culture of the student can mediate the feedback effects, the importance of disconfirmation as well as confirmation, and the necessity for the climate of the learning to encourage 'errors' and entice students to acknowledge misunderstanding – and particularly the power of peers in this process. When assessments (tests, questions, and so on) are considered as a form of gaining feedback such that teachers modify, enhance, or change their strategies, there are greater gains than when assessment is seen as more about informing students of their current status. This is all the essence of formative assessment.

Note that there is no discussion in this chapter on feedback relating to marking or grading. This is because the messages are about 'feedback in motion', primarily assisting all to move forward based on correctives and information that reduces the gap between where students are and where they need to be. Too often, comments on essays or other work are too late, too ineffectual, and ignored. As Kohn (2006: 41) noted: 'Never mark students while they are still learning.' Students see the mark, so often, as the 'end' of the learning. The major reason relating to the nature and structure of these pieces of work that are graded is that they are the outputs of lessons and learning is more likely to occur during rather than after the learning is finished (or 'handed in'). Students soon realize the poverty of the feedback from such work other than a summative grading of the work: they look to the grade, and then to their friend's grades. The comments can provide justification for the grade, but there is little evidence that the comments lead to changes in student learning behaviours, or greater effort, or more deliberate practice – mainly because students see the 'work' as finished.

It should be clear that there are many complexities when aiming to maximize the feedback received by students. Students differ in the receptivity and willingness to understand feedback relative to their cultural backgrounds, their reaction to confirmation and disconfirmation, their experience of handling error, the way in which tests and assessments have proven useful for moving forward, how successfully they have taught to maximize the usefulness of feedback, and the role of peer feedback.

There is an exciting future for research on feedback. That feedback is critical to raising achievement is becoming well understood, but that it is so absent in classrooms (at least in terms of being received by students) should remain an important conundrum. It could be powerful to move research beyond descriptions of types of feedback towards discovering how to embed 'best fit' feedback not only in instruction, but also to help students to seek it, evaluate it (especially when provided by peers and the Internet), and use it in their learning – and towards teachers receiving feedback from students such that they then modify their teaching. This may require a move from talking less about how we teach to more about how we learn, less about reflective teaching and more about reflective learning, and more research about how to embed feedback into the learning processes. It probably requires better understanding of classroom dynamics, and providing ways for teachers to see learning other than merely through their own eyes and reflection, but instead through the eyes of the students.

Shute (2008) provided nine guidelines for using feedback to enhance learning:

- focus feedback on the task not the learner;
- provide elaborated feedback (describing the 'what', 'how', and 'why');
- present elaborated feedback in manageable units (for example, avoid cognitive overload);
- be specific and clear with feedback messages;
- keep feedback as simple as possible, but no simpler (based on learner needs and instructional constraints);
- reduce uncertainty between performance and goals;
- give unbiased, objective feedback, written or via computer (more trustworthy sources are more likely to be received);
- promote a learning goal orientation via feedback (move focus from performance to the learning, welcome errors); and
- provide feedback after learners have attempted a solution (leading to more self-regulation).

She also noted interactions with the level of student achievement: use immediate, directive or corrective, scaffolded feedback for low-achieving students, and delayed, facilitative, and verification feedback for high-achieving students.

Sadler (2008) claimed that in order for feedback to be effective and useful, three conditions have to be met: the learner needs the feedback; the learner receives the feedback and has time to use it; and the learner is willing and is able to use the feedback. So why do students not receive the feedback that teachers claim amply to provide? Dunning (2005) has studied this problem extensively and offers some fascinating explanations. First, for students, feedback is at best probabilistic: there is no guarantee of getting it – especially when it is needed; it is often incomplete – students often cannot know outcomes from alternatives; it is often hidden – and thus the consequences may not be obvious; it can be ambiguous – what is the action that led to the feedback?; and it is biased – it so often includes praise.

Secondly, students (like us all) have biases towards receiving feedback that they want: we seek positive co-occurrences; we create self-fulfilling prophecies; we fail to recognize mistakes in hindsight; we seek feedback consistent with self-image; we accept the positive and scrutinize the negative; we code positive broadly and negative narrowly; we attribute positive to self and negative to anything else; and we misremember feedback.

No wonder giving feedback that is then appropriately received is so difficult.

Exercises

1. As per Exercise 5 in Chapter 6, have a colleague observe your class through the eyes of the students. For example, have this colleague sit in the room, take a script of everything that you say and do, and, most critically, choose two students and note all that they do, react to, and talk about (as far as your colleague can hear). At the end, print out the script and together identify each occasion on which the teacher provided feedback, and *each* occasion when the two students received and acted upon any feedback.

2. Interview five teachers and five students about what 'Feedback looks like and sounds like', and give an example of useful and not so useful instances of feedback. Share these with other teachers who have completed this task. Are there commonalities in terms of corrective or formative feedback?

3. Take a video of one of your classes. Review the lesson and consider where there were opportunities for the students to gain more effective feedback about their progress in the lesson. Practise these opportunities with colleagues and then aim to find occasions in your next classes on which to enact them.

4. After the next administration of a test in your class, detail what you have learned from interpreting the results, what you would do differently, and what you would re-teach. In light of these details, ask whether the assessment served its purpose in providing feedback to you as a teacher. If not, change the assessment to maximize these opportunities.

5. Practise giving each student rapid formative assessment and practise inviting the students to seek feedback about their progress on at least three occasions each during the lesson. Evaluate the value of this intervention.

6. Discuss the following things, which I would argue are true.

   a. Norm-reference tests are optimized when the students get, on average, 50 per cent of the items correct; criterion-referenced tests are optimized when each student gets 50 per cent of the items correct.

   b. A teacher is responsible primarily for ensuring that every student makes at least one year's progress for one year's input than for bringing students up to expected proficiency levels.

   c. Feedback is more powerful when it is sought by the teacher about his or her teaching than by the student about his or her learning.

   d. Formative interpretations cannot be accomplished without including some form of assessment.

   e. 'Errors' relate as much to gifted as to struggling students and should be seen as opportunities.

   f. The major reason for administering tests in classrooms is for teachers to find out what they taught well or not, who they taught well or not, and where they should focus next. If a test does not lead to a teacher evaluating these claims, it was probably a waste of everybody's time and effort.

   g. The teacher's role in testing is to help students to exceed their expected grade on the test.

   h. If a teacher prints out the test results, it is probably too late to change instruction!

8

The end of the lesson

The lesson with the students is completed, but the story continues. So often, the plea now is for reflection – but this is not my message. Reflection quickly turns into post-hoc justification. I have watched so many teachers talk about their lessons or react to videos of their teaching, and they can certainly wax lyrical about what happened, why they did this rather than that – and when asked to consider how to do better, so often they then focus on what they should do more in the future. When they watch the same class through the eyes of the student, they are much more silent! The surprise of what teaching looks like through videos from the students' perspective makes them realize that they had not seen learning – they had seen only teaching. The aim must be to see the *effect* of our actions and teaching, and not to confuse this with those actions and teaching.

This is why I never allow teachers or school leaders to visit classrooms to observe teachers; I allow them to observe only students – the reactions that students have to incidents, to teaching, to peers, to the activity. Then, they interview and listen to the student about what the student was doing, thinking, and not understanding. Such observation adds another pair of eyes to help the teacher to see the effect of his or her teaching, and moves the discussion away from the teaching towards the *effect* of the teaching. Otherwise, observers come up with pleasant ways of telling teachers how to 'teach like me'. . .

The starting point is to review the climate in the class, and then to ask a series of questions relating to the teacher's effect on the students: are you aware of each student's progress on his or her learning journey from his or her starting point to the point at which he or she attains the success criteria? How close is each student to attaining the success criteria? What now needs to occur to help him or her to move closer to meeting the success criteria? As importantly, does each student know where he or she is on his or her learning pathway from his or her starting point to the point at which he or she will have attained success?

The lesson experience from the student's perspective

VISIBLE LEARNING – CHECKLIST FOR THE END OF THE LESSON

39. Teachers provide evidence that all students feel as though they have been invited into their class to learn effectively. This invitation involves feelings of respect, trust, optimism, and intention to learn.

While we can learn without knowing it (commonly called 'tacit knowing'), for most of us there needs to be a deliberate attempt to assimilate or accommodate new learning. That means that a major precursor to learning is engagement in the learning. As William Purkey (1992) has so eloquently put it, we as teachers need to 'invite' our students into learning. So often, many students come to the class simply because it is the next class to which they have to go. His argument is that such an invitation conveys respect, trust, optimism, and intentionality by the teachers.

He identified four major patterns, and the first task was to consider the lesson just held and to ask which of the following *the students would consider* was the dominant pattern.

a. *The lesson was intentionally disinviting* Students would claim that they were made to feel incapable and worthless; the teacher was busy with many distractions and focused on students' shortcomings.

b. *The lesson was unintentionally disinviting* Students would claim that the teacher was well-meaning, but condescending, obsessed with policies and procedures, and unaware of the students' feelings; there was too much labelling and stereotyping, non–verbal signals were negative, and there was a low level of student input.

c. *The lesson was unintentionally inviting* The teacher was involving, but inconsistent when considering what the students were bringing to the lesson; the teacher was not as successful at making intentions transparent, but carried the lesson by good nature and likeability.

d. *The lesson was intentionally inviting* The teacher explicitly invited students to take part in the flow of the lesson, made intentions and success transparent to students, and bothered to check that students were aware of these; the teacher was optimistic that all students would attain success, and was respectful of student errors, travails, and progress.

The key dimensions in evaluating whether the students were invited to learn included the following.

■ *Respect* 'Did you demonstrate to all students that they were able, valuable, and responsible, and did you treat them accordingly?'

■ *Trust* 'Did the lesson lead to cooperative, collaborative engagement in the learning, such that the process of learning was seen by all students to be as important as the product of the lesson?'

- *Optimism* 'Did the students get the message from you that they possess untapped potential in learning what is being taught today?'
- *Intentionality* 'Was the way in which you created and maintained the flow of the lesson specifically designed to invite learning?'

Invitational learning requires a transparent commitment to promote learning for all, and consideration of a student's prior learning and of what each student brings to the lesson. It requires a sense of fairness and openness to allow students to learn, to make errors, and to collaborate in the success of the learning. It allows for a dialogue among teachers and students related to understanding the concepts in the lesson. Further, invitational learning requires the teacher to be proficient in establishing and maintaining such an environment, and transparently demonstrating high expectations for all students.

This notion of how the student experiences the lesson is critical to engagement and success in participating in learning – more so for adolescents than for elementary students (who are more content to be 'busy'). Cornelius-White (2007) completed one of the more important meta-analyses – on student-centred teaching. He located 119 studies and estimated 1,450 effects, based on 355,325 students, 14,851 teachers, and 2,439 schools. Overall, the effect was $d = 0.64$ between person-centred teacher variables and cognitive student outcomes, and $d = 0.70$ with affective or behavioural student outcomes. The key in this student-centred teaching was what Cornelius-White termed the 'facilitative relationship' – that is, the way in which caring teachers approach their students. The student-centred teacher is passionate about each student engaging with and succeeding in what is being taught, and the teacher is aware of each student's progress from the start to the end of teaching the learning intention. (Note that it is important not to confuse the student-centred teacher with particular methods of teaching, such as collaboration learning, individualized learning, and so on.)

The essence of the student-centred teacher is fourfold: a student-centred teacher has warmth, trust, empathy, and positive relationships.

1. *Warmth: the foundational contributor* While it may be common for teachers to think that they are caring (for example, they work hard, they want to succeed, and so on), the key is whether students can cite evidence of this warmth. Warmth is demonstrated in acceptance, affection, unconditional respect, and positive regard for students. The idea is that teachers must show warmth in observable ways rather than simply intend to do so or believe that it is important.

2. *Trust: the optimistic and high expectations contributor* Trust means students seeing that the teacher believes in them – especially when they are struggling.

> It means showing them that you understand their view of things even if it may seem simplistic to you as an adult. You need to have the expectation that they will be able to make it through it or that what they want to learn is worth learning.
>
> (Cornelius-White, 2007: 36)

As noted earlier, high expectations and encouragement are essential not only from teachers, but also from parents and peers.

3. *Empathy: the 'get to know students' contributor*

> Students learn in their own particular ways. Teachers need to understand and take the perspective of students if they are to get through to them. How does a particular kid understand the material? On which part does she get confused? When does she understand it creatively in a way that a teacher does not?
>
> (Cornelius–White, 2007: 38)

Can the teacher stand in the shoes of the student and see his or her perspective of the learning? When this is understood, a teacher can know the optimal feedback to provide to move the student forward.

4. *Positive relationships: the contributors together* One simple way in which to turn students off learning is for them to have a poor relationship with the teacher. The essence of positive relationships is the student seeing the warmth, feeling the encouragement and the teacher's high expectations, and knowing that the teacher understands him or her.

The lesson experience from the teacher's perspective

VISIBLE LEARNING – CHECKLIST FOR THE END OF THE LESSON

40. Teachers collect evidence of the student experience in their classes about their success as change agents, about their levels of inspiration, and about sharing their passion with students.

The good news is that that inspiration and passion are two–way: the aim of deliberate change agents (the teacher) is to make as many students as possible inspired and passionate in learning the subject – and this requires a teacher to inspire that passion. Yes, for some, it is about getting students to move from novice to be at least capable, rather than proficient and full of passion, but for students to become 'capable' still requires a teacher to believe passionately that these students *can* become capable. Steele (2009) has shown that this passion does not necessarily mean bubbly exuberance, but a sense of 'with–it–ness', involvement in each student's learning, and evaluating your effect on each student.

One powerful, but most unused, method is student evaluations of teachers (SETs). Students are more than passive observers of teachers. As the theme in this book indicates, the relations and perceptions that they have of a teacher's impact on their learning is critical to being involved in the discipline of learning: for all students, the basic principle is that there needs to be a reason to be at school. So often, students are omitted in the quest for new innovations and plans for transforming schools – and motivated and engaged students are central to lasting school improvement (Pekrul and Levin, 2007).

Wilson and Corbett (2007) interviewed many students who had not performed so well in school. The students were adamant that teachers not be allowed to find excuses to not teach them, not leave them alone if they did not participate, and not to allow students to decide on their work or whether to work or not. There were six major characteristics of the type of teacher whom students wanted to see in their classroom:

1. someone who stayed on with students to complete their assignments;

2. someone who was able to control student behaviour without ignoring the lesson;

3. someone who went out of his or her way to provide help;

4. someone who explained things until the 'light bulb went on' for the whole class;

5. someone who provided students with a variety of ways through which to learn; and

6. someone who understood students' situations and factored that into his or her lessons.

Student evaluations are often a hotchpotch of questions relating to course effectiveness or improvement, or teacher effectiveness or improvement. Irving (2004) looked at things the other way around. Using the dimensions from the National Board for Professional Teaching Standards (see Chapter 2), he identified, wrote, and compiled 470 questions that related to the 470 statements in the mathematics standards. He ran many focus groups (groups of teachers who rated the items for agreement with the standards) to whittle the items to a smaller number that still ensured that the essence of each standard was well represented, and he also administered the items to large samples of high-school students. From the Delphi and factor analysis, he created a 51-item SET (see Appendix F for the best subset of 24 items), the underlying dimensions of which were:

1. commitment to students and their learning;

2. mathematical pedagogy;

3. student engagement with the curriculum;

4. family and community; and

5. relating mathematics to the real world.

To evaluate the validity of this questionnaire and factor model, he administered the SET to over 1,000 students from the 32 National Board Certified teachers (NBCs) and 26 experienced non-NBC colleagues. He achieved a more than 70 per cent success rate in correctly classifying the NBC status of the teachers by using the student responses!

The seven items that best distinguished the accomplished teacher from the experienced teachers were that the teacher:

- challenged students to think through and solve problems, either by themselves or as a group;
- encouraged students to place a high value on maths;
- helped students to construct an understanding of the language and processes of maths;
- got students to think about the nature and quality of the work;
- developed students' abilities to think and reason mathematically, and to have a mathematical point of view;
- encouraged students to try different techniques to solve problems; and
- showed students interesting and useful ways of solving problems.

These items could well form a set of prompts for teachers to evaluate their level of inspiration and passion. Of course, seeing it through the students' eyes is a more compelling way in which to triangulate these evaluations (see Exercise 1 at the end of this chapter). As has been noted, the hallmarks of the passionate and inspired teacher are a commitment to challenge, engagement, understanding, quality, reasoning, and developing learning strategies.

The lesson experience from the curricular perspective

VISIBLE LEARNING – CHECKLIST FOR THE END OF THE LESSON

41. Together, teachers critique the learning intentions and success criteria, and have evidence that:
    a. students can articulate the learning intentions and success criteria in a way that shows that they understand them;
    b. students attain the success criteria;
    c. students see the success criteria as appropriately challenging; and
    d. teachers use this information when planning their next set of lessons/learning.

The critical part when evaluating the lesson(s) is a review of the learning intentions and success criteria. You need to start by asking: 'Did the students know these?'; 'Could they articulate them in a manner that demonstrated that they understood?'; and 'Did they see the learning intentions and success criteria as appropriately challenging?' As importantly, what changes were made to the learning intentions and success criteria in light of the class experience? Not all learning can be pre-scripted, and there needs to be an opportunity for teachers and students to suggest other learning intentions and success criteria – provided that they are related to the mission of the lessons. As Hastie (2011) showed (see Chapter 4), it may be worth asking students to keep a work diary that details what they think they are learning, indicators of their progress, how confident they are that they will achieve these learning intentions in the time available, and their perception of their degree of success. The students could also be asked whether they consider the learning intentions involved to be attainable and worthwhile challenges – that is, does achieving the success criteria for the learning intentions lead them to progress beyond what they already knew? This is only knowable for students at the end of the lesson.

Another method is to ask colleagues to critique your learning intentions and success criteria – preferably before you implement them, although it is also worth reviewing them at the end of the lesson(s). This can be done alongside examples of students' work to evaluate the level of attainment of the success criteria and to assist in addressing the question: 'Where to next?' Or, you could provide the examples of planning from the lesson including the learning intentions, and ask colleagues to comment on what they see as the success criteria (and maybe also the quality of the learning intention in light of the examples of student work): do they match your success criteria?

Do your colleagues need to know the learning intention or success criteria to do this task? Sometimes 'yes'; sometimes 'no'. Michael Scriven (1991) has long talked about 'goal-free evaluation'. By not knowing the teacher's intentions and success criteria, a colleague can evaluate the students' reactions and claims about these (through interviews), can ask what was actually learnt rather than what was intended to be learnt (through examples of student work), and not have the tunnel vision that can come from looking for evidence for the intended goals and thus overlook many positive or negative unintended side effects. Scriven noted that merit is determined by relating program effects to the relevant needs of the affected population – in this case, the students. The teacher may then see what the students experienced, and reflect on how close this was to his or her own intentions and notions of success.

The lesson experience from a formative and summative perspective

VISIBLE LEARNING – CHECKLIST FOR THE END OF THE LESSON

42. Teachers create opportunities for both formative and summative interpretations of student learning, and use these interpretations to inform future decisions about their teaching.

One major mistake is to consider that the notions of 'formative' and 'summative' have something to do with tests; in fact, there is no such thing called summative or normative tests. 'Formative' and 'summative' refer to *the time at which* a test is administered and, more importantly, to the nature of the interpretations made from the tests. If the interpretations from the test are used to modify the instruction while it is ongoing, it is formative; if the interpretations from the test are used to sum up the learning at the end of the teaching, it is summative – as illustrated by Bob Stake's maxim: 'When the cook tastes the soup, it is formative; when the guests taste the soup, it is summative.'

In the same way that the goal of the cook is to make the best soup possible for the guests, it is imperative that teachers have excellence summative evaluation in place in their classes, because that can be among the most powerful evidence that there is likely to be excellent formative evaluation in place. If a school has poor summative assessment in place, then it is unlikely that teachers will have the ability, purpose, or wherewithal to be concerned with formative interpretations. Serving poor soup to the guests is probably the best indicator that the cook was lousy at tasting it during the preparations. Too much reliance on tasting the soup, as well, may lead to inattention to the goals – with the result, for example, that the soup is cold when the guests arrive.

Many systems are emerging that help teachers in their assessments, although most tend to be summative. Even the so-called 'predictive' tests tend to be more about what the student is supposed to know at the end of the lessons, and thus can be less effective in providing information that can lead to change during the instruction. Tests that are most powerful for formative interpretations tend to be those created to measure what is to be taught in a series of lessons (not a whole term or year), drawn from a large item pool that references the learning intentions from the curricula, and that aim for *each* student to get 50 per cent correct and 50 per cent incorrect – because, in that way, the students and teacher can know what has been accomplished and what still needs to be accomplished. This may mean adaptive assessment (the computer choosing the optimal set of items to administer to each student), but the emphasis needs to be on the quality of interpretations made from the assessments for this to have an effect on what the teacher and student do next.

Our own system, as one example, was developed less as a repository of 'tests' and more as a reporting engine – which made us concentrate on providing worthwhile and dependable interpretations to teachers about who they taught well, what they taught well, their strengths and weaknesses, their effects and progress, and what they could do next to enhance levels of performance and progress (Hattie, 2009).

While these kinds of reporting engine are not inexpensive, schools need to make a decision about the best reporting engine to use or whether to devise their own school report about how successful teachers are teaching all students, both in terms of students' progress and their levels of performance – with the proviso that the system needs to be available during, and not only at the end of, instruction.

The notion suggested here is for a report for teachers (and students) to monitor a teacher's effect, progress, and success with each student – for example, by using data teams to share interpretations across the school to ensure maximum effect. Unlike many more public reports, the essence of the suggested reports relates to informing teachers' overall judgements in a collaborative manner: if we cannot inform and enhance these judgements, we are missing the components that have a major effect on students – the teacher's expectations and notions of challenge and progress.

Conclusions

The lesson does not end when the bell goes! It ends when teachers interpret the evidence of their impact on students during the lesson(s) relative to their intended learning intentions and initial criteria of success – that is, when teachers review learning through the eyes of their students. What was the impact, with whom, about what, and how efficiently? Often, answering these questions requires help from others observing and thus providing extra 'eyes' into student learning, video analyses to provide extra 'eyes', and various forms of informal and formal assessment to provide extra 'eyes'. Did the lesson 'invite' students to participate, engage, and progress? Were there sufficient starting points, given the various phases of prior achievement and learning of the students? Were there any unintended consequences of your teaching? How many students gained the criteria of success – and for those that did not, what is now needed to assist them to meet the criteria? Underlying these questions is whether the students became active partners in evaluating their progress. As evaluators of the teaching impacts on their learning, students are at least as effective as teachers – and often well ahead of most administrators and parents.

A key question when reviewing the effect of the teacher and lessons is not only effectiveness, but also efficiency. Could there have been more efficient methods for having an effect on the learning and achievement of all students? 'Efficiency', in this context, does not necessarily mean 'speed', but rather, more cognitive efficiency. Such efficiency comes from many sources – especially the use of diverse learning strategies. Such versatility in the use of learning strategies can lead to less time taken, greater effort invested, reduced error rates, and opportunities for the further development of a multiplicity of strategies.

Exercises

1. Use the Invitational Teaching Survey (http://www.invitationaleducation.net/ie/ITS.pdf) to see how inviting your students see you.

2. Check each department, or across school years, for the degree of co-planning and critique. Do teachers know what other teachers are teaching, recognize the difficulty of what is taught, and appreciate the concept of 'challenge'? Do they share in determining the quality and nature of success criteria and learning intentions, and regularly review together their effect on students?

3. Invite groups of teachers to share their marking of assignments – which aims to help teachers to see how their concepts of challenge and standards are being realized. In some cases, share the learning intentions and success criteria, and ask for comment on how examples of student work is demonstrating these; in other cases, do not share the intentions and criteria, but ask colleagues to comment on what they consider the learning intentions and success criteria to be based on the evidence in the students' work.

4. Develop a bank of lesson plans to be shared across teachers, identifying the learning intentions and success criteria, including evaluation comments from many sources as to the impact of the lesson(s) on students for consideration in future teaching, and making suggestions for modification in light of these evaluations.

5. Revisit the class and ask students what they now see as the learning intentions and success criteria from these lessons. What did and did they not understand in the lessons? What did they do when they did not understand? Did they seek help (or not)? What were the reactions from their peers to their learning? Did they believe that they were listened to by this teacher? What was the nature of discussions among students during the lessons? What questions did they ask and what would they now still wish to ask? Were there multiple opportunities to learn, re-learn, and re-learn again? What do they now understand by success in these lessons? Finally, how close do the students think they are to the success criteria?

6. Revisit the staffroom and ask teachers if they know what other teachers are teaching at the moment, what other teachers' concepts of challenge are in relation to this teaching, and whether there are high levels of relational trust (for example, respect for each person's role in learning, respect for expertise, personal regard for others, and high levels of integrity) when making policy and teaching decisions. Ask about the degree to which this school carries out collaborative evaluation of the effect of its teachers.

7. Revisit leadership in the school and ask about the common understanding of the school's self-review of programs, the quality of this review program, and, most importantly, the degree to which the interpretations from this review process are having on how all in the school are increasing their impact on students.

8. Administer the Irving Student Evaluation of Teaching to your class (see Appendix F). Share your results with fellow teachers and work out strategies to increase the students' perceptions of your commitment to the students' learning, your teaching effectiveness, the level of engaging students with the curriculum, and how you relate the learning to the real world.

PART

3

Mind frames

Mind frames of teachers, school leaders, and systems

A major theme of this book and of *Visible Learning* is that the quality of teaching makes all the difference. Yes, it would be nice to have eager, well-groomed, invested students with financially gifted parents, but our neighbourhood schools must take all who walk through the gates. We could ask that students need to be 'ready' and motivated, and come to school well fed, having been supported at home to do their homework, and are attentive and calm. This would be wonderful, but a major role of schooling is to help students to acquire these habits; we should not discriminate against students whose parents may not know how to help them to do so. We could remonstrate about the quality of teacher selection, preparation, promotion and so on – but the chances of making differences in these matters has thwarted so many for so long with little evidence of change. These issues are important, but history has shown that resolving them has not made much difference to student learning to the degree that is required. For example, there is not a lot of evidence that improving teacher education colleges has improved the overall quality of teaching (but, of course, this is not to say that we should stop trying to find better ways in which to educate teachers to have these impacts). We have used tests to measure the surface knowledge and used these data to name, shame, and blame – and teachers have learnt to play this game – but playing the testing game even more smartly will not make the difference. We have spent billions on buildings, restructured curricula to align with tests and vice versa, and engaged in wonderful debates on the peripheries of what really makes the difference. We love to talk about the things that do not really matter. Perhaps the greatest resistance to change of the current system is that we have asked millions of teachers to improve this system – and they have applied their creative thoughts, and thus improved and sustained the current model far beyond its use-by date.

We know that the major source of controllable variance in our system relates to the teacher, and that even the best teacher has variability in the effect that he or she has on his or her students. The message in this book is that teachers, schools, and systems need to be consistently aware, and have dependable evidence of the effects that all are having on their students – and from this evidence make the decisions about how they teach and what they teach. The message is that the evidence is about student learning – particularly progress – provided that the learning intentions and success criteria are worthwhile, challenging, and become meaningful to and understood by the students. It can be done – as is the case in so many classrooms around the world every day. Our role is to make this learning more transparent, so that it can be critical in driving decisions.

This chapter starts at the top of the system and asks what some of the implications are for the system level; it then asks what some of the implications are for school leaders and goes on to outline a model of change that may lead to the optimal impact on student learning. Finally, it elaborates on the all-important, key, underlying mind frames suggested for all. It is these mind frames that need to pervade our thinking about teaching and learning, because it is these ways of viewing our world that then lead to the optimal decisions for the particular contexts in which we work.

A model for systems

One of the more powerful books that has influenced me is Ben Levin's *How to Change 5,000 Schools* (2008). Levin is not only a successful academic, but has also been a deputy minister for education in two Canadian provinces. He starts from the premise that the heart of school improvement rests in improving daily teaching and learning practices in schools, balanced with the notion that the school is the appropriate unit of evaluation – that is, that everyone in the school needs to collaborate to ensure that the daily teaching and learning practices are the focus of the school, and all are responsible for its success. This ties directly to the claim in this book that teachers and school leaders are fundamentally evaluators. It ties with claims that the culture of the school is the essence of sustained success. Elmore (2004) also reiterates this claim – that the school leaders are responsible for cultural changes in schools; they do not change by mandate, but by specific displacement of existing norms, structures, and processes by others – 'the process of cultural change depends fundamentally on modelling the new values and behaviours that you expect to displace the existing ones' (p. 11). It is about how the way in which we think leads to the changes that we want. It is about our mind frames in relation not only to having major impacts on students in our schools, but also knowing about the magnitude and nature of these impacts.

Improvements relate to building a collective capacity of teachers in a school to show success – not only in achievement, but also in making learning a valued outcome, by retaining students' interest in learning, in making students respect themselves and others, by recognizing and esteeming diversity, and by building community. Students are never 'owned' by a teacher, but by the school. Collectively, schools need to agree about the key knowledge, skills, and disposition to be learnt, to agree about how all will know the impact and effects of their teaching and the school on students (in a regular and dependable way), to have a specific person responsible for 'student success across the school', to have plans in place to identify when students are not learning or when they are excelling in learning, to ensure that all provide multiple opportunities to learn and to demonstrate learning, and most importantly to share errors, share successes, and constantly share the passion of teaching. Christine McAulliffe, the astronaut, summed up this underlying passion of teaching perfectly: 'I have touched the future: I teach.'

Levin calls for 'Lasting and sustaining improvement in student outcomes' – both in a broad range of important areas, but also in greatly reducing the gaps in outcomes among different populations, so that all in society can benefit from public education. He is clear about what does *not* work. It does *not* work to assume that:

- a single change can create improvement in a short time frame;
- a few strong leaders can force a school to improve by itself;
- simplistic application of incentives will be a successful strategy;
- the starting place is governance and policy;
- new curriculum and standards can, by themselves, foster betterment; and
- an accountability system with oodles of data will create improvement.

Instead, he argues for a balance between focusing on a few key outcomes that relate to better teaching and learning (minimizing the distractions), putting effort into building capacity for improvement, building motivation by taking a positive approach, and increasing support for an effective, thoughtful, and sustained program of improvement – focusing on the will (motivation) and skill. He advocates nine essential practices for improved outcomes:

- high expectations for all students;
- strong personal connections between students and adults;
- greater student engagement and motivation;
- a rich and engaging formal and informal curriculum;
- effective teaching practices in all classrooms on a daily basis;
- effective use of data and feedback by students and staff to improve learning;
- early support with minimum disruption for students in need;
- strong positive relationships with parents; and
- effective engagement with the broader community.

Within a school, we need to collaborate to build a team working together to solve the dilemmas in learning, to collectively share and critique the nature and quality of evidence that shows our impact on student learning, and to cooperate in planning and critiquing lessons, learning intentions, and success criteria on a regular basis. Yes, this takes time to work together, but maybe less debate about other structural concerns (lower class size; different tracking methods; professional development sessions not related to these debates) could make way for financing more teacher planning and review time – together.

Michael Fullan (2011) also has written on choosing the right drivers for whole systems reform. One of his major messages is that the right drivers are those that work directly on changing the culture so that students are achieving better measurable results.

> The glue that binds the effective drivers together is the underlying attitude, philosophy, and theory of action. The mindset that works for whole system reform is the one that inevitably generates individual and collective motivation and corresponding skills to transform the system.
>
> (Fullan, 2011: 5)

He identified four 'wrong' drivers: accountability (using test results to appraise, punish, or reward); promoting individual teacher and leadership solutions; assuming that technology will carry the day; and fragmented strategies. His four 'right' drivers are: creating a powerful centrality of the learning–instruction–assessment nexus; using the group to accomplish this learning–instruction culture; going all out to power new teaching innovations with technology (not the other way around); and building systematic synergy between these first three drivers. These four drivers are among the core of the messages reiterated in this book, but to these we add a fifth: the system needs to provide resources to help schools to know their impact; those schools that have sufficient impact can then earn a degree of autonomy.

One of the roles of the system is to provide mandates about these matters, but also to provide resources to enable schools to efficiently know their impact. What is not suggested is more tests: schools are awash with tests and data that, in whatever language they are packaged, lead only to more summative than formative interpretations. Instead, what is requested are more formative interpretations. The asTTle package that we designed for schools in New Zealand was based on 'backward design' principles – that is, we started with the various interpretations that we considered teachers and schools should be making about their impact. We then devised interpretative reports that passed two tests: did the teachers accurately make the interpretations that we wanted them to make from the reports, and what were their consequences from interpreting the reports? When we started, it took us more than 80 focus groups to satisfy these two tests, but we become more efficient over time (see Hattie, 2010b). After creating seven reports, we then began to back-fill with items, but at all times gave teachers much control over the choice of tests – because one of the key aims of our reporting engine was to ensure that assessment related both to what the teacher was aiming to teach and to what the curriculum meant for this teaching. After initial exposure, it takes teachers a few minutes to set the parameters (for example, length of test, curricular objectives, difficulty of test, method [paper, on-screen, computer-adaptive], plus many other choices) and the linear programming engine takes about 7–10 seconds to build the optimal test from the 12,000+ calibrated items. Most importantly, upon completion, teachers get instant feedback about whom they taught well or not, about what, about their strengths and weaknesses, and so on. The system is voluntary, but the uptake is high in elementary and primary schools. Last year alone, over a million tests were sat (there are about 750,000 students in New Zealand), and the message is that teachers welcome feedback about their impact – provided that it relates to what they are teaching now, and provided that there is a lot of help offered in interpreting the measures. The reporting engine rarely shows a number (because numbers are often the stopping point for interpretation and consequences), is rich in detail while highlighting the main ideas, and has been used in many schools to help to drive teacher debates about their impact on students. The more pleasing use is by students, many as young as 7–9 years old, who can interpret the reports about their own learning, and know how to then create discussions with peers and teachers about 'Where to next?'.

The message is not to introduce more tests for accountability or 'predictive' means, but to introduce more resources to assist in the interpretation of formative information to allow school leaders, teachers, and students (and parents) to see 'learning in progress' and to concentrate more on 'Where to next?', in light of dependable information about where we are now.

New Zealand has now gone a step further, in that contracts for offering professional development in schools must demonstrate agreed effect size gains. This has meant a closer alignment of professional development, more coaching and less telling, a shared responsibility for professional development having an impact on students (and not only on teachers), and a renewed urgency to create more debates about learning. A lot of my own work is spent helping systems and schools to devise 'dashboards' of what success looks like and where on the pathway to this success is the school. The emphasis on a daily basis is more on progress and less on levels of proficiency, but the targets of proficiency are clearly exhibited in the dashboards. As always, the key component is providing quality evidence to create the right debates; the systems do not resolve the debates. Professional judgement is key and it is important to focus the accountability more on the overall teacher judgements that are made about progress. The two key questions here are: what is the quality of evidence that informs the teacher judgement, and what is the quality of the consequences for the teaching and learning from this evidence? Note that the attention is not on the data, not on reports of the data, but on the professional judgements and consequences of the key person in the student learning debate over whom we have some influence: the teacher. The sobering comment is that some schools do not like these debates about their impact – because it is easier not to know.

As has been noted, the reward is teachers knowing, in a dependable and public manner, the quality of their impact (see Amabile & Kramer, 2011), and the New Zealand system rewards schools that are engaging in their debates with 'earned or supported autonomy'. There is a quasi-inspection system (the Educational Review Office, or ERO), which visits schools and then provides a public report on the quality of the school in many aspects. If the inspection finds major evidence of schools having dependable systems about their impact and they are having positive impact, then the school earns a degree of autonomy – that is, inspection every four or five years; if not, the inspection is more frequent (in one case, every four months, and the ERO provides direction for these schools to improve knowing their impact). This is the focus that was referred to in early chapters: a focus on having dependable knowledge of the impact on student learning by evaluating and esteeming the quality of the teachers' professional judgements.

A model for school leaders

A major reason why teachers stay in a school or stay in teaching relates to the support by the school leaders so that teachers can have a positive impact. Think of reasons why a teacher would stay in teaching: teacher autonomy; leadership; staff relations; the nature of the students; facilities; and safety. The factor that explains the decision to stay or not – by a long way – relates to the nature of leadership (Boyd et al., 2011; Ladd, 2011). It is the leaders' motivation of teachers and students, identifying and articulating high expectations for all, consulting with teachers before making decisions that affect teachers, fostering communication, allocating resources, developing organizational structures to support instruction and learning, and regularly collecting and reviewing with teachers data on student learning. Learning leadership is the most powerful incentive to stay in teaching.

To give permission to teachers to engage in evaluating their impact and then using this evidence to enhance their teaching requires leaders who consider that this way of thinking and acting is valuable. The core lever with which to create schools that lead to enhanced impact is the leader's beliefs about his or her role. There are many ways in which we can consider how school leaders think and work. Two well-used ways are 'transformational' and 'instructional' leaders.

- *Transformational* leaders are attuned to inspiring teachers to new levels of energy and commitment towards a common mission, which develops the school's capacity to work together to overcome challenges and reach ambitious goals, and then to ensure that teachers have time to conduct their teaching.

- *Instructional* leaders attend to the quality and impact of all in the school on student learning, ensure that disruption to learning is minimized, have high expectations of teachers for their students, visit classrooms, and are concerned with interpreting evidence about the quality and nature of learning in the school.

Robinson, Lloyd, and Rowe (2008) conducted a meta-analysis comparing these two forms of leadership. Based on 22 studies and 2,883 principals, the impact of transformation leadership on student achievement was 0.11, whereas the impact of instructional leadership was 0.42. The effects were strongest on promoting and participating in teacher learning and development (0.84), establishing goals and expectations (0.42), planning, coordinating, and evaluating teaching and the curriculum (0.42), aligning resource selection and allocation to priority teaching goals (0.31), and then ensuring an orderly and supportive environment (0.27). The authors concluded that the reason for these enhanced effects is that transformational leaders are more focused on the relationship between leaders and teachers, and that the quality of these relationships is not predictive of the quality of student outcomes. In contrast, instructional leaders are more focused on the quality and impact of teaching in the school, and on building appropriate trust and a safe climate in which teachers can seek and discuss this evidence of impact.

These findings align with the fundamental argument in this book that leaders in schools (teachers, principals, boards) need to be fundamentally concerned with evaluation of the impact of all in the school. In schools that regularly have evidence of high levels of impact on students, the leadership can be more indirect in supporting teachers in their work towards higher levels of impact. Conversely, schools with lower levels of impact are more in need of direct leaders creating an orderly and safe environment, working directly with teachers in the school to set appropriate goals and expectations, and explicitly providing resources that help teachers to know their impact and to discuss the consequences for change to improve this impact (Bendikson, Robinson, & Hattie, 2011; Robinson, 2011).

The argument is that such instructional leaders can truly make the difference, and it is the beliefs and construction of their role that serves to make this difference and inspire all in their schools. The important distinction, however, is to move from the notion of 'instructional leaders' (which places too much emphasis on the instruction) to 'learning leaders' (which places the emphasis on student and adult learning). The focus is not 'Was it taught?' and 'How was it taught?', but 'Did students acquire essential knowledge and skills?', 'How do we know?', and 'How can we use that evidence of student learning to improve instruction?'

A key role of learning leaders is to construct the learning of the adults in the schools. There are features of teacher learning or professional development that we know have an impact on student achievement. Such features include coaching over an extended time, the use of data teams, a focus on how students learn subject matter content, and teachers working collaboratively to plan and monitor lessons based on evidence about how students learn in light of this planning (see Bausmith & Barry, 2011). Timperley, Wilson, Barrar, and Fung (2007) completed a synthesis of the effective professional development systems, and they promoted a five-step process (see also Timperley, 2012).

1. What knowledge and skills do our students need?
2. What knowledge and skills do we, as teachers, need?
3. How can we deepen our professional knowledge and refine our skills?
4. How can we engage students in new learning experiences?
5. What has been the impact of our changed actions?

The arguments in this book are aligned with this process – except that we work the other way around. Instead, we *start* with discussions and evidence about the impact of our actions, and then move to the other dimensions.

The topic of staffroom conversation needs to move towards a collective understanding of the adult's effect on the students rather than the 'presentism', privacy, and personal preferences that are so often the norm. This notion of 'presentism', coined by Jackson (1968), relates to the relative emphasis on current and immediate classroom needs, problems, and satisfactions instead of on long-term impact and plans. Jackson noted, as did Lortie (1975), the way in which teachers relied on their own independent observations of their students to gauge how well they were doing, and that there was little significant sharing of common understanding and techniques (see Hargreaves, 2010). Hence the importance of school leaders creating an atmosphere of trust and collegiality to allow the debates to turn to the evidence of the effect on student learning – on a regular basis. It requires strong 'learning leaders' to permit, encourage, and sustain the discussions on impact.

I witnessed one large high school begin this journey, during which the principal took some two or three years to convince teachers that the focus was on student learning and improving every student in the school. If there had been one whiff of accountability, the mood would have turned counter-productive. He provided a school-based reporting engine to help teachers to keep track of their effects on individual students, provided resources to help teachers to build graphs of the individual trajectories of all students from the previous five years through to the end of the current year, at the start of the year created targets for the end of the year for each student based on these trajectories, and created time for teachers to meet to prepare common assessments and then monitor their individual effects on students. This led to rich conversations in which these teachers had engaged and the school is now renowned for the quality of evidence about its success in raising achievement.

I have worked closely with one elementary school, close to my home, over the past eight years. The impact of these teachers is stunning, and every year I see their effect sizes of 1 and 2 for all students; well in excess of the $d = >0.40$ for which I am asking in this book. I know the dedication, the commitment to each student in this school, the absolutely driven hard work that all put in at this school. Most critically, the group most committed to getting the effects are the students. Many of them know more about assessment than university students. They know how to interpret assessments, know about standard error, know how to set tests for themselves, and are constantly seeking answers to 'Where to next?' The school impact is so well known that our prime minister frequently visits the school, and even brings international guests and other leaders to the school; it is one of the more impressive schools that I have visited. On my visits, the students interrogate me, have asked for improvements to the resources that we have provided, and exhibit so much pleasure in their 'known' success.

Developing a defensible model for change is important if the messages in this book are to be achieved. It is important to note that there is nothing new in this book or in *Visible Learning*. The messages and evidence are based on a study of prior literature, on what has worked successfully in so many classrooms. As noted in the introduction, there is no new program, no new acronym, no new 'Gee whiz, let's do this for a while!'; instead, it is a recognition of the critical importance of understanding how excellent teachers think! It is about change, leading to all teachers in the schools thinking in powerful ways about their role, their impact, and their collegiality in assisting all to have high expectations of success. It is about having multiple sources of evidence about impact on all students, and esteeming – and publicly and privatively valuing – this evidence of impact.

The good news is that teachers are often driven by having information about their impact. Amabile and Kramer (2011: 22) noted that 'of all the things that can boost emotions, motivation, and perceptions during a workday, the single most important is making progress in meaningful work'. They noted the power of catalysts (actions directly supporting work – especially from fellow workers) and nourishers (events – again especially from others – that show respect and words of encouragement). Negative influences include inhibitors (actions that fail to support or actively hinder work), and toxins (discouraging or undermining events). The notion of meaningful work for teachers, I would argue, is having positive impacts on students learning. Yes, some may see it more as getting through the curriculum, keeping kids busy until the bell rings, doing one's best . . . Effective school leaders, however, support teachers in their daily progress in this meaningful work, and thus set a positive feedback loop into motion. Amabile and Kramer (2011: 80) concluded that if leaders:

> facilitate their steady progress salient to them, and treat them well, they will experience the emotions, motivations, and perceptions necessary for great performance. Their superior work will contribute to organizational success. And here's the beauty of it: They will love their jobs.

Fullan (2012: 52) echoes this claim: 'It is the actual experience of being more effective that spurs them to repeat, and build on the behaviour.'

A model for change

Learning leaders need clear processes for implementing the mind frames outlined in this book. So often, we spend too much time on saying what leaders ought to be, ought to do, and ought to value; instead, we need to spend more time considering how to effectively create schools in which leaders are responsible for, allow, and encourage all to know about and have positive impacts on student learning. So many good ideas fail due to low levels of degree of implementation, fidelity, or dosage. Michael Barber (2008) has developed a most effective set of methods with which to accomplish successful delivery of such missions, unfortunately termed 'deliverology'. While there has been criticism of the policies that may have been introduced via this method, the method is the message. The following is based on the principles developed by Barber and it is worth reading more about them (because, of course, there is no one way in which to achieve 'deliverology' – see Barber, Moffit, & Kihn, 2011). There are four steps, as follows, to which I add a fifth.

a. Develop a foundation for delivery

1. *Define an aspiration*. In this case, that aspiration is knowing and valuing the impact that all in the school have on the learning of the students. The recommendation is: 'To ensure that all students gain at least $d = >0.40$ each year in this school on valued learning.' This also means that schools need to address some key prior questions: 'What do we want our students to learn?'; 'Why does that learning matter?'; 'What do you want your students to do or produce?'; 'How well do you want them to do it?'; 'How will you know how well the students are understanding?' (Gore, Griffiths, & Ladwig, 2004). *Know thy impact*.

2. *Review the current state of delivery*. As with all learning, knowing prior achievement and what the student brings to the class (from his or her culture, motivation, expectations) is critical for moving forward, and particularly for setting defensible and reasonable targets for enhancing student achievement. This step may entail a needs assessment and a review of current evidence (its quality, appropriateness for the mission, strengths and gaps), but also knowing about whether all in the school understand the delivery challenge and whether there is a culture of delivery.

3. *Build the delivery unit*. This is not about accountability methods or external imperatives, but about a commitment to action to achieve the aspiration. The unit is not necessarily the teachers or school leaders, but a small group responsible for ensuring delivery. The question arises: who is in charge of ensuring success in this school – that is, who is the 'dean of success'? Of course, the answer is 'everyone', but the delivery unit is more focused on ensuring that all systems are going to meet the targets. Barber recommends that the unit be small, reside outside the school hierarchy (because it must influence the school as well), and have time and sufficient resources to ensure delivery.

4. *Establish a guiding coalition that can remove barriers to change, influence and support the unit's work at crucial moments, and provide counsel and advice*. This does not need to be a formal group and may change in membership, with all aiming to help to ensure a maximum probability of success. The coalition is essential for developing the trust that is so important in school change.

b. Understand the delivery challenge

1. *Evaluate past and present performance*. What is the evidence most indicative of performance? How dependable and credible is this evidence to the teachers, school leaders, students, and parents (and whomever else)? What are the target indicators? What are the correlates of these target indicators, and the indicators of unintended consequences? Does the school share a program logic of how learning occurs in this school?

2. *Understand drivers of performance and relevant systems activities*. Do all in the school understand the drivers of student learning? Are they drivers over which they have some control? Are there mindsets that inhibit the impact that we need to have on learning (for example, 'Give me bright students and I can achieve'; 'But it is all about poverty and the home'; 'If they do not come to class prepared, that's not my fault'; 'We know

that Group X are underachievers and do not value education'), or do the teachers in the school see themselves as change agents, recognizing that all students can learn, that they can have marked positive impacts on all students, and that they are tasked primarily with knowing their impact on students?

c. Plan for delivery

1. *Determine your reform strategy.* Strategy is primarily the role of the school leader, and the role of the delivery leader is to inform this strategy. There is no magic formula, no program, and no quick way in which to achieve systematic, genuine, and identifiable impacts on student learning. Doing so requires all in the school to want to have this impact, to adopt theories of change that allow the best ways of getting there, to build capacity, capability, and culture, and to evaluate strategies. Remember: in education, everything works if $d = >0$ is desired; so evaluating strategy against the higher benchmark is required and removing some past practices that have met $d = >0$, but not $d = >0.40$, may be needed. This usually entails changing the way in which teachers see the nature, quality, and acceptability of evidence of their impact.

2. *Set targets and trajectories.* Setting challenging and defensible targets is critical for all levels in the school – from the front office, through school leaders, teachers, and students. The advice earlier in this book was to set targets at each student level and work forward, and certainly not the other way around. School-wide targets are often averaged across all students and thus leave many students behind – this is the flaw of the average. Decide on the trajectories to attain these targets, and then devise systems to evaluate the success in this trajectory. Given that there are likely to be many targets (please, other than test scores), it is also necessary to agree on the nature, quality, and acceptability of the evidence.

3. *Produce delivery plans.* Planning is everything: it is a work in progress, and it requires revision, rework, and realistic support. This is where school leadership comes to the fore.

d. Drive delivery

1. *Establish routines to drive and monitor performance.* This is where effort exceeds expectations by having all being aware of their roles in the plan to the targets, planning stock takes, and being transparent in reporting progress or otherwise in a timely manner, being aware of the challenges, and creating the trust in the culture of the methods to attain the mission.

2. *Solve problems early and rigorously.* In a sense, every student's progress is a 'problem', and if every student is allowed a major problem each year, in a typical school this means at least one major problem a day! Accepting that the problem is real for the person with the problem is important; there is then a need to reassess the priority and severity, and evaluate the criticalness for solving the problem relative to the delivery of the target.

3. *Sustain and continually build momentum.* Momentum is very much a product of the quality of the routines, the willingness to problem-solve, and the evidence of success

along the trajectory. There is a need to persist during distractions, to manage those who resist change, to challenge the status quo, and, most importantly, to celebrate success.

e. Develop, identify, and esteem success

This is the fifth step that I add to the above four.

1. Given the mission, all students should attain $d = >0.40$ in learning within a year, but there are many opportunities for failure: so often, those in schools are quick to recognize such failures and there may be 1,000 reasons why we do not succeed. The problem that I see in many schools is the opposite: so often, there are poor systems with which to identify success in attaining such targets (particularly in a timely manner). We quietly go on assuming that it is 'normal' to be above average (for example, all students $d = >0.40$) and to have success at challenging targets. Throughout the year, there needs to be systems in place to identify where each student, teacher, school leader is on his or her trajectory to the targets, and to pause to reflect, change, esteem, and problem-solve. This can help to develop a culture of improvement rather than blame, which is the true meaning of continuous learning, and to create a cohesive group of educators, students, and families committed to supporting and valuing learning in a school. Attestation, test scores, and voting by parents will not do it; evidence of systematic impact, using multiple forms of evidence, is the only way in which to identify those who are having an impact on our students.

These processes of change are powerful, but they are 'destination-free'. The destination in the current case is very much related to having major and positive impacts on student learning in our schools. The essence underlying these changes is the ways in which the participants think about their role, their impact, and their success. This is moving from the mechanisms of change towards the meaning and purpose of change.

Eight mind frames

The major argument in this book underlying powerful impacts in our schools relates to how we think! It is a set of mind frames that underpin our every action and decision in a school; it is a belief that we are evaluators, change agents, adaptive learning experts, seekers of feedback about our impact, engaged in dialogue and challenge, and developers of trust with all, and that we see opportunity in error, and are keen to spread the message about the power, fun, and impact that we have on learning.

Teachers do have 'theories of practice', which most often centre on how to manage and engage students, how to teach particular content, and how to do it all within the available time and resources. They also have theories about the context enablers and barriers to this process – such as beliefs about the kind of community that they wish to encourage in their class, the effects of family and cultural factors, and the structural needs for them to efficiently teach this content. As teachers become more experienced, these theories become more convincing to them, and sometimes changing them requires a major disruption and high levels of convincing power of the effect of alternative theories of action. Bishop (2003), in his work to change teachers to see that high expectations can also relate to minority students, started by showing teachers students' stories of what it was like for them in these teachers' classes. To encourage teachers to adopt some of the 'theories of practice' outlined in this book requires not lecturing or hectoring them, but starting with listening to these theories of practice, and then seeing how their own theories can be modified or enhanced to consider the fundamental message about them knowing their impact – as the starting point for having theories (not the end point). In working with many teachers and school leaders, it does not take long to show them the power of starting with the evaluation questions about knowing their impact, but it requires a lot of change to sustain and embed this mind frame. As many have said: 'It was easier not to know.'

These mind frames, or ways of thinking, are identified based on the claims made in the preceding chapters. The claim is that teachers and school leaders who develop these ways of thinking are more likely to have major impacts on student learning.

Mind frame 1: Teachers/leaders believe that their fundamental task is to evaluate the effect of their teaching on students' learning and achievement

Among the most powerful of all interventions is feedback or formative evaluation – providing information to the teacher as to where he or she is going, how he or she is going there, and where he or she needs to go next. The key factor is for teachers to have mind frames in which they seek such feedback about their influences on students and thus change, enhance, or continue their teaching methods. Such a mind frame – that is, seeking evidence relating to the three feedback questions ('Where am I going?'; 'How am I going there?'; 'Where to next?') – is among the most powerful influences on student achievement that we know.

Knowing what is optimal does not always mean deciding on a teaching method, resources, sequence, and so on, and then implementing these to the best of our abilities. It does not mean a prescription of the 'seven best strategies to use', 'what works', and so on. Instead, what is optimal means altering the instruction 'on the fly' during the class, with the many students at differing stages of knowing and understanding on the basis of feedback to the teacher about the value and magnitude of their teaching decisions. Hence the importance of seeking feedback about our effects both in a formative and summative manner.

The interactions between what we do as educators and what students are doing as learners is the key: it is the interaction – and being tuned into the nature and impact of these interactions – that is critical. This means evaluating what we are doing and what the student is doing, and seeing learning through the eyes of students, as well as evaluating the effect of our actions on what the student does *and* the effect of what the student does on what we then need to do – and, together, this is the essence of excellent teaching.

The operative notion is that of 'evaluating'. Teachers need to enhance their evaluation skills about the effects that they are having on students. Only then are teachers best equipped to know what to do next to enhance students' improvement. Over a series of lessons, if the typical impact is not high (that is, at least $d = >0.40$), then change in the teaching methods is likely to be necessary. Offering 'more' is probably the worst solution; what is needed is more likely to be 'different' methods. This is a 'win–stay, lose–shift' strategy.

The key questions underlining Mind frame 1 are as follows.

■ 'How do I know that this is working?'

■ 'How can I compare "this" with "that"?'

■ 'What is the merit and worth of this influence on learning?'

■ 'What is the magnitude of the effect?'

■ 'What evidence would convince me that I was wrong in using these methods and resources?'

■ 'Where is the evidence that shows that this is superior to other programs?'

■ 'Where have I seen this practice installed where it has produced effective results (which would convince me and my colleagues on the basis of the magnitude of the effects)?'

■ 'Do I share a common conception of progress with other teachers?'

Mind frame 2: Teachers/leaders believe that success and failure in student learning is about what they, as teachers or leaders, did or did not do . . . We are change agents!

This proposition is *not* making the claim that students are not involved in the learning equation, or that all success or failure is indeed the responsibility of the teacher; rather, it is claiming that the greatest impact relates the teacher's mindset. Some of the positive beliefs that need to be fostered include the following.

■ 'All students can be challenged.'

■ 'It's all about strategies, never styles.'

■ 'It is important to develop high expectations for all students relative to their starting point.'

■ 'It is important to encourage help-seeking behaviours.'

■ 'It is important to teach multiple learning strategies to all students.'

■ 'It is important to develop assessment-capable students.'

■ 'Developing peer interactions is powerful for improving learning.'

■ 'Critique, error, and feedback are powerful opportunities for improving learning.'

■ 'Developing student self-regulation and developing "students as teachers" are powerful mechanisms for improving learning.'

■ 'Don't blame the kids.'

■ 'Handicaps of social class and home resources are surmountable.'

■ 'There is no place for deficit thinking – that is, there is no labelling of students, nor are there low expectations of students.'

Teachers need to see themselves as change agents – not as facilitators, developers, or constructivists. Their role is to change students from what they are to what we want them to be, what we want them to know and understand – and this, of course, highlights the moral purposes of education. It is about teachers believing that achievement is changeable or enhanceable and is never immutable or fixed, that the role of a teacher is as an enabler not as a barrier, that learning is about challenge and not about breaking down material into easier chunks, and it is about teachers seeing the value of both themselves and students understanding learning intentions and success criteria.

There has been a longstanding debate between those who argue that teachers need to be facilitative and less intrusive, and those who support teachers as activators in the classroom (Taber, 2010). The answer is clear, but it seems that, every few years, we rediscover this notion (see Mayer, 2004, 2009). Alrieri, Brooks, Aldrich, and Tenenbaum (2011) conducted a meta-analysis on this question. They showed the value of directed over undirected discovery learning. From 580 effects based on 108 studies, the average effect was 0.38 in favour of the former over the latter. They then compared more specific, but explicit, methods of teaching: requiring students to generate rules, strategies, etc. ($d = 0.30$); elicited explanation requiring learners to explain their learning or target material ($d = 0.36$); scaffolding or regular feedback ($d = 0.50$). They concluded that:

> unassisted discovery generally does not benefit learning . . . . teaching practices should employ scaffolded tasks that have support in place as learners attempt to reach some objective, and/or activities that require learners to explain their own ideas. The benefits of feedback, worked examples, scaffolding, and elicited explanation can be understood to be part of a more general need for learners to be redirected . . . . unguided discovery activities were too ambiguous to allow learners to transcend the mere activity and to teach the level of constructivism intended.
>
> (Alrieri et al., 2011: 12)

The message in this book certainly supports the direct approach. Too often, the distinction is not made starkly enough, but I mince no words: teachers are change agents; they need to be activators; and they are responsible for enhancing student learning. There are many others also responsible (the student, parents, and so on), but the teacher is employed to be a change agent. As I noted in *Visible Learning*, this places a high obligation on the moral aspects of teaching – especially what is taught and knowing the effects of the teacher on what is taught. It also places an obligation on all then to esteem this expertise – in the staffroom, in the home, in the community, and in the profession.

Mind frame 3: Teachers/leaders want to talk more about the learning than the teaching

I have almost reached the point at which I lose interest in discussion about teaching – not because it is not important, but because it is often prevents important discussions about learning. So many professional development sessions are about best practice, new methods of teaching, interrogation of assessment far too late to make a difference today or tomorrow – and we seem to like these safe and non-threatening topics. Where is the debate about how we learn, evidence of students' learning in their multiple ways, how to learn differently? Can you name three competing theories of learning? To have these collegial debates about learning and about our impact on this learning requires school leaders that are supportive of teachers being learners and evaluators. Teachers need to be adaptive learning experts, to know multiple ways of teaching and learning, to be able to coach and model different ways of learning, and to be the best error detectors in the business.

Mind frame 4: Teachers/leaders see assessment as feedback about their impact

Of all of the influences on student learning, feedback is among the top-ranked – and this is also the case for teacher learning. Teachers need feedback about their effects on each student; hence the notions of assessment as teacher feedback, teachers as evaluators, and teacher colleagues and students as peers in the feedback equation. Teachers, like students, need to debate and agree about where they are going, how they are going, and where they are going next.

Of course, the assessment is about the student, but the power of interpretation and the consequences of assessment are more in the hands of teachers. We need to move from the prepositional divide of assessment as 'assessment of' and 'assessment for' to assessment as feedback for teachers. The critical questions are as follows.

- 'Who did you teach well and who not so well?'
- 'What did you teach well and what not so well?'
- 'Where are the gaps, where are the strengths, what was achieved, and what has still to be achieved?'
- 'How do we develop a common conception of progress with the students and with all of the teachers in our school?'

Mind frame 5: Teachers/leaders engage in dialogue not monologue

While there is a need for teachers to impart information, while the lecture format is indeed efficient, and while teachers do and should know more than students, there is a major need for teachers also to *listen* to the students' learning. This listening can come from listening to their questions, their ideas, their struggles, their strategies of learning, their successes, their interaction with peers, their outputs, and their views about the teaching. The current dominance of monologue may cause less damage for the brighter students, who can engage in learning with their typically greater access to learning strategies and self-talk about the learning. Monologue is less satisfactory for the struggling, the disengaged, and the confused, and is powerful for the brighter students.

There is a need for more research about the optimal proportions of dialogue and monologue – particularly when one is preferred more than the other – and which is best for surface and deep learning. There is also a great need to find out more about the effects of the nature of the dialogue. One form of dialogue can enhance the language of a subject such that students begin to talk the language of the subject, or the language of the 'correct procedures' to use when studying the subject, or the language of more lucid explanations or justification when interacting with the subject. Clarke (2010) videoed mathematics classes in many countries and noted marked differences in the language used in the class-rooms. He concluded that:

> it is clearly the case that some mathematics teachers value the development of a spoken mathematical vocabulary and some do not. If the goal of classroom mathematical activity was fluency and accuracy in the use of written mathematics, then the teacher may give little priority to students developing any fluency in spoken mathematics. On the other hand, if the teacher subscribes to the view that student understanding resides in the capacity to justify and explain the use of mathematical procedures, in addition to tech-nical proficiency in carrying out these procedures in solving mathematical problems, then the nurturing of student proficiency in the spoken language of mathematics will be prioritized, both for its own sake as valued skill and also because of the key role that language plays in the process whereby knowledge is constructed.
>
> (Clarke, 2010: 35)

A recent newspaper heading about my presentation on this topic read 'Researcher claims teachers should shut up' (although I liked the letter to the editor the next day headed 'Teacher claims researcher should shut up'). While the heading may have captured the spirit, the major message is more about the balance of talking and listening. What is not suggested is that teachers 'shut up' and then students engage in busy work, complete endless trials of similar tasks, fill in worksheets, or talk among themselves. There is not a lot of evidence that reducing teacher talk and increasing student talk necessarily leads to greater achievement gains (Murphy, Wilkinson, Soter, Hennessey, & Alexander, 2009). It may be that a particular type of talk is needed to promote surface and deeper comprehension; it may that a particular type of listening is needed to better understand how and whether students are learning; and it may be that a particular type of reaction to this listening (for example, using rapid formative feedback) is the essence of the power of 'shutting up'. As Carl Rogers, the famed psychotherapist, demonstrated, active listening means that we demonstrate to the other that we not only have listened, but also that we have aimed to understand and show that we have listened. Providing formative feedback helping the student to know what to do next is among the most powerful ways in which to demon-strate to that student that we have listened.

Mind frame 6: Teachers/leaders enjoy the challenge and never retreat to 'doing their best'

Every day in most class's life is a challenge – and we need to embrace this challenge and make it the challenge that we want it to be. The art of teaching is that what is challenging to one student may not be to another; hence the constant attention to the individual differences and seeking the commonality so that peers can work together with the teacher to make the difference. The teachers' role is not to decide on the challenge and then 'break it down' into manageable bits so that it is easier for students; instead, his or her role is to decide on how to engage students in the challenge of the learning. This is why learning intentions and success criteria have been emphasized so strongly, because when students understand these, they can see the purposes of the challenges that are so critical to success in learning.

Mind frame 7: Teachers/leaders believe that it is their role to develop positive relationships in classrooms/staffrooms

So often, we are concerned about the classroom climate, but forget the purpose of warm, trustworthy, empathetic climates. The primary purpose is to allow students to feel okay about making mistakes and not knowing, and to establish a climate in which we welcome error as opportunities. Learning thrives on error: a fundamental role for teachers is to seek out misconceptions, misunderstandings, and lack of knowledge. While teachers may have warm interpersonal interactions, this is not the point. The point is: do the students believe that the climate of the class is fair, empathetic, and trustworthy? Can students readily indicate that they do not know, do not understand – without getting snide comments, looks, and sneers from peers? The power of peers is pervasive, and much about creating the right classroom climate is about creating a safe harbour for welcoming error and thence learning; in the same way, it is critical for school leaders to create a safe staffroom climate, so that all teachers can talk about teaching and their impact on student learning.

Mind frame 8: Teachers/leaders inform all about the language of learning

In many aspects of daily interactions, we take on many roles that are formally undertaken by professionals. We are travel agents, bank tellers, store assistants, bloggers of news, and so on. Such co-production is becoming more common, but it has hardy dented schools. We still see parents as those who receive biannual reports, supervise homework (or not), provide accommodation, and feed and look after students in the other eight hours of their waking lives.

While all parents want to find ways in which to help to co-educate their children, not all parents know how to do this. A major barrier for these latter parents is that they are often not familiar with the language of learning and schools. For many of them, school was not always the most pleasant experience. In our multi-year evaluation of five of the schools in the lowest socio-economic area in New Zealand, we found many positive consequences when teaching parents the language of schooling (Clinton, Hattie, & Dixon, 2007). The Flaxmere Project involved a series of innovations related to improving home–school relations, and included giving a sample of families computers and employing former teachers as 'home–school liaison persons' to help the families to learn how to use the computers. The evaluation demonstrated that it was these former teachers who were informing the parents about the language of schooling that made big differences – that is, the parents learned the language about the nature of learning in today's classrooms, learned how to help their children to attend and engage in learning, and learned how to speak with teachers and school personnel. Parents who co-understand the importance of deliberate practice, concentration, the difference between surface and deep knowing, and the nature of the learning intentions and success criteria are more able to have dialogue with their children. Teaching parents the language of learning led to enhanced engagement by students in their schooling experiences, improvements in reading achievement, greater skills and jobs for the parents, and higher expectations, higher satisfaction, and higher endorsement of the local schools and the Flaxmere community (the effect sizes ranged from $d = 0.30$ to $d = 0.60$ and occasionally were much higher across many outcomes).

When this co-learning occurs, then more evidence about the impact on learning can be understood and potentially acted upon by all. The involvement in homework, in esteeming and promoting schools based on evidence of impact on progress of their children, and in providing support and opportunities to engage in worthwhile challenges in the home can all assist in progressing students to become critical evaluators and learned citizens.

These eight mind frames are the essence of creating schools that can claim they have 'visible learning inside'. They are the core notions on which schools need to focus if there is to be success at having major impacts on all students in their learning and achievement. It is a way of thinking that makes the difference and we need to turn away from finding the 'thing' – the program, the resource, the teaching method, or the structure. When we become the 'evaluators of our impact', then we have the basis for the greatest single improvement in our schools.

Where to start this change process?

In the above three sections, the agents, processes, and purposes for change have been outlined, but the most common question that I am asked is: 'Where do I start?' The start-ing point is evaluating whether you and your school are 'ready' for change in the directions outlined in this book. I do not suggest running sessions lecturing staff about what is going to happen – because this ignores the mind frames that teachers currently have about the success of their own teaching. War stories are so often the currency of defence. Instead, I suggest inviting teachers to evaluate their own mind frames and to see whether they are shared across other teachers. For example, it is worthwhile starting by asking about teachers' and students' conceptions of feedback (see Exercise 2 in Chapter 8); it is also worth using currently available standardized assessment to calculate effect sizes on the school, each class, and each student – and asking about the value of the interpretations of these effect sizes (see Chapter 6 and Appendix E).

This introduction to 'visible learning inside' takes time, cannot be rushed, and requires that much groundwork be done before you can drive delivery. The mind frames of the senior management are critical, because if there is any sense of accountability, it is highly likely to fail; they need to be learning leaders. This is a developmental, shared concept of excellence and impact, which needs to involve all staff in shared success of the effects on all students in the school. The process must be seen as supportive of teachers, provide opportunities for teachers to discuss their beliefs and concerns about the nature of the evidence and the meaning of the ways in which the school decides to 'know its impact,' and see the value and esteem that comes from engaging in this process.

One of the concerns that will soon become evident as a school starts this journey is that much of the data that drowns most schools may not be of much use – because so often it is administered too late, because we collected it these past years, and because it is too broad (a mile wide and an inch deep). It is so often of little use for formative interpretations. A place to start is to consider the nature and quality of the learning intentions and success criteria, and how these relate to the different levels of surface and deep understanding desired. The question is then: how would you be convinced that the student has attained these success criteria relative to where he or she began at the start of the lessons? Simply creating the end-of-lesson assessments and administering them (or a sample of them) at the start and again at the end can provide a worthwhile basis for beginning to estimate the effects.

These are suggested starting points – because these can help you to understand the delivery challenge and help you to decide on plans for delivery.

Conclusions

Once again, I am not claiming that it is teachers that make the difference. This mantra ignores that there are as many teachers who have impact on learning below as above the mean of $d = 0.4$. As I wrote in *Visible Learning*, this mantra:

> has become a cliché that masks the fact that the greatest source of variance in our system relates to teachers – they can vary in many ways. Not all teachers are effective, not all teachers are experts, and not all teachers have powerful effects on students.
>
> (Hattie, 2009: 22)

That we do have so many teachers who can regularly attain above average impact and attain above the typical growth within their classrooms is to be acknowledged, esteemed, and should be the essence of teaching as a profession. Allowing the notion that 'everything goes' de-professionalizes teaching: if anyone with a pulse can teach and be allowed to show success if they exceed the typical low threshold of demonstrating $d = > 0$, then this means that there is no practice of teaching, there is no professional set of skills and understandings that allows more positive impacts (for example, $d = > 0.40$), and that we might as well open the classroom doors to anybody. Sometimes, this seems already to be occurring and the argument in this book is that this is detrimental to the enormous number of teachers who are systematically having high positive impacts on student learning.

As noted earlier, this book is not about a new program that entails fundamental change in what most schools are doing; it is about a frame of reference for thinking about the effects or consequences of what occurs in a school. It is asking for more evaluation by all (teachers, leaders, students) of the effects that the key personnel are having in schools. It is not about asking for more measurement, but about asking for more evaluation of the effects of this measurement (and if the measurement is not having much evaluation value, then maybe it should be reduced, modified, or dropped). The key factor is the mind frames that teachers and school leaders have about the quality of evidence of their impact, their understandings about the nature of this impact, and the way in which they decide on consequences from this evidence of impact.

As Michael Fullan (2012) has so long argued, teachers are not unfamiliar with change – change is their life to the point at which many are inured to it – but so often schools are asked to change programs, to introduce new resources, or to try a new assessment scheme. This is not the change requested in this book; rather, it is asking for a change in the way in which we think about our role, and that we then engender high levels of collaboration, confidence, and commitment to evaluating our effect on students. School leaders and systems must take the lead in this evaluation process, and create a safe and rewarding environment in which the evaluation process can occur.

The major message in this book is that enhancing teacher quality is one of the keys – and the way in which to achieve this is through ensuring that every teacher in the school has the mind frame that leads to the greatest positive effect on student learning and achievement. This is not going to happen with short-term interventions, by naming and blaming, by more testing, by more accountability, by new curricula, or by new resources. It is going to happen through enacting deliberate policies to support schools with the resources to know about their impact, and esteem them when they (the schools) demonstrate their impact on all of their students.

We need policies that make the school the 'unit of evaluation' and we need to help each school to get its staff to work collaboratively on determining the key outcomes that it wishes to evaluate. We need to help schools to collect dependable evidence of the current levels and the desired levels of achievement for each student, and, critically, to monitor the progression from the current to desired levels. It then requires that teachers work together with all students in a school to attend to this monitoring – what to change, what to keep, what to share, what to put in place to give second and third chances, who to advance, and how to constantly challenge, engage, and give confidence to students that they can do better, do more, and can attain the goals. Most importantly, there needs to be recognition and esteem when these progression targets are met, and such success needs to be made public to the school community.

Further, we need to create space in which this can happen. It is not about asking for more professional learning circles or communities of practice, because so often these are dominated by matters that do not make the difference – that is, they are but means. What is needed is more space for teachers to interpret the evidence about their effect on each student. This may require some major rethinking of teachers' work. For example, in much of the Western world, teachers spend about 1,100 hours a year in front of students. This is 36 per cent more time in front of classes when compared to 30 nations in the Organisation for Economic Co-operation and Development (OECD) review: in Japan, for example, they spend about 500 hours in front of students – and the school is structured differently to allow this to happen; the mind frame in Japan is different. Darling-Hammond (2010: 193) argued that the countries that have made the greatest progress in achievement allow teachers with:

> 15 to 25 hours a week . . . to plan cooperatively and engage in analyses of student learning, lesson study, action research, and observation of one another's classrooms that help them continually improve their practice.

I want them to spend such time working together to plan and critique lessons, interpret and deliberate in light of evidence about their impact on each student's learning, in each other's classes observing student learning, and continually evaluating the evidence about how 'we as teachers in this school' can optimize worthwhile outcomes for all students – and share the errors, the enjoyments, the successes about the impact. As a profession, we are excellent at critique; let's use this critique to evaluate whether we are having sufficiently high impacts on all students, whether the nature of how we impact on this learning can be made more effective and efficient, and to make decisions about what we do based on this positive impact on learning – together.

So often, in schools, when time is created for teachers to be out of their classes, teachers want to spend the time marking, preparing, and seeking resources. These are not unimportant activities – but what is asked for here is a culture in which teachers spend more time *together* pre-planning and critiquing this pre-planning, and working in teacher groups to interpret the evidence about their effect on students. What is needed is an attention to both the short-term and the longer-term effects that we have on students, a move from seeing the effect of one teacher on a student in one year towards seeing the effect of many teachers on students over many years (which requires more longitudinal interpretations), a move from teachers seeing their professionalisms in terms of autonomy (which usually means 'Just leave me alone to teach as I wish') towards seeing professionalism in terms of the positive effects that so many teachers already have on so many students. We need to replace 'presentism', conservatism, and individualism with the longer-term school effects of those teachers who are 'evidence-informed' and who take collective responsibility for the success of our schools.

What is asked is not a restructuring, but a recapturing, of schools to optimize and esteem the positive impacts that all can have on student learning. It is not a 'one size fits all' solution; there are many evaluation processes and models, and it takes time and a climate of safety to implement and nurture these changes. It needs attention to and an esteeming of teacher judgements, because it is these judgements that the evaluation process is aiming to influence. It is using the preponderance of evidence to make professional judgements and to see, as far as possible, beyond reasonable doubt that all in a school are having a sufficiently high impact on all of the students. It also means that there is a powerful criterion of success for all of our teachers and school leaders – that is, that success is learning from evaluating our effect. You can all do this . . . You can focus . . . You can deeply implement . . . You can

Know thy impact

Exercises

1. Administer the Checklist in Appendix A to all in the school and then use it as the basis for discussion about the future goals for the school, and to monitor your progress towards becoming a 'visible learning inside' school.

2. Administer the following personal health check to yourself. Share the results with your coach.

YOUR PERSONAL HEALTH CHECK FOR VISIBLE LEARNING

1. I am actively engaged in, and passionate about teaching and learning.
2. I provide students with multiple opportunities for learning based on surface and deep thinking.
3. I know the learning intentions and success criteria of my lessons, and I share these with students.
4. I am open to learning and actively learn myself.
5. I have a warm and caring classroom climate in which errors are welcome.
6. I seek regular feedback from my students.
7. My students are actively involved in knowing about their learning (that is, they are assessment-capable).
8. I can identify progression in learning across multiple curricular levels in my student work and activities.
9. I have a wide range of teaching strategies in my day-to-day teaching repertoire.
10. I use evidence of learning to plan the next learning steps with students.

---

3. Consider the following ten questions that I have used to help parents and students to identify great schools. Consider them in relation to your own school.

   a. In the playground, do the students look each other in the eye? Or do they avoid each other or sit in cliques?

   b. Diversity breeds fresh thinking. Can the parents and students show you genuine evidence that it is encouraged?

   c. How do parents and the students measure success? By the achievements of the few or of the many?

   d. Ask to meet the best teacher. If the parents and students tell you that they're all good, they're not thinking clearly.

   e. To whom do students turn to? Every student should have someone who knows how they are doing and who will spend time with them.

   f. Do new students make friends in the first month? It is a critical indicator for success: how does the school make sure that it happens with all students?

   g. Do students like mistakes? Learning starts from not knowing, so do they embrace that? Do students feel confident enough to talk about errors or not knowing something?

   h. Are students 'assessment-capable' in this school? Can they talk about how well they are doing, and where they are going next?

   i. Does the school use acceleration for all? Are students enabled to learn at different speeds?

   j. What feedback do students get? Ask one: 'What did you get told about your work today?'

4. Look at the following books and see how they complement the arguments in this one. (Many provide more specific examples of the concepts developed in these pages.)

Alton-Lee, A. (2003). *Quality teaching for diverse students in schooling: Best evidence synthesis iteration.* Wellington, New Zealand: Ministry of Education, available online at http://www.educationcounts.govt.nz/publications/series/2515/5959

Ayers, W. (2010). *To teach: The journey of a teacher* (3rd ed.). New York: Teachers College Press.

Clarke, S. (2011). *Active learning through formative assessment.* London: Hodder.

Dinham, S. (2008). *How to get your school moving and improving.* Camberwell: ACER Press.

DuFour, R., & Marzano, R.J. (2011). *Leaders of learning: How district, school, and classroom leaders improve student achievement.* Bloomington, IN: Solution Tree Press.

Higgins, S., Kokotsaki, D., & Coe, R. (2011). *Toolkit of strategies to improve learning: Summary for schools spending the pupil premium.* London: Sutton Trust, available at: http://www.suttontrust.com/research/toolkit-of-strategies-to-improve-learning/ (retrieved 26 May 2011).

Petty, G. (2009a) *Evidence based teaching: A practical approach* (2nd ed.). Cheltenham: Nelson Thornes.

— (2009b) *Teaching today: A practical guide* (4th ed.). Cheltenham: Nelson Thornes.

Robinson, V.M.J. (2011). *Student-centred leadership.* San Francisco, CA: Jossey- Bass.

Steele, C.F. (2009). *The inspired teacher: How to know one, grow one, or be one.* Alexandria, VA: ASCD.

Willingham, D.T. (2009). *Why don't students like school? A cognitive scientist answers questions about how the mind works and what it means for the classroom.* San Francisco, CA: John Wiley & Sons.

References

Absolum, M., Flockton, L., Hattie, J.A.C., Hipkins, R., & Reid, I. (2009). *Directions for assessment in New Zealand: Developing students' assessment capabilities.* Wellington: Ministry of Education, available online at http://assessment.tki.org.nz/Assessment-in-the-classroom/Directions-for-assessment-in-New-Zealand-DANZ-report

Adams, G.L., & Engelmann, S. (1996). *Research on direct instruction: 20 years beyond DISTAR.* Seattle, WA: Educational Achievement Systems.

Alexander, P.A. (2006). *Psychology in learning and instruction.* Columbus, OH: Prentice-Hall.

Alexander, R.J. (2008). *Towards dialogic teaching: Rethinking classroom talk* (4th ed.). York: Dialogos.

Alrieri, L., Brooks, P.J., Aldrich, N.J., & Tenenbaum, H.R. (2011). Does discovery-based instruction enhance learning? *Journal of Educational Psychology, 103*(1), 1–18.

Alton-Lee, A. (2003). *Quality teaching for diverse students in schooling: Best evidence synthesis iteration.* Wellington: Ministry of Education, available online at http://www.educationcounts.govt.nz/publications/series/2515/5959

Alton-Lee, A.G., & Nuthall, G.A. (1990). Pupil experiences and pupil learning in the elementary classroom: An illustration of a generative methodology. *Teaching and Teacher Education: An International Journal of Research and Studies, 6*(1), 27–46.

Amabile, T.S., & Kramer, S.J. (2011). The power of small wins. *Harvard Business Review, 89*(5), 70–90.

Anderman, L.H., & Anderman, E.M. (1999). Social predictors of changes in students' achievement goal orientations. *Contemporary Educational Psychology, 24*(1), 21–37.

Anderson, K. (2010). *Data team success stories, Vol. 1.* Englewood, CO: The Leadership and Learning Center.

Anderson, K. (2011). *Real-time decisions: Educators using formative assessment to change lives now!* Englewood, CO: The Leadership and Learning Center.

Andersson, H., & Bergman, L.R. (2011). The role of task persistence in young adolescence for successful educational and occupational attainment in middle adulthood. *Developmental Psychology, 47*(4), 950–60.

Angus, M., McDonald, T., Ormond, C., Rybarcyk, R., Taylor, A., & Winterton, A. (2009). *Trajectories for classroom behaviour and academic progress.* Perth: Edith Cowan University, available online at http://www.pipelineproject.org.au/Results

Aronson, E. (2008). *Jigsaw classroom,* available online at http://www.jigsaw.net

Au, R., Watkins, D.W., Hattie, J.A.C., & Alexander, P. (2009). Reformulating the depression model of learned hopelessness for academic outcomes. *Educational Research Review, 4,* 103–17.

Ausubel, D.P. (1968). *Educational psychology: A cognitive view.* New York: Holt, Rinehart, and Winston.

Ayers, W. (2010) *To teach: The journey of a teacher* (3rd ed.). New York: Teachers College Press.

Bakhtin, M.M. (1981) *The dialogic imagination: Four essays*. Ed. Michael Holquist. Trans. Caryl Emerson & Michael Holquist. Austin, TX and London: University of Texas Press.

Barber, M. (2008). *Instruction to deliver: Fighting to transform Britain's public services* (2nd ed.). London: Methuen.

Barber, M., Moffit, A., & Kihn, P. (2011). *Deliverology: A field guide for educational leaders*. Thousand Oaks, CA: Corwin Press.

Bausmith, J.M., & Barry, C. (2011). Revisiting professional learning communities to increase college readiness: The importance of pedagogical content knowledge. *Educational Researcher, 40*(40), 175–8.

Becker, L.E. (2009). Effect size calculators, available online at http://www.uccs.edu/~faculty/lbecker/

Bendikson, L., Robinson, V.M.J., & Hattie, J.A. (2011). Identifying the comparative academic performance of secondary schools. *Journal of Educational Administration, 49(4)*, 433–49.

Bereiter, C. (2002). *Education and mind in the knowledge age*. Hillsdale, NJ: Lawrence Erlbaum Associates.

Berthold, K., Nückles, M., & Renkl, A. (2007). Do learning protocols support learning strategies and outcomes? The role of cognitive and metacognitive prompts. *Learning and Instruction, 17*(5), 564–77.

Biggs, J.B., & Collis, K.F. (1982). *Evaluating the quality of learning: The SOLO taxonomy (structure of the observed learning outcome)*. New York: Academic Press.

Bishop, R. (2003). Changing power relations in education: Kaupapa Māori messages for 'mainstream' education in Aotearoa/New Zealand. *Comparative Education, 39*(2), 221–38.

Black, P., Harrison, C., Hodgen, J., Marshall, M., & Serret, N. (2010). Validity in teachers' summative assessments. *Assessment in Education, 17*(2), 215–32.

Black, P., Harrison, C., Lee, C., Marshall, B., & Wiliam, D. (2003). *Assessment for learning: Putting it into practice*. Maidenhead: Open University Press.

Black, P.J., & Wiliam, D. (1998). Assessment and classroom learning. *Assessment in Education, 5*(1), 7–73.

Black, P.J., & Wiliam, D. (2009). Developing the theory of formative assessment. *Educational Assessment, Evaluation and Accountability, 21*(1), 5–31.

Boyd, D., Grossman, P., Ing, M., Lankford, H., Loeb, S., & Wyckoff, J. (2011). The influence of school administrators on teacher retention decisions. *American Educational Research Journal, 48*, 303–33.

Bransford, J., Brown, A.L., & Cocking, R.R. (2000). *How people learn: Brain, mind, experience, and school* (Expanded ed.). Washington, DC: National Academy Press.

Brock, P. (2004). *A passion for life*. Sydney: Australian Broadcasting Corporation.

Brooks, G. (2002). *What works for children with literacy difficulties? The effectiveness of intervention schemes (RR380)*. London: HMSO.

Brown, G., Irving, S.E., & Peterson, E.R. (2009, August). *The more I enjoy it the less I achieve: The negative impact of socio-emotional purposes of assessment and feedback on academic performance*. Paper presented at EARLI conference, Amsterdam.

Brualdi, A.C. (1998). *Classroom questions: ERIC/AE Digest*, ERIC Digest Series No. EDO-TM-98–02, Los Angeles, CA: ERIC Clearinghouse for Community Colleges, University of California at Los Angeles.

Brutus, S., & Greguras, G.J. (2008). Self-construals, motivation, and feedback-seeking behaviors. *International Journal of Selection and Assessment, 16*(3), 282–91.

Bryan, W. L., & Harter, N. (1898). Studies in the physiology and psychology of the telegraphic language. *Psychological Review, 4*, 27–53.

Bryk, A.S., & Schneider, B.L. (2002). *Trust in schools: A core resource for improvement.* New York: Russell Sage Foundation.

Burnett, P.C. (2003). The impact of teacher feedback on student self-talk and self-concept on reading and mathematics. *Journal of Classroom Interaction, 38*(1), 11–16.

Burns, C., & Myhill, D. (2004). Interactive or inactive? A consideration of the nature of interaction in whole class teaching. *Cambridge Journal of Education, 34*(1), 35–49.

Burns, M.K. (2002). Comprehensive system of assessment to intervention using curriculum-based assessments. *Intervention in School and Clinic, 38*(1), 8–13.

Butler, R. (2007). Teachers' achievement goal orientations and associations with teachers' help seeking: Examination of a novel approach to teacher motivation. *Journal of Educational Psychology, 99*(2), 241–52.

Carless, D. (2006). Differing perceptions in the feedback process. *Studies in Higher Education, 31*(2), 219–33.

Carroll, A., Houghton, S., Durkin, K., & Hattie, J.A.C. (2009). *Adolescent reputations and risk: Developmental trajectories to delinquency.* New York: Springer.

Case, R. (1987). The structure and process of intellectual development. *International Journal of Psychology, 5*(6), 571–607.

Case, R. (1999). Conceptual development in the child and the field: A personal view of the Piagetian legacy. In E. Scholnick, K. Nelson, S. Gelman, & P. Miller (Eds.), *Conceptual development: Piaget's legacy* (pp. 23–51). Hillsdale, NJ: Lawrence Erlbaum Associates.

Cazden, C. (2001). *Classroom discourse: The language of teaching and learning.* Portsmouth, NH: Heinemann.

Chan, C.Y.J. (2006). *The effects of different evaluative feedback on student's self-efficacy in learning.* Unpublished doctoral dissertation, University of Hong Kong.

Clarke, D.J. (2010). The cultural specificity of accomplished practice: Contingent conceptions of excellence. In Y. Shimizu, Y. Sekiguchi, & K. Hino (Eds.), *In search of excellence in mathematics education* (pp. 14–38). Proceedings of the 5th East Asia Regional Conference in Mathematics Education. Tokyo: Japan Society of Mathematical Education.

Clarke, S. (2011). *Active learning through formative assessment.* London: Hodder.

Clarke, S., Timperley, H., & Hattie, J.A.C. (2003). *Unlocking formative assessment: Practical strategies for enhancing students' learning in the primary and intermediate classroom* (1st New Zealand ed.). Auckland: Hodder Moa Beckett.

Clements, D.H., & Sarama, J. (2009). *Learning and teaching early math: The learning trajectories approach.* New York: Routledge.

Clinton, J., Hattie, J.A.C., & Dixon, R. (2007). *Evaluation of the Flaxmere Project: When families learn the language of school.* Wellington: Ministry of Education.

Coe, R. (2002). 'It's the effect size, stupid': What effect size is and why it is important, available online at http://www.leeds.ac.uk/educol/documents/00002182.htm

Coffield, F., Moseley, D.V.M., Ecclestone, K., & Hall, E. (2004). *Learning styles and pedagogy: A systematic and critical review.* London: Learning and Skills Research Council.

Cohen, J. (1977). *Statistical power analysis for the behavioral sciences* (Rev. ed.). New York: Academic Press.

Confrey, J., & Maloney, A. (2010, October). *The building of formative assessments around learning trajectories as situated in the CCSS.* Paper presented at the SCASS FAST Fall meetings, Savannah, GA.

Coogan, P., Hoben, N., & Parr, J. (2003). *Written language curriculum framework and map: Levels 5–6.* (Project asTTle Tech. Rep. No. 37). Auckland: University of Auckland, available online at http://www.tki.org.nz/r/asttle/pdf/technical-reports/techreport37.pdf

Cooper, H.M. (1989). *Homework.* New York: Longman.

Cooper, H.M. (1994). *The battle over homework.* Thousand Oaks, CA: Corwin Press.

Cooper, H.M., Robinson, G.C., & Patall, E.A. (2006). Does homework improve academic achievement? A synthesis of research, 1987–2003. *Review of Educational Research, 76*(1), 1–62.

Cornelius-White, J. (2007). Learner-centered teacher–student relationships are effective: A meta-analysis. *Review of Educational Research, 77*(1), 113–43.

Darling-Hammond, L. (2006). *Powerful teacher education: Lessons from exemplary programs.* San Francisco, CA: Jossey-Bass.

Darling-Hammond, L. (2010). *The flat world and education: How America's commitment to equity will determine our future.* New York: Teachers College Press.

Daro, P., Mosher, F.A., & Corcoran, T. (2011). *Learning trajectories in mathematics: A foundation for standards, curriculum, assessment, and instruction.* Philadelphia, PA: Consortium for Policy Research in Education (CRPE).

Davis, E.A. (2003). Prompting middle school science students for productive reflection: Generic and directed prompts. *The Journal of Learning Sciences, 12*, 91–142.

Davis, E.A., & Linn, M.C. (2000). Scaffolding students' knowledge integration: Prompts for reflection in KIE. *International Journal of Science Education, 22*(8), 819–37.

Day, C. (2004). *A passion for teaching.* London: Routledge Falmer.

DeBaz, T.P. (1994). *A meta-analysis of the relationship between students' characteristics and achievement and attitudes toward science.* Unpublished Ph.D., Ohio State University, United States.

Dinham, S. (2008). *How to get your school moving and improving.* Camberwell: ACER Press.

DuFour, R., DuFour, R., & Eaker, R. (2008). *Revisiting professional learning communities at work.* Bloomington, IN: Solution Tree Press.

DuFour, R., & Marzano, R.J. (2011). *Leaders of learning: How district, school, and classroom leaders improve student achievement.* Bloomington, IN: Solution Tree Press.

Dunning, D. (2005). *Self-insight: Roadblocks and detours on the path to knowing thyself.* New York: Psychology Press.

Duschl, R.A., & Osborne, J. (2002). Supporting and promoting argumentation discourse in science education. *Studies in Science Education, 38*, 39–72.

Dweck, C. (2006). *Mindset.* New York: Random House.

Elmore, R.F. (2004). *School reform from the inside out: Policy, practice, and performance.* Cambridge, MA: Harvard Education Press.

Elmore, R.F., Fiarmen, S., & Teital, L. (2009). *Instructional Rounds in Education.* Cambridge, MA: Harvard Education Press.

English, L.D. (Ed.). (2002). *Handbook of International Research in Mathematics Education.* Hillsdale, NJ: Lawrence Erlbaum Associates.

Ericsson, K.A. (2006). The influence of experience and deliberate practice on the development of superior expert performance. In K.A. Ericsson, N. Charness, P. Feltovich, & R.R. Hoffman (Eds.), *Cambridge handbook of expertise and expert performance* (pp. 685–706). Cambridge: Cambridge University Press.

Falchikov, N., & Goldfinch, J. (2000). Student peer assessment in higher education: A meta-analysis comparing peer and teacher marks. *Review of Educational Research, 70*(3), 287–322.

Fletcher, R.B., & Hattie, J.A.C. (2011). *Intelligence and intelligence testing.* London: Routledge.

Fullan, M. (2011). *Choosing the wrong drivers for whole system reform.* Melbourne: Centre for Strategic Education.

Fullan, M. (2012). *Change leader: Learning to do what matters most.* New York: John Wiley.

Fullan, M., Hill, P., & Crévola, C. (2006). *Breakthrough.* Thousand Oaks, CA: Corwin Press.

Gage, N. L., & Berliner, D.C. (1998). *Educational psychology* (6th ed.). Boston, MA: Houghton Mifflin.

Galton, M., Morrison, I., & Pell, T. (2000). Transfer and transition in English schools: Reviewing the evidence. *International Journal of Educational Research, 33*, 341–63.

Galton, M., & Patrick, H. (Eds.). (1990). *Curriculum provision in small primary schools.* London: Routledge.

Gan, M. (2011). *The effects of prompts and explicit coaching on peer feedback quality.* Unpublished doctoral dissertation, University of Auckland, available online at https://researchspace.auckland.ac.nz/handle/2292/6630

Gardner, H. (2009). Reflections on my works and those of my commentators. In B. Shearer (Ed.), *MI at 25* (pp. 113–120). New York: Teachers College Press.

Gates Foundation (2010). *Learning about teaching: Initial findings from the Measures of Effective Teaching Project,* available online at http://www.gatesfoundation.org/college-ready-education/Documents/preliminary-findings-research-paper.pdf

Gawande, A. (2009). *The checklist manifesto.* New York: Henry Holt Publishers.

Gickling, E.E. (1984, October). *Operationalizing academic learning time for low achieving and handicapped mainstreamed students.* Paper presented at the Annual Meeting of the Northern Rocky Mountain Educational Research Association, Jackson Hole, WY.

Gladwell, M. (2008). *Outliers: The story of success.* New York: Little, Brown, and Company.

Glass, G.V., McGaw, B., & Smith, M.L. (1981). *Meta-analysis in social research.* Beverly Hills, CA: Sage.

Glasswell, K., Parr, J., & Aikman, M. (2001). *Development of the asTTle writing assessment rubrics for scoring extended writing tasks.* (Tech. Rep. No. 6). Auckland: University of Auckland, Project asTTle.

Goldstein, L. (2006). Feedback and revision in second language writing: Contextual, teacher, and student variables. In K. Hyland & F. Hyland (Eds.), *Feedback in second language writing: Contexts and issues* (pp. 185–205). New York: Cambridge University Press.

Gore, J.M., Griffiths, T., & Ladwig, J.G. (2004). Towards better teaching: Productive pedagogy as a framework for teacher education. *Teaching and Teacher Education, 20*(4): 375–87.

Graesset, A.C., Halpern, D.F., & Hakel, M. (2008). *25 principles of learning.* Washington, DC: Taskforce on Lifelong Learning at Work and at Home, available online at www.psyc.memphis.edu/learning/whatweknow/index.shtml

Griffin, P. (2007). The comfort of competence and the uncertainty of assessment. *Studies in Educational Evaluation, 33*(1), 87–99.

Hardman, F., Smith, F., & Wall, K. (2003). Interactive whole class teaching in the National Literacy Strategy. *Cambridge Journal of Education, 33*(2), 197–215.

Harelli, S., & Hess, U. (2008). When does feedback about success at school hurt? The role of causal attributions. *Social Psychology in Education, 11*, 259–72.

Hargreaves, A. (2010). Presentism, individualism, and conservatism: The legacy of Dan Lortie's 'Schoolteacher: A Sociological Study'. *Curriculum Inquiry, 40*(1), 143–54.

Harks, B., Rokoczy, K., Hattie, J.A.C., Klieme, E., & Besser, M. (2011). Self regulation mediates the impact of feedback, forthcoming publication.

Hastie, S. (2011). *Teaching students to set goals: Strategies, commitment, and monitoring.* Unpublished doctoral dissertation, University of Auckland, New Zealand.

Hattie, J.A.C (1992). *Self-concept.* Hillsdale, NJ: Lawrence Erlbaum Associates, p. 304.

Hattie, J.A.C. (2007). The status of reading in New Zealand schools: The upper primary plateau problem (PPP3). *Reading Forum, 22*(2), 25–39.

Hattie, J.A.C. (2008). Processes of integrating, developing, and processing self information. In H.W. Marsh, R. Craven, & D.M. McInerney (Eds.), *Self-processes, learning, and enabling human potential: Dynamic new approaches* (Vol. 3). Greenwich, CN: Information Age Publishing.

Hattie, J.A.C. (2009). *Visible learning: A synthesis of 800+ meta-analyses on achievement*. London: Routledge.

Hattie, J.A.C. (2010a). The validity of reports. *Online Educational Research Journal*, available online at http://www.oerj.org/View?action=viewPaper&paper=6

Hattie, J.A.C. (2010b, May). *The differences in achievement between boys and girls*. Presentation to the Boys Schools Annual Conference, Wellington.

Hattie, J.A.C., Biggs, J., & Purdie, N. (1996). Effects of learning skills interventions on student learning: A meta-analysis. *Review of Educational Research*, *66*(2), 99–136.

Hattie, J.A.C., & Brown, G.T.L. (2004). *Cognitive processes in asTTle: The SOLO taxonomy*. asTTle Technical Report (No. 43). Auckland: University of Auckland and the Ministry of Education.

Hattie, J.A.C., Brown, G.T.L., & Keegan, P.J. (2003). A national teacher-managed, curriculum-based assessment system: Assessment Tools for Teaching & Learning (asTTle). *International Journal of Learning*, *10*, 771–8.

Hattie, J.A.C., & Clinton, J.M. (2011). School leaders as evaluators. In *Activate: A leader's guide to people, practices and processes* (pp. 93–118). Englewood, CO: The Leadership and Learning Center.

Hattie, J.A.C., Clinton, J.M., Nagle, B., Kelkor, V., Reid, W., Spence, K., Baker, W., & Jaeger, R. (1998). *The first year evaluation of Paideia*. Guilford County: Bryan Foundation and Guilford County Schools.

Hattie, J.A.C., & Masters, D. (2011). *The evaluation of a student feedback survey*. Auckland: Cognition.

Hattie, J.A.C., & Purdie, N. (1998). The SOLO model: Addressing fundamental measurement issues. In B.C. Dart & G.M. Boulton-Lewis (Eds.), *Teaching and learning in higher education* (pp. 145–176). Camberwell, Victoria, Australia: Australian Council of Educational Research.

Hattie, J.A.C., Rogers, H.J., & Swaminathan, H. (2010). The role of meta-analysis in educational research. In A. Reid, P. Hart, M. Peters, & C. Russell (Eds.), *A companion to research in education*. UK: Springer.

Hattie, J.A.C. and team (2009). *Generation II: e-asTTle. An internet computer application*. Wellington: Ministry of Education.

Hattie, J.A.C., & Timperley, H. (2006). The power of feedback. *Review of Educational Research*, *77*(1), 81–112.

Hays, M.J., Kornell, N., & Bjork, R.A. (2010). Costs and benefits of feedback during learning. *Psychonomic Bulletin and Review*, *17*(6), 797–801.

Hedges, L.V., & Olkin, I. (1985). *Statistical methods for meta-analysis*. Orlando, FL: Academic Press.

Heimbeck, D., Frese, M., Sonnentag, S., & Keith, N. (2003). Integrating errors into the training process: The function of error management instructions and the role of goal orientation. *Personnel Psychology*, *56*, 333–62.

Heubusch, J.D., & Lloyd, J.W. (1998). Corrective feedback in oral reading. *Journal of Behavioral Education*, *8*, 63–79.

Higgins, R., Hartley, P., & Skelton, A. (2001). Getting the message across: The problem of communicating assessment feedback. *Teaching in Higher Education*, *6*(2), 269–74.

Higgins, S., Kokotsaki, D., and Coe, R. (2011) *Toolkit of strategies to improve learning: Summary for schools spending the pupil premium*. London: Sutton Trust, available online at http://www.sutton trust.com/research/toolkit-of-strategies-to-improve-learning/

Hill, C.J., Bloom, H.S., Black, A.R., & Lipsey, M.W. (2008). Empirical benchmarks for interpreting effect sizes in research. *Child Development Perspectives*, *2*(3), 172–7.

Holt, C.R., Denny, G., Capps, M., & De Vore, J. (2005). Teachers' ability to perceive student learning preferences: 'I'm sorry, but I don't teach like that.' *Teachers College Record*, available online at www.tcrecord.org/printContent.asp/Content ID=11767

Hunter, J.E., & Schmidt, F.L. (1990). *Methods of meta-analysis: Correcting error and bias in research findings*. Newbury Park, CA: Sage.

Hyde, J.S. (2005). The gender similarities hypothesis. *American Psychologist, 60*(6), 581–92.

Hyland, F., & Hyland, K. (2001). Sugaring the pill: Praise and criticism in written feedback. *Journal of Second Language Writing, 10*(3), 185–212.

Hyland, K., & Hyland, F. (Eds.), (2006). *Feedback in second language writing: Contexts and issues*. Cambridge: Cambridge University Press.

Ingvarson, L., & Hattie, J. (Eds.). (2008). *Assessing teachers for professional certification: The first decade of the National Board for Professional Teaching Standards*. Advances in Program Evaluation Series #11, Oxford: Elsevier.

Inoue, N. (2007). Why face a challenge? The reason behind intrinsically motivated students' spontaneous choice of challenging tasks. *Learning and Individual Differences, 17*(3), 251–9.

Irving, S. E. (2004). *The development and validation of a student evaluation instrument to identify highly accomplished mathematics teachers*. Unpublished Ph.D., University of Auckland.

Jackson, P.W. (1968). *Life in classrooms*. New York: Holt, Rinehart and Winston.

James, W. (1897/1927). *The will to believe*. London: Longmans, Green and Co.

Joyce, B., & Showers, B. (1995). *Student achievement through staff development: Fundamental of school renewal* (2nd ed.). New York: Longman Press.

Kamins, M.L., & Dweck, C.S. (1999). Person versus process praise and criticism: Implications for contingent self-worth and coping. *Developmental Psychology, 35*(3), 835–47.

Kang, S., McDermott, K.B., & Roediger, H. L. (2007). Test format and corrective feedback modulate the effect of testing on memory retention. *The European Journal of Cognitive Psychology, 19*, 528–58.

Kennedy, M.M. (2010). Attribution error and the quest for teacher quality. *Educational Researcher, 39*(8), 591–8.

Kessels, U., Warner, L.M., Holle, J., & Hannover, B. (2008). Threat to identity through positive feedback about academic performance. *Zeitschrift fur Entwicklungspsychologie und Padagogische Psychologie, 40*(1), 22–31.

Kluger, A.N., & DeNisi, A. (1996). The effects of feedback interventions on performance: A historical review, a meta-analysis, and a preliminary feedback intervention theory. *Psychological Bulletin, 119*(2), 254–84.

Kobayashi, K. (2005). What limits the encoding effect of note-taking? A meta-analytic examination. *Contemporary Educational Psychology, 30*(2), 242–62.

Kohn, A. (2006). *The homework myth: Why our kids get too much of a bad thing*. Cambridge, MA: Da Capo Press.

Kulhavy, R. W. (1977). Feedback in written instruction. *Review of Educational Research, 47*(2), 211–32.

Kung, M.C. (2008). *Why and how do people seek success and failure feedback? A closer look at motives, methods and cultural differences*. Unpublished doctoral dissertation, Florida Institute of Technology.

Ladd, H.F. (2011). Teachers' perceptions of their working conditions: How predictive of planned and actual teacher movement? *Educational Evaluation and Policy Analysis, 33*(2), 235–61.

Lavery, L. (2008). *Self-regulated learning for academic success: An evaluation of instructional techniques*. Unpublished Ph.D., University of Auckland.

Leahy, S., & Wiliam, D. (2009). *Embedding assessment for learning: A professional development pack*. London: Specialist Schools and Academies Trust.

Levin, B. (2008). *How to change 5000 schools*. Cambridge, MA: Harvard Education Press.

Levin, H., Belfield, C., Muennig, P., & Rouse, C. (2006). *The costs and benefits of an excellent education for all of America's children*. New York: Teachers College.

Lingard, B. (2007). Pedagogies of indifference. *International Journal of Inclusive Education*, *11*(3), 245–66.

Lipsey, M.W., & Wilson, D.B. (2001). *Practical meta-analysis*. Applied Social Research Methods Series (Vol. 49). Thousand Oaks, CA: Sage.

Lortie, D.C. (1975). *School teacher: A sociological study*. Chicago, IL: University of Chicago Press.

Luque, M.F., & Sommer, S.M. (2000). The impact of culture on feedback-seeking behavior: An integrated model and propositions. *The Academy of Management Review*, *25*(4), 829–49.

Maguire, T.O. (1988, December). *The use of the SOLO taxonomy for evaluating a program for gifted students*. Paper presented at the Annual Conference of the Australian Association for Research in Education, Armidale, NSW.

Mansell, W. (2008, 21 November). Pupil self-assessment is top way to improve. *Times Educational Supplement*, p. 21.

Marsh, H.W., Seaton, M., Trautwein, U., Lüdtke, O., Hau, K.T., O'Mara, A.J., & Craven, R.G. (2008). The big-fish-little-pond-effect stands up to critical scrutiny: Implications for theory, methodology, and future research. *Educational Psychology Review*, *20*, 319–50.

Martin, A.J. (2006). Personal bests (PBs): A proposed multidimensional model and empirical analysis. *British Journal of Educational Psychology*, *76*, 803–25.

Mayer, R.E. (2004). Should there be a three-strikes rule against pure discovery learning? The case for guided methods of instruction. *American Psychologist*, *59*, 14–19.

Mayer, R.E. (2009). Constructivism as a theory of learning versus constructivism as a prescription for instruction. In S. Tobias & T.M. Duffy (Eds.), *Constructivist theory applied to instruction: Success or failure?* (pp. 184–200). New York: Taylor & Francis.

Mayer, R. E., Stull, A., DeLeeuw, K., Almeroth, K., Bimber, B., Chun, D., Bulger, M., Campbell, J., Knight, A., & Zhang, H. (2009). Clickers in college classrooms: Fostering learning with questioning methods in large lecture classes. *Contemporary Educational Psychology*, *34*(1), 51–7.

McIntyre, D., Pedder, D., & Rudduck, J. (2005). Pupil voice: Comfortable and uncomfortable learnings for teachers. *Research Papers in Education*, *20*(2), 149–68.

McNulty, B.A., & Besser, L. (2011). *Leaders make it happen! An administrator's guide to data teams*. Englewood, CO: The Leadership and Learning Center.

Meehan, H. (1979). *Learning lessons*. Cambridge, MA: Harvard University Press.

Mercer, N., & Littleton, K. (2007). *Dialogue and the development of children's thinking*. London: Routledge.

Miller, P. (2010). *The smart swarm: How understanding flocks, schools, and colonies can make us better at communicating, decision making, and getting things done*. London: Penguin Group.

Moseley, D., Baumfield, V., Higgins, S., Lin, M., Miller, J., Newton, D., Robson, S., Elliott, J., and Gregson, M. (2004). *Thinking skill frameworks for post-16 learners: An evaluation*. London: Learning and Skills Research Centre.

Murphy, P.K., Wilkinson, I.A.G., Soter, A.O., Hennessey, M.N., & Alexander, J.F. (2009). Examining the effects of classroom discussion on students' comprehension of text: A meta-analysis. *Journal of Educational Psychology*, *101*(3), 740–64.

Neiderer, K. (2011). *The BFLPE: Self-concepts of gifted students in a part-time, gifted program*. Unpublished doctoral dissertation, University of Auckland.

Neumann, A. (2006) Professing passion: Emotion in the scholarship of professors at research universities, *American Educational Research Journal*, *43*(3), 381–424.

Newton, P., Driver. R., & Osborne, J. (1999). The place of argumentation in the pedagogy of school science. *International Journal of Science Education*, *21*(5), 553–76.

Nickerson, R.S. (1998). Confirmation bias: A ubiquitous phenomenon in many guises. *Review of General Psychology*, *2*, 175–220.

Nuckles, M., Hubner, S., & Renkl, A. (2009). Enhancing self-regulated learning by writing learning protocols. *Learning and Instruction*, *19*, 259–71.

Nussbaum, E.S. (2010). *Not for profit: Why democracy needs the humanities.* Princeton, NJ: Princeton University Press.

Nuthall, G.A. (2005). The cultural myths and realities of classroom teaching and learning: A personal journey. *Teachers College Record*, *107*(5), 895–934.

Nuthall, G.A. (2007). *The hidden lives of learners.* Wellington: New Zealand Council for Educational Research.

Ornstein, P., Coffman, J., McCall, L., Grammer, J., & san Souci, P. (2010). Linking the classroom context and the development of children's memory skills. In J.L. Meece & J.S. Eccles (Eds.), *Handbook on research on schools, schooling, and human development* (pp. 42–59). New York: Routledge.

Parker, W.B. (2006). Public discourses in schools: Purposes, problems, possibilities. *Educational Researcher*, *35*(8), 11–18.

Paschal, R. A., Weinstein, T., & Walberg, H. J. (1984). The effects of homework on learning: A quantitative synthesis. *Journal of Educational Research*, *78*(2), 97–104.

Pashler, H., McDaniel, M., Rohrer, D., & Bjork, R. (2009). Learning styles: Concepts and evidence. *Psychological Science in the Public Interest*, *9*(3), 105–19.

Peeck, J., van den Bosch, A.B., & Kreupeling, W.J. (1985). Effects of informative feedback in relation to retention of initial responses. *Contemporary Educational Psychology*, *10*(4), 303–13.

Pekrul, S., & Levin, B. (2007). Building student voice for school improvement. In D. Thiessen & A. Cook-Sather (Eds.), *International handbook of student experience in elementary and secondary school* (pp. 711–26). Dordrecht: Springer.

Petty, G. (2006). *Evidence-based teaching: A practical approach.* Cheltenham: Nelson Thornes.

Petty. G. (2009a) *Evidence-based teaching: A practical approach* (2nd ed.). Cheltenham: Nelson Thornes.

Petty, G. (2009b) *Teaching today: A practical guide* (4th ed.). Cheltenham: Nelson Thornes.

Piaget, J. (1970). *Genetic epistemology.* New York: Columbia University Press.

Plant, E.A., Ericsson, K.A., Hill, L., & Asberg, K. (2005). Why study time does not predict grade point average across college students: Implications of deliberate practice for academic performance. *Contemporary Educational Psychology*, *30*, 96–116.

Popham, J. (2011, April). *How to build learning progressions: Keep them simple, Simon.* Paper presented at the annual meeting of the American Educational Research Association, New Orleans, LA.

Pratt, S., & George, R. (2005). Transferring friendship: Girls' and boys' friendships in the transition from primary to secondary school. *Children & Society*, *19*(1), 16–26.

Purkey, W.W. (1992). An introduction to invitational theory. *Journal of Invitational Theory and Practice*, *1*(1), 5–15.

Reeves, D. (2009). Level-five networks: Making significant changes in complex organizations. In A. Hargreaves & M. Fullan (Eds.), *Change wars* (pp. 185–200). Bloomington, IN: Solution Tree Press.

Reeves, D. (2010). *Transforming professional development into student results.* Alexandria, VA: ACSD.

Reeves, D. (2011). *Finding your leadership focus.* New York: Teachers College Press.

Retelsdorf, J., Butler, R., Streblow, L., & Schiefele, U. (2010). Teachers' goal orientations for teaching: Associations with instructional practices, interest in teaching, and burnout. *Learning and Instruction*, *20*(1), 30–46.

Riener, C., & Willingham, D. (2010). The myth of learning styles. *Change*, Sept/Oct, 32–6.

Roberts, T., & Billings, L. (1999). *The Paideia classroom: Teaching for understanding.* Larchmont, NY: Eye on Education.

Robinson, V.M.J. (2011). *Student-centred leadership.* San Francisco, CA: Jossey Bass.

Robinson, V.M.J., Lloyd, C., & Rowe, K.J. (2008). The impact of educational leadership on student outcomes: An analysis of the differential effects of leadership types. *Education Administration Quarterly, 41,* 635–74.

Roseth, C.J., Fang, F., Johnson, D.W., & Johnson, R.T. (2006, April). *Effects of cooperative learning on middle school students: A meta-analysis.* Paper presented at the Annual Meeting of the American Educational Research Association, San Francisco, CA.

Rubie-Davies, C.M. (2007). Classroom interactions: Exploring the practices of high- and low-expectation teachers. *British Journal of Educational Psychology, 77,* 289–306.

Rubie-Davies, C., Hattie, J.A.C., & Hamilton, R. (2006). Expecting the best for students: Teacher expectations and academic outcomes. *British Journal of Educational Psychology, 76,* 429–44.

Sadler, D.R. (1989). Formative assessment and the design of instructional systems. *Instructional Science, 18*(2), 119–44.

Sadler, D.R. (2008). Beyond feedback: Developing student capability in complex appraisal. *Assessment and Evaluation in Higher Education, 35*(5), 535–50.

Schagen, I., & Hodgen, E. (2009). *How much difference does it make? Notes on understanding, using, and calculating effect sizes for schools,* available online at www.educationcounts.govt.nz/publications/schooling/36097/36098

Schunk, D.H. (1996). Goal and self-evaluative influences during children's cognitive skill learning. *American Educational Research Journal, 33,* 359–82.

Schunk, D.H. (2008). *Learning theories: An educational perspective* (4th ed.). Upper Saddle River, NJ: Merrill/Prentice Hall.

Scriven, M. (1991). Pros and cons about goal-free evaluation. *American Journal of Evaluation, 12*(1), 55–62.

Scriven, M. (2005). *The logic and methodology of checklists,* available online at www.wmich.edu/evalctr/checklists

Shayer, M. (2003). Not just Piaget; not just Vygotsky, and certainly not Vygotsky as alternative to Piaget. *Learning and Instruction, 13,* 465–85.

Shayer, M., & Adey, P.S. (1981). *Towards a science of science teaching.* London: Heinemann Educational Books.

Sherman, S., & Frea, A. (2004). The Wild West of executive coaching. *Harvard Business Review, 82*(11), 82–90.

Shernoff, D.J., & Csikszentmihalyi, M. (2009). Flow in schools: Cultivating engaged learners and optimal learning environments. In R.C. Gilman, E.S. Heubner, & M.J. Furlong (Eds.), *Handbook of positive psychology in schools* (pp. 131–45). New York: Routledge.

Shields, D.L. (2011). Character as the aim of education. *Phi Delta Kappan, 92*(8), 48–53.

Shute, V.J. (2008). Focus on formative feedback, *Review of Educational Research, 78*(1), 153–89.

Simon, H.A., & Chase, W.G. (1973). Skill in chess. *American Scientist, 61*(4), 394–403.

Sitzmann, T., & Ely, K. (2011). A meta-analysis of self-regulated learning in work-related training and educational attainment: What we know and where we need to go. *Psychological Bulletin, 137*(3), 421–42.

Skipper, Y., & Douglas, K. (2011). Is no praise good praise? Effects of positive feedback on children's and university students' responses to subsequent failures. *British Journal of Educational Psychology.*

Slater, H., Davies, N., & Burgess, S. (2009). *Do teachers matter? Measuring the variation in teacher effectiveness in England.* Centre for Market and Public Organisation Working Series No. 09/212, available online at www.bristol.ac.uk/cmpo/publications/papers/2009/wp212.pdf

Sluijsmans, D.M.A., Brand-Gruwel, S., & van Merrienboer, J.J.G. (2002). Peer assessment training in teacher education: Effects on performance and perceptions. *Assessment and Evaluation in Higher Education, 27*(5), 443–54.

Smith S.L. (2009). *Academic target setting: Formative use of achievement data.* Unpublished doctoral dissertation, University of Auckland.

Smith, T.W., Baker, W.K., Hattie. J.A.C., & Bond, L. (2008). A validity study of the certification system of the National Board for Professional Teaching Standards. In L. Ingvarson & J.A.C. Hattie (Eds.), *Assessing teachers for professional certification: The first decade of the National Board for Professional Teaching Standards* (pp. 345–80). Advances in Program Evaluation Series #11, Oxford: Elsevier.

Snowling, M.J., & Hulme, C. (2010). Evidence-based interventions for reading and language difficulties: Creating a virtuous circle. *British Journal of Educational Psychology, 81*(1), 1–23.

Steedle, J.T., & Shavelson, R.J. (2009). Supporting valid interpretations of learning progression level diagnoses. *Journal of Research in Science Teaching, 46*(6), 699–715.

Steele, C.F. (2009). *The inspired teacher: How to know one, grow one, or be one.* Alexandria, VA: ASCD.

Taber, K.S. (2010, 6 July). Constructivism and direct instruction as competing instructional paradigms: An essay review of Tobias and Duffy's constructivist instruction: Success or failure? *Education Review, 13*(8), available online at http://www.edrev.info/essays/v13n8index.html

Timperley, H. (2012). *Realising the power of professional learning.* Maidenhead: Open University Press.

Timperley, H., Wilson, A., Barrar, H., & Fung, I. (2007). *Teacher professional learning and development: Best evidence synthesis on professional learning and development.* Wellington: Ministry of Education, available online at http://www.educationcounts.govt.nz/publications/series/2515/15341

Tomlinson, C.A. (1995). *How to differentiate instruction in mixed-ability classrooms.* Alexandria, VA: ASCD.

Tomlinson, C.A. (2005). *Differentiation in practice: A resource guide for differentiating curriculum, grades 9–12.* Alexandria, VA: ASCD.

Van de Pol, J., Volman, M., & Beishuizen, J. (2010). Scaffolding in teacher–student interaction: A decade of research. *Educational Psychological Review, 22*, 271–96.

Van den Bergh, L., Ros, A., & Beijaard, D. (2010). *Feedback van basisschoolleerkrachten tijdens actief leren: de huidige praktijk.* ORD-paper ORD, Enschede.

van Gog, T., Ericsson, K.A., Rikers, R.M.J.P., & Paas, F. (2005). Instructional design for advanced learners: Establishing connections between theoretical frameworks of cognitive load and deliberate practice. *Educational Technology Research and Development, 53*(3), 73–81.

Weinstein, R.S. (2002). *Reaching higher: The power of expectations in schooling.* Cambridge, MA: Harvard University Press.

Wetzels, S.A.J., Kester, L., van Merrienboer, J.J.G., & Broers, N.J. (2011). The influence of prior knowledge on the retrieval-directed function of note taking in prior knowledge activation. *British Journal of Educational Psychology, 81*(2), 274–91.

Wickens, C. (2002). Situation awareness and workload in aviation. *Current Directions in Psychological Science, 11*(4), 128–33.

Wiggins, G.P., & McTighe, J. (2005). *Understanding by design* (Expanded 2nd ed.). Alexandria, VA: ASCD.

Wiliam, D. (2011). *Embedded formative assessment.* Bloomington, IN: Solution Tree Press.

Wiliam, D., Lee, C., Harrison, C., & Black, P. (2004). Teachers developing assessment for learning: Impact on student achievement. *Assessment in Education: Principles, Policy, and Practice, 11*(1), 49–65.

Wiliam, D., & Thompson, M. (2008). Integrating assessment with instruction: What will it take to make it work? In C.A. Dwyer (Ed.), *The future of assessment: Shaping teaching and learning* (pp. 53–92). Hillsdale, NJ: Lawrence Erlbaum Associates.

Wilkinson, I.A.G., Parr, J.M., Fung, I.Y.Y., Hattie, J.A.C., & Townsend, M.A.R. (2002). Discussion: Modeling and maximizing peer effects in school. *International Journal of Educational Research*, *37*(5), 521–35.

Wilkinson, S.S. (1980). *The relationship of teacher praise and student achievement: A meta-analysis of selected research.* Unpublished doctoral dissertation, University of Florida.

Willingham, D.T. (2009). *Why don't students like school? A cognitive scientist answers questions about how the mind works and what it means for the classroom.* San Francisco, CA: John Wiley & Sons.

Wilson, B.L., & Corbett, H.D. (2007). Students' perspectives on good teaching: Implications for adult reform behavior. In D. Thiessen & A. Cook-Sather (Eds.), *International handbook of student experience in elementary and secondary school* (pp. 283–314). Dordrecht: Springer.

Winne, P.H., & Hadwin, A.F. (2008). The weave of motivation and self-regulated learning. In D.H. Schunk & B.J. Zimmerman (Eds.), *Motivation and self-regulated learning: Theory, research, and applications* (pp. 297–314). Hillsdale, NJ: Lawrence Erlbaum Associates.

Wittgenstein, L. (1958). *Philosophical investigations* (G.E.M. Anscombe, Trans. 2nd ed.). Oxford: Blackwell.

Yair, G. (2000). Educational battlefields in America: The tug-of-war over students' engagement with instruction. *Sociology of Education*, *73*(4), 247–69.

Yeh, S.S. (2011). *The cost-effectiveness of 22 approaches for raising student achievement.* Charlotte, NC: Information Age.

Zehm, S.J., & Kottler, J.A. (1993). *On being a teacher: The human dimension.* Thousand Oaks, CA: Corwin Press.

Checklist for 'visible learning inside'

Photocopying of this appendix is permitted.

It is valuable for personnel in the school to use this checklist at the start, and during, their journey towards 'visible learning inside' to plot their own progress. The meaning of each part of the checklist is elaborated in each of the chapters, and needs to be understood by reading the appropriate sections.

Be sure that all understand the meaning of each checklist, and then independently rate each and review the results as a school by circling the number that best represents your feelings about the statement.

STRONGLY DISAGREE	GENERALLY DISAGREE	PARTLY DISAGREE	PARTLY AGREE	GENERALLY AGREE	STRONGLY AGREE
1	2	3	4	5	6

Inspired and passionate teaching

1. **All adults in this school recognize that:**

   a. there is variation among teachers in their impact on student learning and achievement; 1 2 3 4 5 6

   b. all (school leaders, teachers, parents, students) place high value on having major positive effects on all students; and 1 2 3 4 5 6

   c. all are vigilant about building expertise to create positive effects on achievement for all students. 1 2 3 4 5 6

2. **This school has convincing evidence that all of its teachers are passionate and inspired – and this should be the major promotion attribute of this school.** 1 2 3 4 5 6

3. **This school has a professional development program that:**

   a. enhances teachers' deeper understandings of their subject(s);   1 2 3 4 5 6

   b. supports learning through analyses of the teachers' classroom interactions with students;   1 2 3 4 5 6

   c. helps teachers to know how to provide effective feedback;   1 2 3 4 5 6

   d. attends to students' affective attributes; and   1 2 3 4 5 6

   e. develops the teacher's ability to influence students' surface and deep learning.   1 2 3 4 5 6

4. **This school's professional development also aims to help teachers to seek pathways towards:**

   a. solving instructional problems;   1 2 3 4 5 6

   b. interpreting events in progress;   1 2 3 4 5 6

   c. being sensitive to context;   1 2 3 4 5 6

   d. monitoring learning;   1 2 3 4 5 6

   e. testing hypotheses;   1 2 3 4 5 6

   f. demonstrating respect for all in the school;   1 2 3 4 5 6

   g. showing passion for teaching and learning; and   1 2 3 4 5 6

   h. helping students to understand complexity.   1 2 3 4 5 6

5. **Professionalism is this school is achieved by teachers and school leaders working collaboratively to achieve 'visible learning inside'.**   1 2 3 4 5 6

Planning

6. **The school has, and teachers use, defensible methods for:**

   a. monitoring, recording, and making available on a 'just-in-time' basis, interpretations about prior, present, and targeted student achievement;   1 2 3 4 5 6

   b. monitoring the progress of students regularly throughout and across years, and this information is used in planning and evaluating lessons;   1 2 3 4 5 6

   c. creating targets relating to the effects that teachers are expected to have on all students' learning.   1 2 3 4 5 6

7. **Teachers understand the attitudes and dispositions that students bring to the lesson, and aim to enhance these so that they are a positive part of learning.**   1 2 3 4 5 6

8. Teachers within the school jointly plan series of lessons, with learning intentions and success criteria related to worthwhile curricular specifications. 1 2 3 4 5 6

9. There is evidence that these planned lessons:

    a. invoke appropriate challenges that engage the students' commitment to invest in learning; 1 2 3 4 5 6

    b. capitalize on and build students' confidence to attain the learning intentions; 1 2 3 4 5 6

    c. are based on appropriately high expectations of outcomes for students; 1 2 3 4 5 6

    d. lead to students having goals to master and wishing to reinvest in their learning; and 1 2 3 4 5 6

    e. have learning intentions and success criteria that are explicitly known by the student. 1 2 3 4 5 6

10. All teachers are thoroughly familiar with the curriculum – in terms of content, levels of difficulty, expected progressions – and share common interpretations about these with each other. 1 2 3 4 5 6

11. Teachers talk with each other about the impact of their teaching, based on evidence of student progress, and about how to maximize their impact with all students. 1 2 3 4 5 6

Starting the lesson

12. The climate of the class, evaluated from the student's perspective, is seen as fair: students feel that it is okay to say 'I do not know' or 'I need help'; there is a high level of trust and students believe that they are listened to; and students know that the purpose of the class is to learn and make progress. 1 2 3 4 5 6

13. The staffroom has a high level of relational trust (respect for each person's role in learning, respect for expertise, personal regard for others, and high levels of integrity) when making policy and teaching decisions. 1 2 3 4 5 6

14. The staffrooms and classrooms are dominated more by dialogue than by monologue about learning. 1 2 3 4 5 6

15. The classrooms are dominated more by student than teacher questions. 1 2 3 4 5 6

16. There is a balance between teachers talking, listening, and doing; there is a similar balance between students talking, listening, and doing. 1 2 3 4 5 6

17. Teachers and students are aware of the balance of surface, deep, and conceptual understanding involved in the lesson intentions.   1 2 3 4 5 6

18. Teachers and students use the power of peers positively to progress learning.   1 2 3 4 5 6

19. In each class and across the school, labelling of students is rare.   1 2 3 4 5 6

20. Teachers have high expectations for all students, and constantly seek evidence to check and enhance these expectations. The aim of the school is to help all students to exceed their potential.   1 2 3 4 5 6

21. Students have high expectations relative to their current learning for themselves.   1 2 3 4 5 6

22. Teachers choose the teaching methods as a final step in the lesson planning process and evaluate this choice in terms of their impact on students.   1 2 3 4 5 6

23. Teachers see their fundamental role as evaluators and activators of learning.   1 2 3 4 5 6

During the lesson: learning

24. Teachers have rich understandings about how learning involves moving forward through various levels of capabilities, capacities, catalysts, and competencies.   1 2 3 4 5 6

25. Teachers understand how learning is based on students needing multiple learning strategies to achieve surface and deep understanding.   1 2 3 4 5 6

26. Teachers provide differentiation to ensure that learning is meaningfully and efficiently directed to all students gaining the intentions of the lesson(s).   1 2 3 4 5 6

27. Teachers are adaptive learning experts who know where students are on the continuum from novice to capable to proficient, when students are and are not learning, and where to go next, and who can create a classroom climate to attain these learning goals.   1 2 3 4 5 6

28. Teachers are able to teach multiple ways of knowing and multiple ways of interacting, and provide multiple opportunities for practice.   1 2 3 4 5 6

29. Teachers and students have multiple strategies for learning.   1 2 3 4 5 6

30. Teachers use principles from 'backward design' – moving from the outcomes (success criteria) back to the learning intentions, then to the activities and resources needed to attain the success criteria.　　1 2 3 4 5 6

31. All students are taught how to practise deliberately and how to concentrate.　　1 2 3 4 5 6

32. Processes are in place for teachers to see learning through the eyes of students.　　1 2 3 4 5 6

During the lesson: feedback

33. Teachers are aware of, and aim to provide feedback relative to, the three important feedback questions: 'Where am I going?'; 'How am I going there?'; and 'Where to next?'　　1 2 3 4 5 6

34. Teachers are aware of, and aim to provide feedback relative to, the three important levels of feedback: task; process; and self-regulation.　　1 2 3 4 5 6

35. Teachers are aware of the importance of praise, but do not mix praise with feedback information.　　1 2 3 4 5 6

36. Teachers provide feedback appropriate to the point at which students are in their learning, and seek evidence that this feedback is appropriately received.　　1 2 3 4 5 6

37. Teachers use multiple assessment methods to provide rapid formative interpretations to students and to make adjustments to their teaching to maximize learning.　　1 2 3 4 5 6

38. Teachers:

    a. are more concerned with how students receive and interpret feedback;　　1 2 3 4 5 6

    b. know that students prefer to have more progress than corrective feedback;　　1 2 3 4 5 6

    c. know that when students have more challenging targets, this leads to greater receptivity of feedback;　　1 2 3 4 5 6

    d. deliberately teach students how to ask for, understand, and use the feedback provided; and　　1 2 3 4 5 6

    e. recognize the value of peer feedback, and deliberately teach peers to give other students appropriate feedback.　　1 2 3 4 5 6

The end of the lesson

39. **Teachers provide evidence that all students feel as though they have been invited into their class to learn effectively. This invitation involves feelings of respect, trust, optimism, and intention to learn.** 1 2 3 4 5 6

40. **Teachers collect evidence of the student experience in their classes about their success as change agents, about their levels of inspiration, and about sharing their passion with students.** 1 2 3 4 5 6

41. **Together, teachers critique the learning intentions and success criteria, and have evidence that:**

    a. students can articulate the learning intentions and success criteria in a way that shows that they understand them; 1 2 3 4 5 6

    b. students attain the success criteria; 1 2 3 4 5 6

    c. students see the success criteria as appropriately challenging; and 1 2 3 4 5 6

    d. teachers use this information when planning their next set of lessons/learning. 1 2 3 4 5 6

42. **Teachers create opportunities for both formative and summative interpretations of student learning, and use these interpretations to inform future decisions about their teaching.** 1 2 3 4 5 6

Mind frames

43. **In this school, the teachers and school leaders:**

    a. believe that their fundamental task is to evaluate the effect of their teaching on students' learning and achievement; 1 2 3 4 5 6

    b. believe that success and failure in student learning is about what they, as teachers or leaders, did or did not do . . . We are change agents! 1 2 3 4 5 6

    c. want to talk more about the learning than the teaching; 1 2 3 4 5 6

    d. see assessment as feedback about their impact; 1 2 3 4 5 6

    e. engage in dialogue not monologue; 1 2 3 4 5 6

    f. enjoy the challenge and never retreat to 'doing their best'; 1 2 3 4 5 6

    g. believe that it is their role to develop positive relationships in classrooms/staffrooms; and 1 2 3 4 5 6

    h. inform all about the language of learning. 1 2 3 4 5 6

The 900+ meta-analyses

NOTE: Meta-analyses added since *Visible Learning* (2009) are shaded.

NO.	DOMAIN	AUTHOR	YEAR	NO. STUDIES	TOTAL NO.	NO. EFFECTS	MEAN	SE	VARIABLE
STUDENT									
		Prior achievement							
1	Student	Boulanger	1981	34		62	1.09	0.039	Ability related to science learning
2	Student	Hattie & Hansford	1983	72		503	1.19		Intelligence and achievement
3	Student	Samson, Graue, Weinstein & Walberg	1983	35		209	0.31		Academic and occupational performance
4	Student	Kavale & Nye	1985	1077		268	0.68		Ability component in predicting special ed students
5	Student	Cohen	1985	108		108	0.37	0.015	College grades and adult achievement

NO.	DOMAIN	AUTHOR	YEAR	NO. STUDIES	TOTAL NO.	NO. EFFECTS	MEAN	SE	VARIABLE
6	Student	McLinden	1988	47	2,220	47	0.61		Blind vs sighted on spatial tasks
7	Student	Bretz	1989	39	26,816	39	0.39		College to adult success
8	Student	Schuler, Funke & Baron-Boldt	1990	63	29,422	63	1.02		High-school grades to university grades
9	Student	Fabram	1991	33	825	275	0.52	0.060	Language ability of special ed students on achievement
10	Student	Rush	1992	100	236,772	404	0.48		Differences in at-risk students
11	Student	Piburn	1993	44		186	0.80		Prior ability on science achievement
12	Student	Ernst	2001	23	1,733	32	0.41		Early cognition and school achievement
13	Student	Kuncel, Hezlett & Ones	2001	1753	82,659	6589	0.52	0.005	High-school grades to university grades
14	Student	Murphy & Alexander	2006	20		50	0.80		Knowledge, beliefs, and interests on conceptual change
15	Student	Trapmann, Hell, Weigand & Schuler	2007	83		83	0.90		High-school grades to university grades
16	Student	Duncan et al.	2007	6		228	0.35		Preschool to first years of schooling
		Piagetian programs							
17	Student	Jordan & Brownlee	1981	51	6,000	65	1.28		Piagetian tasks and reading and maths
		Self-reported grades							
18	Student	Mabe & West	1982	35	13,565	35	0.93		Self-evaluation of achievement
19	Student	Falchikov & Boud	1989	57	5,332	96	0.47		Self-assessment in college
20	Student	Ross	1998	11		60	1.63		Self-assessment in second language

#		Reference	Year						Description
21	Student	Falchikov & Goldfinch	2000	48	4,271	56	1.91		Self-assessment in college
22	Student	Kuncel, Crede & Thomas	2005	29	56,265	29	3.10	0.026	Self-assessment of college GPA
23	Student	Kuncel, Crede & Thomas	2005	29		29	0.60	0.034	Differences between self and recorded grades

Creativity

#		Reference	Year						Description
24	Student	Kim	2005	21	45,880	447	0.35		Relationship between creativity and achievement

Attitudes and dispositions

Personality

#		Reference	Year						Description
25	Student	Hattie & Hansford	1983	115		1197	0.07	0.007	Personality on achievement
26	Student	O'Connor & Paunonen	2007	23		108	0.10		Big Five and achievement
27	Student	Poropat	2009	80	341,385	634	0.21		Big Five and achievement
28	Student	Chu, Saucier & Hafner	2010	164		164	0.21		Wellness on achievement
29	Student	Clarke	2006	9		9	0.24		Active coping on achievement
30	Student	Trapmann, Hell, Hirn & Schuler	2007	58	17,493	258	0.05		Big Five and achievement with university students
31	Student	Boyd	2007	50		130	0.06		Extraversion on achievement
32	Student	Lyubomirsky, King & Diener	2005	46		46	0.54		Happiness on achievement

Self-concept

#		Reference	Year						Description
33	Student	Hansford & Hattie	1980	128	202,823	1136	0.41		Self-concept
34	Student	Muller, Gullung & Bocci	1988	38		838	0.36		Self-concept
35	Student	Holden, Moncher, Schinke & Barker	1990	25		26	0.37		Self-efficacy
36	Student	Multon, Brown & Lent	1991	36	4,998	38	0.76		Self-efficacy
37	Student	Carpenter	2007	48	12,466	48	0.70		Self-efficacy
38	Student	Wickline	2003	41	48,038	41	0.35		Self-concept

NO.	DOMAIN	AUTHOR	YEAR	NO. STUDIES	TOTAL NO.	NO. EFFECTS	MEAN	SE	VARIABLE
39	Student	Valentine, DuBois & Cooper	2004	56	50,000	34	0.32	0.010	Self-concept
		Motivation							
40	Student	Uguroglu & Walberg	1979	40	36,946	232	0.34	0.070	Motivation
41	Student	Findley & Cooper	1983	98	15,285	275	0.36	0.039	Internal locus of control
42	Student	Whitley & Frieze	1985	25		25	0.56		Success vs failure attributions
43	Student	Ross	1988	65		65	0.73	0.093	Controlling one's study
44	Student	Schiefel, Krapp & Schreyer	1995	21		121	0.65	0.02	Interest and achievement
45	Student	Kalechstein & Nowicki	1997	78	58,142	261	0.23	0.010	Internal locus of control
		Concentration/persistence/engagement							
46	Student	Feltz & Landers	1983	60	1,766	146	0.48		Mental practice on motor skill learning
47	Student	Datta & Narayanan	1989	23		45	0.61		Concentration on achievement
48	Student	Kumar	1991	16	4,518	102	1.09	0.035	Engagement in science
49	Student	Cooper & Dorr	1995	19	6,684	26	0.21	0.030	Race on need for achievement
50	Student	Mikolashek	2004	28		268	0.03		Resilience for at-risk students
		Reducing anxiety							
51	Student	Hembree	1988	46	28,276	176	0.22		Reduced test anxiety
52	Student	Seipp	1991	26	36,626	156	0.43		Reduction of anxiety on achievement
53	Student	Bourhis & Allen	1992	23		728	0.37		Lack of communication apprehension
54	Student	Ma	1999	26	18,279	37	0.56		Reducing anxiety towards maths and achievement

Attitude to content domains

55	Student	Willson	1983	43	638,333	280	0.32		Attitudes to science
56	Student	Bradford	1991	102		241	0.29		Attitude to mathematics
57	Student	Petscher	2010	32	224,615	118	0.32		Attitude to reading and achievement
58	Student	Ma & Kishor	1997	143	94,661	143	0.47		Attitude to mathematics

Physical influences

Pre-term birth weight

59	Student	Bhutta, Cleves, Casey, Cradock & Anand	2002	15	3,276	15	0.73		Full vs pre-term birth weight
60	Student	Barre, Morgan, Doyle & Anderson	2011	12		36	0.53	0.029	Full vs pre-term birth weight
61	Student	Corbett & Drewett	2004	31	1,213	121	0.34		Thriving and failure to thrive in infancy

Illness

62	Student	Sharpe & Rossiter	2002	7		7	0.20		Chronic illness (lack of) on achievement
63	Student	Vu, Babikian & Asarnow	2011	18		36	0.41		Non vs brain injury on achievement
64	Student	Gaudieri, Chen, Greer & Holmes	2008	19	2,144	19	0.13		Non-diabetic vs diabetes on achievement
65	Student	Schatz	2003	6		6	0.25		Non vs sickle cell disease on achievement

Diet

66	Student	Kavale & Forness	1983	23	125		0.12	0.037	Reduction of artificial food colours

NO.	DOMAIN	AUTHOR	YEAR	NO. STUDIES	TOTAL NO.	NO. EFFECTS	MEAN	SE	VARIABLE
		Exercise/relaxation							
67	Student	Moon, Render & Pendley	1985	20		36	0.16	0.088	Relaxation and achievement
68	Student	Etnier, Salazar, Landers, Petruzzelo, Han & Nowell	1997	134		1260	0.25	0.019	Physical fitness and exercise
69	Student	Sibley & Etnier	2002	36		104	0.36		Physical activity on achievement
70	Student	Etnier, Nowell, Landers & Sibley	2006	37	1,306	571	0.34	0.013	Aerobic fitness and cognitive performance
		Drugs							
71	Student	Ottenbacher & Cooper	1975	61	1,972	61	0.47	0.038	Stimulant medication on achievement
72	Student	Kavale	1982	135	5,300	984	0.58	0.019	Stimulant drug treatment for hyperactivity
73	Student	Thurber & Walker	1983	20	1,219	20	0.23	0.038	Stimulant medication on achievement
74	Student	Kavale & Nye	1984	70		401	0.30	0.038	Drug treatment
75	Student	Crenshaw	1997	36	1,030	36	0.29	0.042	Drugs treatment (ADHD) on cognitive outcomes
76	Student	DuPaul & Ekert	1997	63	637	63	0.31	0.038	School-based interventions on ADHD
77	Student	der Oord, Prins, Oosterlaan & Emmelkamp	2008	7		7	0.19	0.038	ADHD drugs on achievement
78	Student	Purdie, Carroll & Hattie	2002	74	2,188	266	0.28	0.038	Drugs treatment (ADHD) on cognitive outcomes

No.		Author	Year						Description
79	Student	Snead	2005	8	815	8	0.20		Beh intervention, medication on achievement
		Gender – achievement (male vs female)							
80	Student	Hattie & Hansford	1980	72		503	-0.02		Gender and achievement
81	Student	Hyde	1981	16	65,193	16	0.43		Gender and cognitive achievement
82	Student	Hyde	1981	27	68,899	27	-0.24		Reading and gender
83	Student	Kahl, Fleming & Malone	1982	169		31	0.12		Pre-college science and achievement
84	Student	Steinkamp & Maehr	1983	83		107	0.19		Gender differences in science
85	Student	Freeman	1984	35		35	0.09	0.050	Gender differences in mathematics
86	Student	Meehan	1984	53		160	0.14		Formal operations and gender
87	Student	Johnson, E	1984	9		9	0.45		Gender in problem-solving
88	Student	Linn & Peterson	1985	172		263	0.40		Spatial achievement and gender
89	Student	Becker & Chang	1986	42		42	0.16		Science and gender
90	Student	Tohidi, Steinkamp & Maehr	1986	70		70	0.32		Cognitive functioning and gender
91	Student	Born, Bleichrodt & Van der Flier	1987	17		772	0.08		Gender in intelligence
92	Student	Hyde & Linn	1988	165	1,418,899	165	-0.11		Gender differences on verbal achievement
93	Student	Friedman	1989	98	227,879	98	0.02	0.016	Maths and gender
94	Student	Hines	1989	30		260	0.01		Maths and gender
95	Student	Becker	1989	29	17,603	67	0.16		Gender differences in science
96	Student	Stumpf & Kliene	1989	18	171,824	18	0.48	0.020	Spatial achievement and gender
97	Student	Hyde, Fennema & Lamon	1990	100	3,217,489	259	0.20		Gender and cognitive achievement
98	Student	Cohn	1991	65	9,000	113	-0.61		Gender on ego enhancement
99	Student	Frost, Hyde & Fennema	1994	100		254	0.15		Maths and gender

NO.	DOMAIN	AUTHOR	YEAR	NO. STUDIES	TOTAL NO.	NO. EFFECTS	MEAN	SE	VARIABLE
100	Student	Daliaz	1994	67	7,026	9	0.26		Gender and achievement
101	Student	Lindberg, Hyde, Petersen & Linn	2010	242	1,286,350	242	0.05		Maths and gender
102	Student	Schram	1996	13	4,134	18	-0.08		Applied statistics and gender
103	Student	Yang	1997	25		25	-0.34	0.054	Maths and gender
104	Student	Lietz	2006	139		139	-0.19		Reading and gender
		Gender – attitudes							
105	Student	Cooper, Burger & Good	1978	10	219	10	-0.10		Control beliefs and gender
106	Student	Haladyna & Shaughnessy	1982	49		17	0.36		Science and gender
107	Student	Hyde, Fenemma, Ryan, Frost & Hopp	1990	70	63,229	126	0.15		Maths and gender
108	Student	DeBaz	1994	67	89,740	25	0.30	0.027	Science and gender
109	Student	Weinburgh	1995	18	6,753	18	0.20		Science and gender
110	Student	Whitley	1997	82	40,491	104	0.23		Computers and gender
111	Student	Etsey & Snetzler	1998	96	30,490	304	-0.01		Maths and gender
		Gender – leadership							
112	Student	Wood	1987	52	3,099	19	0.38		Group performance and gender
113	Student	Wood	1987	52	3,099	45	0.39		Group performance and gender
114	Student	Eagly & Johnson	1990	370	32,560	370	-0.11		Leadership and gender
115	Student	Pantili, Williams & Fortune	1991	10		47	0.18		Assessment centres and gender
116	Student	Eagly, Karau & Johnson	1992	50	8,375	125	-0.01		Principal leadership and gender

Gender – motor outcomes									
117	Student	Eaton & Enns	1986	90	8,636	127	0.49	0.040	Motor activity and gender
118	Student	Thomas & French	1985	64	100,195	445	0.62		Motor activity and gender
Gender – behaviour outcomes									
119	Student	Gaub & Carlson	1997	18		17	0.13		ADHD and gender
120	Student	Hall	1980	42		75	-0.32		Emotional cues and gender
121	Student	Lytton & Romney	1991	172		717	-0.02		Socialization and gender
Ethnicity									
122	Student	Allen, Bradford, Grimes, Cooper & Howard	1999	9	2661	9	0.32	0.003	Positive view of own ethnicity
Preschool interventions									
Early intervention									
123	Student	Exceptional Child Center	1983	156		1436	0.43	0.023	Handicapped and disadvantaged students
124	Student	Harrell	1983	71		449	0.42		Head start programs
125	Student	Collins	1984	67		271	0.27		Head start programs
126	Student	Horn & Packard	1985	58	59,998	138	0.90		Early prediction of learning problems
127	Student	Casto & White	1985	126		663	0.43	0.040	At-risk children
128	Student	Ottenbacher & Petersen	1985	38	1,544	118	0.97	0.083	Early intervention for disabled students
129	Student	White & Casto	1985	326		2266	0.52		Handicapped
130	Student	White & Casto	1985	162		1665	0.44	0.026	Handicapped and disadvantaged
131	Student	McKey, Condelli, Ganson, Barrett, McConkey & Plantz	1985	72		17	0.31		Head start programs
132	Student	Casto & Mastropieri	1986	74		215	0.68	0.050	Handicapped

NO.	DOMAIN	AUTHOR	YEAR	NO. STUDIES	TOTAL NO.	NO. EFFECTS	MEAN	SE	VARIABLE
133	Student	Murphy	1991	150		104	0.46		*Sesame Street*
134	Student	Innocenti & White	1993	155		797	0.60		Early intervention
135	Student	Kim, Innocenti & Kim	1997	80		659	0.25	0.024	Early intervention
136	Student	Mentore	1999	77	16,888	319	0.48	0.040	Early intervention
137	Student	Crosby	2004	44	2,267	196	0.14		Early intervention with disabled or delayed children
138	Student	Bakermans-Kranenburg, van Ijzendoorn & Bradley	2005	48	7,350	56	0.20		Early intervention in the home
		Preschool programs							
139	Student	Snyder & Sheehan	1983	8		182	0.48		Preschool programs
140	Student	Goldring & Presbrey	1986	11	1,267	11	0.25		Preschool programs
141	Student	Chambers, Cheung, Slavin, Smith & Laurenzano	2010	38		38	0.15		Preschool programs
142	Student	La Paro & Pianta	2000	70	7,243	63	1.02	0.370	Preschool to first years of schooling
143	Student	Applegate	1986	13		114	0.42	0.094	Day care
144	Student	Lewis & Vosburgh	1988	65	3,194	444	0.43		Kindergarten-based
145	Student	Nelson	1994	21		135	0.42	0.037	Parent ed programs
146	Student	Fusaro	1997	23		23	1.43		Full vs half-day kindergarten
147	Student	Gilliam & Zigler	2000	13		22	0.17		Preschool across 13 states
148	Student	Violato & Russell	2000	101	32,271	101	0.14		Day vs home care
149	Student	Camilli, Vargas, Ryan & Barnett	2010	81		306	0.23		Kindergarten vs not kindergarten on school achievement
150	Student	Jones	2002	22		22	0.56		All-day kindergarten

No.	Category	Author	Year	Studies	N	ES	SE	Description
151	Student	Nelson, Westhues & Macleod	2003	34		721	0.53		Preschool prevention programs
152	Student	Timmerman	2006	47	7,800	47	0.10		Family vs day care

HOME

No.	Category	Author	Year	Studies	N	ES	SE	Description
		Socio-economic status						
153	Home	White	1982	101		620	0.66		Socio-economic status and achievement
154	Home	Fleming & Malone	1983	273		21	0.50		Student characteristics and science achievement
155	Home	van Ewijka & Sleegers	2010	30		30	0.32		Peer socio-economic status on achievement
156	Home	Daliaz	1994	67	47,001	9	0.50		Availability of resources in the home
157	Home	Sirin	2005	58	129,914	307	0.61	0.016	Relation between socio-economic status and achievement
		Welfare policies						
158	Home	Gennetian, Duncan, Knox, Clark-Kauffman & London	2004	8		8	−0.12	0.030	Families receiving welfare on school achievement
		Family structure						
159	Home	Falbo & Polit	1986	115		115	0.17	0.023	Only vs non-only children
160	Home	Salzman	1987	137	9,955,118	273	0.26		Father present vs father absent
161	Home	Amato & Keith	1991	39		39	0.16		Both parents vs divorced families
162	Home	Wierzbicki	1993	66		31	0.13	0.041	Adoptee vs non-adoptive achievement
163	Home	Kunz	1995	65		65	0.30		Both parents vs divorced families

NO.	DOMAIN	AUTHOR	YEAR	NO. STUDIES	TOTAL NO.	NO. EFFECTS	MEAN	SE	VARIABLE
164	Home	fbeelm	1999	63	14,471	52	0.12		Resident vs non-resident fathers
165	Home	Amato & Gilbreth	1999	52		52	0.07		Father's presence in family
166	Home	Amato	2001	67		177	0.29		Resident vs non-resident fathers
167	Home	Reifman, Villa, Amans, Rethinam & Telesca	2001	35		7	0.16		Children of intact vs divorced parents
168	Home	Pong, Dronkers, Hampden-Thompson	2003	22		22	0.13		Single vs two-parent family on maths and science
169	Home	Ijzendoorn, Juffer, Poelhuis	2005	55		52	0.19		Non-adopted vs adopted children
170	Home	Jeynes	2006	61	370,000	61	0.25		Intact vs remarried families on achievement
171	Home	Goldberg, Prause, Lucas-Thompson & Himsel	2007	68	178,323	1483	0.06		Maternal employment on achievement
172	Home	Jeynes	2007	61		78	0.22		Intact vs parental remarriage on achievement
		Home environment							
173	Home	Iverson & Walberg	1982	18	5,831	92	0.80		Home environment and school learning
174	Home	Stron & Baker	2007	13	24,047	13	0.42		Home communicative support
175	Home	Gottfried	1984	17		17	0.34		Home environment and early achievement
		Television							
176	Home	Williams, Haertel, Haertel & Walberg	1982	23		227	−0.12		Leisure time television

177	Home	Neuman	1986	8		8	-0.15		TV on reading
178	Home	Razel	2001	6	1,022,000	305	-0.26	0.178	TV on achievement
		Parental involvement							
179	Home	Graue, Weinstein & Walberg	1983	29		29	0.75		Effects of home instruction
180	Home	Casto & Lewis	1984	76		754	0.41		Parent involvement in infant and preschool programs
181	Home	Crimm	1992	57		57	0.39		Parent involvement and achievement
182	Home	White, Taylor & Moss	1992	205		205	0.13		Moderate to extensive parent involvement
183	Home	Rosenzweig	2000	34		474	0.31		Parent involvement and achievement
184	Home	Fan & Chen	2001	92		92	0.52		Parent involvement and achievement
185	Home	Comfort	2003	94		43	0.56		Parent training on cognitive/language
186	Home	Hill & Tyson	2009	32		32	0.36	0.030	Parent involvement in middle school
187	Home	Jeynes	2005	41	20,000	41	0.74		Parental involvement in urban areas – primary
188	Home	Senechal	2006	14		14	0.68		Family involvement in reading
189	Home	Earhart, Ramirez, Carlson & Beretvas	2006	22		22	0.70		Parent involvement and achievement
190	Home	Jeynes	2007	52	300,000	52	0.38		Parental involvement in urban areas – high
		Home visiting							
191	Home	Black	1996	11		11	0.39		Home visiting of learning disabled
192	Home	Sweet & Applebaum	2004	60		41	0.18		Home visiting

SCHOOL

School effects

NO.	DOMAIN	AUTHOR	YEAR	NO. STUDIES	TOTAL NO.	NO. EFFECTS	MEAN	SE	VARIABLE
193	School	Scheerens & Bosker	1997	168		168	0.48	0.019	School effects

Finances

NO.	DOMAIN	AUTHOR	YEAR	NO. STUDIES	TOTAL NO.	NO. EFFECTS	MEAN	SE	VARIABLE
194	School	Childs & Shakeshaft	1986	45	2,205,319	417	0.00		Educational expenditure
195	School	Murdoch	1987	46	71,698	46	0.06		Financial aid on persistence at college
196	School	Hedge, Laine & Greenwald	1994	38		38	0.70		Effect of $500 per student on achievement
197	School	Greenwald, Hedges & Laine	1996	60		180	0.14		Effect of $500 per student on achievement

Systems accountability systems

NO.	DOMAIN	AUTHOR	YEAR	NO. STUDIES	TOTAL NO.	NO. EFFECTS	MEAN	SE	VARIABLE
198	School	Lee	2008	14		76	0.31		Accountability systems of testing on achievement

Types of school

Charter schools

NO.	DOMAIN	AUTHOR	YEAR	NO. STUDIES	TOTAL NO.	NO. EFFECTS	MEAN	SE	VARIABLE
199	School	Miron & Nelson	2001	18		18	0.20		Charter schools

Religious schools

NO.	DOMAIN	AUTHOR	YEAR	NO. STUDIES	TOTAL NO.	NO. EFFECTS	MEAN	SE	VARIABLE
200	School	Jeynes	2002	15	54,060	15	0.25		Religious vs public schooling on achievement
201	School	Jeynes	2004	56		56	0.20		Religious commitment on achievement

		Summer school						
202	School	Cooper, Charlton, Valentine, Muhlenbruck & Borman	2000	41	26,500	385	0.28		Remedial summer programs
203	School	Cooper, Charlton, Valentine, Muhlenbruck & Borman	2000	7	2,200	60	0.23		Acceleration summer programs
204	School	Kim	2002	57		155	0.17		Academic summer programs
		School compositional effects						
		Desegregation						
205	School	Krol	1980	71		71	0.16	0.049	Desegregated vs segregated classes in USA
206	School	McEvoy	1982	29		29	0.20		Desegregated vs segregated classes in USA
207	School	Miller & Carlson	1982	19		34	0.19	0.028	Desegregated vs segregated classes in USA
208	School	Walberg	1982	19		19	0.88		Desegregated vs segregated classes in USA
209	School	Armor	1983	19		51	0.05		Desegregated vs segregated classes in USA
210	School	Bryant	1983	31		31	0.45	0.122	Desegregated vs segregated classes in USA
211	School	Crain & Mahard	1983	93		323	0.08	0.013	Desegregated vs segregated classes in USA
212	School	Wortman	1983	31		98	0.45	0.089	Desegregated vs segregated classes in USA
213	School	Stephan	1983	19		63	0.15		Desegregated vs segregated classes in USA
214	School	Goldring & Addi	1989	4	6,731	4	0.15		Desegregated vs segregated classes in Israel

NO.	DOMAIN	AUTHOR	YEAR	NO. STUDIES	TOTAL NO.	NO. EFFECTS	MEAN	SE	VARIABLE
		College halls of residence							
215	School	Blimling	1999	10	11,581	23	0.05		College halls of residence
		Diversity of students							
216	School	Bowman	2010	17	77,029	58	0.05		Diversity of students in college on achievement
		School size							
217	School	Stekelenburg	1991	21		120	0.43		High school size on achievement
		Summer vacation							
218	School	Cooper, Nye, Charlton, Lindsay & Greathouse	1996	39		62	−0.09		Summer vacation on achievement
219	School	Cooper, Valentine, Charlton & Melson	2003	39	44,000	649	0.06		Modified school year vs longer summer breaks
		Mobility							
220	School	Jones	1989	93	51,057	141	−0.50		Mobility and achievement
221	School	Mehana	1997	26	2,889	45	−0.24		Mobility and achievement
222	School	Diaz	1992	62	131,689	354	−0.28	0.005	Moving from community college to four-year institutions
		Out-of-school experiences							
223	School	Lauer, Akiba, Wilkerson, Apthorp, Snow & Martin-Glenn	2006	30	15,277	24	0.10		After-school programs on reading and maths
224	School	Lauer, Akiba, Wilkerson, Apthorp, Snow & Martin-Glenn	2006	22	15,277	26	0.07		Summer school programs on reading and maths

225	School	Whiston, Tai, Rahardja & Eder	2009	150		84	0.30		Counselling on cognitive outcomes
226	School	Reese, Prout, Zirkelback & Anderson	2010	65		28	0.23		Counselling on cognitive outcomes
227	School	Prout & Prout	1998	17	550	6	0.00		Counselling on cognitive outcomes

Principals/school leaders

228	School	Neuman, Edwards & Raju	1989	126		238	0.159	0.034	Organizational development interventions
229	School	Pantili, Williams & Fortune	1991	32	10,773	32	0.41		Assessment ratings of principals and job performance
230	School	Gasper	1992	22		25	0.81		Transformational leadership
231	School	Bosker & Witziers	1995	21		65	0.04		Principals on student achievement
232	School	Brown	2001	38		339	0.57	0.028	Leadership on student achievement
233	School	Bulris	2009	30	3,378	152	0.70		Leadership school culture on outcomes
234	School	Wiseman	2002	59	16,326	59	−0.26		Instructional management on achievement
235	School	Witziers, Bosker & Kruger	2003	61		377	0.02		Principals on student achievement
236	School	Waters, Marzano & McNulty	2003	70	1,100,000	70	0.25		Principals on student achievement
237	School	Waters & Marzano	2006	27	6,558	27	0.49		District superintendents on achievement
238	School	Chin	2007	21		11	1.12		Transformational leadership
239	School	Robinson, Lloyd & Rowe	2008	14		14	0.39		Principals on student achievement

Classroom compositional effects

NO.	DOMAIN	AUTHOR	YEAR	NO. STUDIES	TOTAL NO.	NO. EFFECTS	MEAN	SE	VARIABLE
		Class size							
240	School	Glass & Smith	1997	77	520,899	725	0.09		Class size
241	School	McGiverin et al.	1999	10		24	0.34		Class size
242	School	Shin & Chung	2009	17		17	0.20		Class size
243	School	Goldstein, Yang, Omar & Thompson	2000	9	29,440	36	0.20		Class size
		Open vs traditional							
244	School	Peterson	1980	45		45	0.12		Trad vs open classrooms
245	School	Madamba	1980	72		72	-0.03		Trad vs open classrooms on reading
246	School	Hetzel	1980	45		45	-0.13		Trad vs open classrooms
247	School	Giaconia & Hedges	1982	153		171	0.06	0.032	Trad vs open classrooms
		School calendar							
248	School	Cooper et al.	2003	47	44,000	644	0.09		Modified school calendar vs traditional calendar
		Ability grouping							
249	School	Kulik	1982	41		41	0.13		Ability grouping on high-school students
250	School	Kulik & Kulik	1982	52		51	0.10	0.045	Ability grouping on high-school students
251	School	Kulik & Kulik	1984	23		23	0.19		Ability grouping in elementary grades

No.	Level	Study	Year	No.	People	No.	ES	Description
252	School	Kulik & Kulik	1985	85		85	0.15	Inter-class ability grouping
253	School	Noland & Taylor	1986	50		720	-0.08	Ability grouping
254	School	Slavin	1987	14		17	0.00	Ability grouping in elementary grades
255	School	Henderson	1989	6		6	0.23	Ability grouping in elementary grades
256	School	Slavin	1990	29		29	-0.02	Ability grouping on high school students
257	School	Gutierrez & Slavin	1992	14		14	0.34	Non-graded elementary schools
258	School	Kulik & Kulik	1992	56		51	0.03	Ability grouping
259	School	Kim	1996	96		96	0.17	Non-graded schools in Kentucky
260	School	Mosteller, Light & Sachs	1996	10		10	0.00	Ability grouping
261	School	Lou, Abrami, Spence, Poulsen, Chambers & d'Apollonia	1996	12		12	0.12	Ability grouping
262	School	Neber, Finsterwald & Urban	2001	12		214	0.33	Homogeneous vs heterogeneous on gifted
		Multi-grade/age classes						
263	School	Veenman	1995	11		11	-0.03	Multi-age classes
264	School	Veenman	1996	56		34	-0.01	Multi-grade classes
265	School	Kim	1998	27		27	0.17	Non-graded vs multi-grade/multi-age classes
		Within-class grouping						
266	School	Kulik	1985	78		78	0.15	Inter-class ability grouping
267	School	Puzio & Colby	2010	15	5,410	28	0.22	Within-class grouping in reading
268	School	Lou, Abrami, Spence, Poulsen, Chambers & d'Apollonia	1996	51	16,073	103	0.17	Within-class grouping

NO.	DOMAIN	AUTHOR	YEAR	NO. STUDIES	TOTAL NO.	NO. EFFECTS	MEAN	SE	VARIABLE
		Small-group learning							
269	School	Springer, Stanne & Donovan	1997	39	3,472	116	0.46		Working in small groups in college
270	School	Springer, Stanne & Donovan	1999	39		39	0.51		Working in small groups in science
		Mainstreaming							
271	School	Carlberg & Kavale	1980	50	27,000	50	0.12	0.092	Regular vs special class placement
272	School	Baker	1994	13	2,532	129	0.08		Regular vs special class placement
273	School	Dixon	1997	70		70	0.65		Regular vs special class placement
274	School	Zumeta	2009	9		9	0.09		Regular vs special class placement
275	School	Baker, Wang & Walberg	1994	6		6	0.20		Regular vs special class placement
276	School	Wang & Baker	1986	11		115	0.33		Regular vs special class placement
		Retention							
277	School	Holmes	1983	7	11,132	527	-0.42		Retained vs non-retained
278	School	Holmes & Matthews	1984	44		575	-0.37		Retention on all students on elementary students
279	School	Holmes	1986	17		217	-0.06		Retained vs non-retained
280	School	Holmes	1989	63		861	-0.15		Retention on all students
281	School	Allen, Chen, Willson & Hughes	2009	22	13,470	207	0.04		High-quality studies on retention

282	School	Yoshida	1989	34		242	-0.38		Retention on elementary students
283	School	Drany & Wilson	1992	22		78	0.66		Retained vs non-retained within same year
284	School	Jimerson	2001	20	2,806	175	-0.39		Retained vs non-retained

School curricula for gifted students

Ability grouping for gifted students

285	School	Kulik & Kulik	1985	25		25	0.25		Classroom organization on gifted
286	School	Goldring	1986	23		146	0.35	0.059	Ability grouping for gifted
287	School	Rogers	1991	13		13	0.43		Grouping on gifted
288	School	Vaughn, Feldhusen & Asher	1991	8		8	0.47	0.070	Pull out programs for gifted
289	School	Kulik & Kulik	1992	56		10	0.02		Classroom organization on gifted

Acceleration

290	School	Kulik & Kulik	1984	26		13	0.88	0.183	On achievement outcomes on gifted
291	School	Steenbergen-Hu & Moon	2011	38		141	0.29		Acceleration on gifted
292	School	Kulik	2004	11	4,340	11	0.87		Acceleration with same age controls on gifted

Enrichment

293	School	Wallace	1989	138	22,908	136	0.57	0.010	Enrichment programs with gifted
294	School	Romney & Samuels	2001	40	13,428	47	0.35	0.025	Feuerstein's instrumental enrichment with gifted
295	School	Shiell	2002	36		360	0.26		Feuerstein's instrumental enrichment with gifted

NO.	DOMAIN	AUTHOR	YEAR	NO. STUDIES	TOTAL NO.	NO. EFFECTS	MEAN	SE	VARIABLE
		Classroom influences							
		Classroom management							
296	School	Marzano	2003	100		5	0.52		Classroom management on achievement
		Classroom cohesion							
297	School	Haertel, Walberg & Haertel	1980	12	17,805	403	0.17	0.016	Classroom climate
298	School	Evans & Dion	1991	27		372	0.92		Group cohesion
299	School	Mullen & Copper	1994	49	8,702	66	0.51		Group cohesion
		Classroom behavioural							
300	School	Bender & Smith	1990	25		124	1.101	0.13	Classroom behaviour of disabled and learning disabilities
301	School	DuPaul & Eckert	1997	63		637	0.58	0.450	School programs for ADHD
302	School	Naso, Siler, Hougland, Lance, Maws & Bridgett	2011	58	8,394	89	0.32		Effortful control
303	School	Frazier, Youngstron, Glutting & Watkins	2007	72		181	0.71		Programs for ADHD
		Decreasing disruptive behaviour							
304	School	Skiba & Casey	1985	41	883	26	0.93		Classroom disruptive behaviour
305	School	Stage & Quiroz	1997	99	5,057	289	0.78	0.034	Decreasing disruptive behaviour
306	Student	Reid, Gonzalez, Nordness, Trout & Epstein	2004	25	2,486	101	-0.69	0.040	Emotional/behavioural disturbance

Peer influences

No.	Level	Author	Year					Influence
307	School	Ide, Parkerson, Haertel & Walberg	1980	12	122	0.53		Peer influences on achievement

TEACHER

Teacher effects

308	Teacher	Mye, Konstantopoulos & Hedges	2004	18	18	0.32	0.020	Overall teacher effects

Teacher training

No.	Level	Author	Year					Influence
309	Teacher	Qu, Becker & Kennedy	2004	24	192	0.08	0.044	Certified vs alternative certified teachers
310	Teacher	Hacke	2010	21	1,989,761	0.09		NBC vs non-NBC teachers
311	Teacher	Qu, Becker & Kennedy	2004	24	76	0.14		Trad vs emergency licensed teachers
312	Teacher	Kelley & Camilli	2007	32	105	0.15		Teacher ed in early childhood
313	Teacher	Sparks	2004	5	18	0.12		Trad vs emergency or probationary training

Micro-teaching

No.	Level	Author	Year					Influence
314	Teacher	Butcher	1981	47	47	0.55		Teacher training on teacher skills
315	Teacher	Yeany & Padilla	1986	183	183	1.18		Teacher training on teacher skills in science
316	Teacher	Bennett	1987	112	126	1.10		Teacher training on teacher skills
317	Teacher	Metcalf	1993	60	83	0.70		Lab experiences in teacher education on teacher skills

Teacher subject matter knowledge

No.	Level	Author	Year					Influence
318	Teacher	Druva & Anderson	1983	65	360	0.06		Teacher background in science
319	Teacher	Ahn & Choi	2004	27	64	0.12	0.016	Teacher knowledge in mathematics

NO.	DOMAIN	AUTHOR	YEAR	NO. STUDIES	TOTAL NO.	NO. EFFECTS	MEAN	SE	VARIABLE
		Quality of teaching							
320	Teacher	Cohen	1980	22		22	0.33		Feedback from student ratings
321	Teacher	Cohen	1981	19		19	0.68		Student rating of teacher
322	Teacher	Cohen	1981	41		68	0.48		Student rating of teacher
323	Teacher	Clayson	2008	17		42	0.66		Student rating of teacher
324	Teacher	Abrami, Leventhal & Perry	1982	12		12	0.29		Expressiveness of teacher
325	Teacher	Cohen	1986	47		74	0.44	0.060	Student rating of teacher
		Teacher–student relationships							
326	Teacher	Cornelius-White	2007	229	355,325	1450	0.72	0.01	Teacher–student relations on achievement
		Professional development							
327	Teacher	Joslin	1980	137	47,000	902	0.81		In-service teacher education
328	Teacher	Harrison	1980	47		47	0.80		Staff development
329	Teacher	Wade	1985	91		715	0.37		In-service teacher education on achievement
330	Teacher	Blank & Alas	2010	16	1,063	21	0.21	0.080	PD in student outcomes
331	Teacher	Lomos, Hofman & Bosker	2011	5		5	0.25	0.031	Professional communities on student outcomes
332	Teacher	Salinas	2010	15		42	0.57	0.130	PD in mathematics
333	Teacher	Yoon, Duncan, Lee & Shapley	2008	9		9	0.54		PD on student outcomes
334	Teacher	Batts	1988	40		101	0.40		Using consultants to coach teachers
335	Teacher	Tinoca	2004	35		37	0.45	0.007	PD in science

336	Teacher	Timperley, Wilson, Barrar & Fung	2007	227	183	0.66	0.060	PD on student outcomes
		Expectations						
337	Teacher	Rosenthal & Rubin	1978	345	345	0.70	0.200	Teacher expectations
338	Teacher	Smith	1980	46	149	0.82		Teacher expectations
339	Teacher	Dusek & Joseph	1983	102	102	0.39		Teacher expectations
340	Teacher	Raudenbush	1984	18	33	0.08	0.044	Teacher expectations
341	Teacher	Harris & Rosenthal	1985	53	53	0.41		Teacher expectations
342	Teacher	Ritts, Patterson & Tubbs	1992	12	12	0.36		Expectations of physical attractiveness and achievement
343	Teacher	Ide, Parkerson, Haertel & Walberg	1995	59	51	0.47	0.042	Physical attractiveness on achievement
344	Teacher	Tenebaum & Ruck	2007	39	39	0.23	0.040	Teacher expectations
		Labelling students						
345	Teacher	Fuchs, Fuchs, Mathes, Lipsey & Roberts	1985	79	79	0.61		Low-achieving non-disabled students vs learning disabled in reading
		Teacher verbal ability						
346	Teacher	Aloe & Becker	2009	21	58	0.22	0.027	Teacher verbal ability on outcomes
		Teacher credibility						
347	Teacher	Finn, Schrodt, Witt, Elledge, Jernberg & Larson	2009	51	14,378	0.90	0.050	Teacher credibility
		Teacher clarity						
348	Teacher	Fendick	1991	na	na	0.75		Teacher clarity on outcomes

NO.	DOMAIN	AUTHOR	YEAR	NO. STUDIES	TOTAL NO.	NO. EFFECTS	MEAN	SE	VARIABLE

CURRICULA

Reading, writing, and the arts

Visual-perception programs

NO.	DOMAIN	AUTHOR	YEAR	NO. STUDIES	TOTAL NO.	NO. EFFECTS	MEAN	SE	VARIABLE
349	Curricula	Kavale	1980	31	4,400	101	0.70	0.102	Auditory-visual integration
350	Curricula	Kavale	1981	106		723	0.767		Auditory perception
351	Curricula	Kavale	1982	161	325,000	1571	0.81	0.008	Visual perceptual skills in reading
352	Curricula	Kavale	1984a	59		173	0.09	0.014	Frostig developmental training in reading
353	Curricula	Kavale	1984c	59		173	0.18	0.028	Visual perceptual skills
354	Curricula	Kavale & Forness	2000	267	50,000	2294	0.76	0.012	Auditory-visual processes

Vocabulary programs

NO.	DOMAIN	AUTHOR	YEAR	NO. STUDIES	TOTAL NO.	NO. EFFECTS	MEAN	SE	VARIABLE
355	Curricula	Kavale	1982	36		240	0.38		Psycholinguistic training
356	Curricula	Stahl & Fairbanks	1986	41		41	0.97	0.127	Vocabulary interventions
357	Curricula	Arnold, Myette & Casto	1986	30		87	0.59	0.090	Language intervention
358	Curricula	Nye, Foster & Seaman	1987	61		299	1.04	0.107	Language intervention
359	Curricula	Marulis & Neuman	2010	67		216	0.88		Vocabulary intervention on word learning
360	Curricula	Abraham	2008	11		11	0.73		Using word glosses on vocabulary learning
361	Curricula	Piasta & Wagner	2011	63	8,468	82	0.43		Alphabet learning on outcomes
362	Curricula	Poirier	1989	61		61	0.5		Language intervention
363	Curricula	Marmolejo	1990	33		33	0.69		Vocabulary interventions
364	Curricula	Klesius & Searls	1990	39		39	0.50		Vocabulary interventions

Phonics instruction

365	Curricula	Wagner	1988	16		1766	0.38		Phonological processing abilities
366	Curricula	Fukkink & de Glopper	1998	12		21	0.43	0.120	Deriving word meaning from context
367	Curricula	Metsala, Stanovich & Brown	1998	17	1,116	38	0.58	0.060	Spelling to sound regularities and reading
368	Curricula	Miller	1999	18	882	18	1.53	0.231	Phonemic awareness programs
369	Curricula	Bus & van IJzendoorn	1999	70	5,843	1484	0.73		Phonological awareness training
370	Curricula	Jeynes	2008	22	5,000	22	0.23		Phonics for minority students
371	Curricula	Sherman	2007	26	1,358	88	0.26		Phonemic awareness and phonics instruction
372	Curricula	Thomas	2000	8	715	10	1.02		Phonemic awareness
373	Curricula	National Reading Panel	2000	52		96	0.53		Phonemic awareness
374	Curricula	National Reading Panel	2000	38		66	0.44		Phonics instruction
375	Curricula	National Reading Panel	2000	14		14	0.41		Fluency
376	Curricula	Ehri, Nunes, Stahl & Willows	2001	34		66	0.41		Systematic phonics instruction
377	Curricula	Ehri, Nunes, Willows, Schuster, Yaghoub-Zadeh & Shanahan	2001	52		72	0.53		Phonemic awareness on reading
378	Curricula	Swanson, Trainin, Necoechea & Hammill	2003	35	3,568	2257	0.93	0.473	Rapid naming, phonological awareness
379	Curricula	Goodwin & Ahn	2010	17		79	0.33	0.070	Morphological teaching
380	Curricula	Bowers, Kirby & Deacon	2010	22	2,652	285	0.32		Morphological teaching
381	Curricula	Weiser & Mathes	2011	11		11	0.78		Encoding instruction
382	Curricula	Camilli, Vargas & Yirecko	2003	40		40	0.24		Phonics instruction
383	Curricula	Torgerson, Brooks & Hall	2006	19		20	0.27		Phonics instruction

NO.	DOMAIN	AUTHOR	YEAR	NO. STUDIES	TOTAL NO.	NO. EFFECTS	MEAN	SE	VARIABLE
		Sentence-combining programs							
384	Curricula	Neville & Searls	1991	24		29	0.09		Sentence-combining on reading
385	Curricula	Fusaro	1993	11		11	0.20	0.087	Effects of sentence-combining
		Repeated reading programs							
386	Curricula	Therrien	2004	33		28	0.65	0.080	Repeated reading
387	Curricula	Chard, Vaughn & Tyler	2002	21		128	0.68		Repeated reading without a model
		Comprehension programs							
388	Curricula	Pflaum, Walberg, Karegiances & Rasher	1980	31		341	0.60		Reading instruction
389	Curricula	Rowe	1985	137		1537	0.70	0.044	Reading comprehension interventions
390	Curricula	Yang	1997	39		162	0.33		Programs to enhance reading fluency
391	Curricula	O'Shaughnessy & Swanson	1998	41	1,783	161	0.61	0.069	Non vs learning disabled on memory processing of information
392	Curricula	Kan & Windsor	2010	28	582	244	0.60		Word learning
393	Curricula	Swanborn & de Glopper	1999	20	2,130	20	0.15		Incidental word learning
394	Curricula	Swanson	1999	112	3,895	334	0.77	0.055	Reading interventions
395	Curricula	Berger & Winner	2000	9	378	10	0.10		Visual arts programs on reading
396	Curricula	Edmonds et al.	2010	29	976	29	0.89		Reading interventions with older students
397	Curricula	Scammaca, Roberts, Vaughn, Edmonds,	2007	31		31	0.95		Reading intervention for older students

#		Authors	Year						
398	Curricula	Wexler, Reutebuch & Torgesen	2010	24	187	35	1.13		Reading instruction for learning disabled students
399	Curricula	Benner, Nelson, Ralston & Mooney	2009	63	22,000	63	0.22		Effective reading programs
400	Curricula	Slavin	2009	37	3,063	44	0.50		Vocabulary interventions
401	Curricula	Elleman, Lindo, Morphy & Compton	2011	30		47	0.18		Family literacy programs
402	Curricula	van Steensel, McElvany, Kurvers & Herppich	2005	15	538	23	1.15		Visual or auditory programs to improve comprehension
403	Curricula	Sencibaugh	2007	11	2,861	75	0.78		Concept-oriented reading program
		Whole language							
404	Curricula	Guthrie, McRae & Klauda	1989	15		117	0.09	0.056	Effects of whole-language instruction
405	Curricula	Stahl & Miller	1993	21		52	0.65		Effects of whole-language instruction
406	Curricula	Gee	1994	14		14	0.15		Effects of whole-language instruction
407	Curricula	Stahl, McKenna & Pagnucco	2000	14	630	14	−0.65		Effects of whole-language instruction
		Jeynes & Littell							
		Exposure to reading							
408	Curricula	Bus, van IJzendoorn & Pellegrini	1995	29	3,410	33	0.59		Joint book reading
409	Curricula	Blok	1999	11		53	0.63	0.140	Reading to young children
410	Curricula	Mol & Bus	2011	99	7,669	383	0.78		Print exposure
411	Curricula	Torgerson, King & Sowden	2002	8	3,183	8	0.19	0.040	Volunteers helping to read
412	Curricula	Yoon	2002	7		7	0.12		Sustained silent reading
413	Curricula	Lewis & Samuels	2005	49	112,000	182	0.10		Time on reading
414	Curricula	Burger & Winner	2005	10		10	0.52		Visual arts on reading readiness

NO.	DOMAIN	AUTHOR	YEAR	NO. STUDIES	TOTAL NO.	NO. EFFECTS	MEAN	SE	VARIABLE
		Second/third-chance programs							
415	Curricula	Batya, Vaughn, Hughes & Moody	2000	16		16	0.66		Reading recovery programs
416	Curricula	D'Agostino & Murphy	2004	36	5,685	1379	0.34		Reading recovery programs
		Writing programs							
417	Curricula	Hillocks	1984	60	11,705	73	0.28	0.020	Teaching writing
418	Curricula	Atkinson	1993	20		55	0.40	0.063	Writing projects
419	Curricula	Gersten & Baker	2001	13		13	0.81	0.031	Expressive writing
420	Curricula	Bangert-Drowns, Hurley & Wilkinson	2004	46	5,416	46	0.26	0.058	School-based writing to learn interventions
421	Curricula	Graham & Perin	2007	123	14068	154	0.43	0.036	Writing programs
		Drama/arts programs							
422	Curricula	Kardash & Wright	1987	16		36	0.67	0.090	Creative dramatics
423	Curricula	Podlozny	2000	17		17	0.31		Drama on reading
424	Curricula	Moga, Burger, Hetland & Winner	2000	8	2,271	8	0.35		Arts programs on creativity
425	Curricula	Winner & Cooper	2000	31		24	0.06		Arts programs on achievement
426	Curricula	Keinanen, Hetland & Winner	2000	527	69,564	527	0.43		Dance on reading
427	Curricula	Butzlaff	2000	30	5,734,878	30	0.35		Music programs on reading
428	Curricula	Hetland	2000	15	1,170	15	0.80		Music programs on spatial reasoning
429	Curricula	Hetland	2000	15		15	0.06		Music programs on intelligence

| 430 | Curricula | Vaughn | 2000 | 20 | | 20 | 0.30 | | Music study/listening and maths |
| 431 | Curricula | Hetland | 2000b | 36 | | 36 | 0.23 | | Listening to music |

Math and sciences

Mathematics

432	Curricula	Athapilly	1978	134		810	0.24	0.030	Modern vs trad maths
433	Curricula	Parham	1983	64		171	0.53	0.099	Manipulative materials
434	Curricula	Sutawidjaja	1987	19		40	0.00		Manipulative materials
435	Curricula	Domino	2010	31	5,288	35	0.50		Manipulative materials
436	Curricula	Slavin	2008	87		87	0.22		Effective maths programs
437	Curricula	Gersten, Chard, Jayanthi, Baker, Morphy, Flojo	2008	44	4,772	108	0.55		Maths programs with learning disabled students
438	Curricula	Rakes, Valentine, McGatha & Ronau	2010	82	22,424	109	0.29	0.139	Algebra strategies
439	Curricula	Fuchs & Fuchs	1985	16		17	0.46	0.009	Use of graphing paper
440	Curricula	Moin	1987	na		na	0.23		Self-paced method of calculus instruction
441	Curricula	Friedman	1989	136		394	0.88		Spatial effects in maths
442	Curricula	LeNoir	1989	45		135	0.19		Manipulative materials
443	Curricula	Mitchell	1987	29		34	0.11	0.083	Discovery methods in mathematics
444	Curricula	Sowell	1989	60		138	0.19		Manipulative materials
445	Curricula	Fischer & Tarver	1997	7	277	22	1.01		Videodisc math
446	Curricula	Lee	2000	61	5,172	97	0.60	0.100	Math programs on learning disabled students
447	Curricula	Baker, Gersten & Lee	2002	15	1,271	39	0.51		Feedback and peer tutoring with low achieving students

NO.	DOMAIN	AUTHOR	YEAR	NO. STUDIES	TOTAL NO.	NO. EFFECTS	MEAN	SE	VARIABLE
448	Curricula	Haas	2005	35		66	0.38	0.141	Teaching methods in algebra
449	Curricula	Malofeeva	2005	29	1,845	29	0.47	0.047	Maths programs for K-2
450	Curricula	Hembree	2005	75		452	0.16		Non-contigent variables
		Use of calculators							
451	Curricula	Hembree & Dessart	1986	79		524	0.14		Use of calculators in pre-college students
452	Curricula	Smith	1996	24		54	0.25		Use of calculators
453	Curricula	Ellington	2000	53		305	0.28		Use of calculators in pre-college students
454	Curricula	Nikolaou	2001	24		103	0.49	0.092	Use of calculators on problem-solving
455	Curricula	Ellington	2006	42		97	0.19		Use of non-CAS graphing calculators
		Science							
456	Curricula	El-Memr	1979	59		250	0.17		Trad vs enquiry method for biology
457	Curricula	Bredderman	1980	50		17	0.12		Textbooks vs process curricula
458	Curricula	Weinstein, Boulanger & Walberg	1982	33	19,149	33	0.31		Science curriculum effects
459	Curricula	Bredderman	1983	57	13,000	400	0.35		Activity-based methods
460	Curricula	Scott, Tolson, Schroeder, Lee, Huang, Hu & Bentz	2005	61	159,695	61	0.67		Science teaching strategies
461	Curricula	Shymansky, Kyle & Alport	1983	105	45,626	341	0.43		New science curricula

No.		Author	Year						Description
462	Curricula	Wise & Okey	1983	160		400	0.34		Science teaching strategies
463	Curricula	Shymansky	1984	47	6,035	43	0.64		Biology science curricula
464	Curricula	Horak	1985	40		472	0.57		Learning science from textual materials
465	Curricula	Guzzetti, Snyder, Glass & Gamas	1993	23		35	0.29		On misconceptions in reading
466	Curricula	Guzzetti, Snyder, Glass & Gamas	1993	70		126	0.81		Conceptual change in science
467	Curricula	Wise	1996	140		375	0.32		Strategies for science teaching
468	Curricula	Rubin	1996	39		39	0.22	0.018	Laboratory component in college science
469	Curricula	Schroeder, Scott, Tolson, Huang & Lee	2007	61	159,695	61	0.67		Teaching strategies in science
Other curricular programs									
Values/moral education programs									
470	Curricula	Schlaefli, Rest & Thoma	1985	55		68	0.28		Effects on moral judgements
471	Curricula	Berg	2003	29	27,064	29	0.20		Character ed programs on knowledge
Perceptual-motor programs									
472	Curricula	Kavale & Mattson	1983	180	13,000	637	0.08	0.011	PM programs on learning disabled
Integrated curriculum programs									
473	Curricula	Hartzler	2000	30		30	0.48	0.086	Integrated curriculum programs
474	Curricula	Hurley	2001	31	7,894	50	0.31	0.015	Integrated science and maths programs

NO.	DOMAIN	AUTHOR	YEAR	NO. STUDIES	TOTAL NO.	NO. EFFECTS	MEAN	SE	VARIABLE
		Tactile stimulation							
475	Curricula	Ottenbacher, Muller, Brandt, Heintzelman, Hojem & Sharpe	1987	19	505	103	0.58	0.145	Tactile stimulation
		Social skills programs							
476	Curricula	Denham & Almeida	1987	70		70	0.62		Social problem-solving programs
477	Curricula	Hanson	1988	63		586	0.65	0.034	Social skill training
478	Curricula	Schneider	1992	79		12	0.19		Enhancing peer relations
479	Curricula	Swanson & Malone	1992	39	3,944	366	0.72	0.043	Social skills of learning disabled and non-disabled students
480	Curricula	Durlak, Weissberg, Dymnicki, Schellinger & Taylor	2011	35	270,034	35	0.34		Social and emotion interventions on achievement
481	Curricula	Beelmann, Pfingsten & Losel	1994	49		23	−0.04		Social competence training on achievement outcomes
482	Curricula	Forness & Kavale	1996	53	2,113	328	0.21	0.034	Social skills with learning difficulties
483	Curricula	Kavale & Forness	1996	152		858	0.65	0.015	Social skills of learning disabled and non-disabled students
484	Curricula	Quinn, Kavale, Mathur, Rutherford & Forness	1999	35	1,123	35	0.20	0.03	Social skills with emotional and behavioural disorders
		Creativity programs							
485	Curricula	Rose & Lin	1984	158		158	0.47	0.054	Long-term creativity programs
486	Curricula	Cohn	1986	106		177	0.55		Creativity training effectiveness
487	Curricula	Bangert-Drowns & Bankert	1990	20		20	0.37		Explicit instruction of creativity

No.	Domain	Study	Year							Description
488	Curricula	Hollingsworth	1991	39			39	0.82		Creativity programs
489	Curricula	Conard	1992	na			na	0.48		Creative dramatics
490	Curricula	Scope	1998	30			40	0.90	0.188	Instructional influences on creativity
491	Curricula	Scott, Leritz & Mumford	2004	70			70	0.64		Creativity programs
492	Curricula	Bertrand	2005	45			45	0.64	0.10	Creativity programs
493	Curricula	Higgins, Hall, Baumfield & Moseley	2005	19			19	0.62		Thinking programs on achievement
494	Curricula	Huang	2005	51			62	0.89	0.098	Creativity programs
495	Curricula	Berkowitz	2006	23	5,000		39	0.46	0.050	Various creative communication strategies
496	Curricula	Abrami, Bernard, Zhang, Borokhovski, Surkes & Wade	2006	124	18,299		168	1.01		Interventions to improve critical thinking skills
		Outdoor programs								
497	Curricula	Cason & Gillis	1994	43	11,238		10	0.61	0.051	Outdoor education on high-school achievement
498	Curricula	Hattie, Marsh, Neill & Richards	1997	96	12,057		30	0.46		Outward Bound
499	Curricula	Laidlaw	2002	48	3,550		389	0.49	0.020	Outdoor education on achievement
		Play								
500	Curricula	Spies	1987	24	2,491		24	0.26		Impact of play on achievement
501	Curricula	Fisher	1992	46	2,565		46	0.74		Impact of play on achievement
		Bilingual programs								
502	Curricula	Powers & Rossman	1984	16	1,257		16	0.12		Bilingual programs
503	Curricula	Willig	1985	16			513	0.10		Bilingual programs

NO.	DOMAIN	AUTHOR	YEAR	NO. STUDIES	TOTAL NO.	NO. EFFECTS	MEAN	SE	VARIABLE
504	Curricula	Oh	1987	54	6,207	115	1.21	0.140	Bilingual programs for Asian students
505	Curricula	Greene	1997	11	2,719	11	0.18		Bilingual programs
506	Curricula	McField	2002	10		12	0.35		Bilingual programs
507	Curricula	Rolstad, Mahoney & Glass	2005	4		43	0.16		Bilingual programs in Arizona
508	Curricula	Slavin & Cheung	2005	17		17	0.45		Bilingual and English-only reading programs
		Extra-curricular activities							
509	Curricula	Scott-Little, Hamann 2002 & Jurs		6			0.18		After-school care programs
510	Curricula	Lewis & Samuels	2004	10		10	0.47	0.101	General activities
511	Curricula	Lewis & Samuels	2004	5		5	0.10	0.058	Sports
512	Curricula	Lewis & Samuels	2004	8		8	-0.01	0.058	Work
513	Curricula	Chappella, Nunneryb, Pribeshc & Hagerd	2011		140,345	801	0.03	0.004	Supplemental education services out of school
514	Curricula	Shulruf	2011	29		148	0.19		Extra-curricular activities
515	Curricula	Conway, Amiel & Gerswein	2009	19	1,193	19	0.43		Service learning
516	Curricula	Durlak, Weisberg & Casel	2007	73		45	0.13		After-school programs
		Career interventions							
517	Curricula	Baker & Popowicz	1983	18		118	0.50	0.050	Evaluating career ed on outcomes
518	Curricula	Oliver & Spokane	1988	58		58	0.48		Career education interventions
519	Curricula	Evans & Burck	1992	67	159,243	67	0.17		Career education interventions

Strategies emphasizing learning intentions

Goals

520	Teaching	Chidester & Grigsby	1984	21	1,770	21	0.44	0.030	Goal difficulty
521	Teaching	Fuchs & Fuchs	1985	18		96	0.64		Long-term vs short-term goals
522	Teaching	Tubbs	1986	87		147	0.58	0.030	Goal difficulty, specificity, and feedback
523	Teaching	Mento, Steel & Karren	1987	70	7,407	118	0.58	0.018	Goal difficulty
524	Teaching	Wood, Mento & Locke	1987	72	7,548	72	0.58	0.149	Goal difficulty
525	Teaching	Wood, Mento & Locke	1987	53	6,635	53	0.43	0.063	Goal specificity
526	Teaching	Wright	1990	70	7,161	70	0.55	0.018	Goal difficulty
527	Teaching	Donovan & Radosevich	1998	21	2,360	21	0.36		Goal commitment
528	Teaching	Klein, Wesson, Hollenbeck & Alge	1999	74		83	0.47		Goal commitment
529	Teaching	Carpenter	2007	48	12,466	48	0.24		Mastery goals on achievement
530	Teaching	Hulleman, Schrager, Bodmann & Harackiewica	2010	243	91,087	243	0.12		Approach goals on achievement
531	Teaching	Burns	2004	55		45	0.82	0.089	Degree of challenge
532	Teaching	Gollwitzer & Sheeran	2007	63	8,461	94	0.72		Goal intentions on achievement

Behavioural objectives/advance organizers

533	Teaching	Kozlow	1978	77		91	0.89	0.017	Advance organizers
534	Teaching	Luiten, Ames & Ackerman	1980	135		160	0.21		Advance organizers
535	Teaching	Stone	1983	29		112	0.66	0.074	Advance organizers
536	Teaching	Lott	1983	16		147	0.24		Advance organizers in science
537	Teaching	Asencio	1984	111		111	0.12		Behavioural objectives

NO.	DOMAIN	AUTHOR	YEAR	NO. STUDIES	TOTAL NO.	NO. EFFECTS	MEAN	SE	VARIABLE
538	Teaching	Klauer	1984	23		52	0.40		Intentional learning
539	Teaching	Rolheiser-Bennett	1987	12	1,968	45	0.80		Advance organizers
540	Teaching	Mahar	1992	50		50	0.44		Advance organizers
541	Teaching	Catts	1992	14		80	-0.03	0.056	Incidental learning
542	Teaching	Catts	1992	90		1065	0.35	0.013	Intentional learning
543	Teaching	Preiss & Gayle	2006	20	1,937	20	0.46		Advance organizers
		Concept mapping							
544	Teaching	Moore & Readence	1984	161		161	0.22	0.050	Graphics organizers in mathematics
545	Teaching	Vazquez & Carballo	1993	17		19	0.57	0.032	Concept mapping in science
546	Teaching	Horton, McConney, Gallo, Woods, Senn & Hamelin	1993	19	1,805	19	0.45		Concept mapping in science
547	Teaching	Kang	2002	14		14	0.79		Graphics organizers in reading with learning disabled
548	Teaching	Campbell	2009	38		46	0.79		Concept mapping in all subjects
549	Teaching	Kim, Vaughn, Wanzek & Wei	2004	21	848	52	0.81	0.081	Graphics organizers in reading
550	Teaching	Nesbit & Adesope	2006	55	5,818	67	0.55	0.040	Concept and knowledge maps
		Learning hierarchies							
551	Teaching	Horon & Lynn	1980	24		24	0.19		Learning hierarchies
		Strategies emphasizing success criteria							
		Mastery learning							
552	Teaching	Block & Burns	1976	45		45	0.83		Mastery learning
553	Teaching	Willett, Yamashita & Anderson	1983	130		13	0.64		Mastery teaching in science

No.		Author	Year						Description
554	Teaching	Guskey & Gates	1985	38	7,794	35	0.78		Group-based mastery learning
555	Teaching	Guskey	1988	43		78	0.61		Mastery learning
556	Teaching	Hefner	1985	8	1,529	12	0.66	0.055	Mastery learning/competency-based methods
557	Teaching	Kulik & Kulik	1986	49		49	0.54		Mastery testing
558	Teaching	Slavin	1987	7		7	0.04		Mastery learning
559	Teaching	Guskey & Pigott	1988	43		78	0.61		Group-based mastery learning
560	Teaching	Hood	1990	23		23	0.56		Mastery learning
561	Teaching	Kulik, Kulik & Bangert-Drowns	1990	34		34	0.52		Mastery learning

Keller Personalized System of Instruction

No.		Author	Year						Description
562	Teaching	Kulik, Kulik & Cohen	1979	61		75	0.49		PSI and achievement
563	Teaching	Willett, Yamashita & Anderson	1983	130		15	0.60		PSI in science
564	Teaching	Kulik, Kulik & Bangert-Drowns	1988	72		72	0.49		PSI in college students

Worked examples

No.		Author	Year						Description
565	Teaching	Crissman	1986	62	3,324	151	0.57	0.042	Worked examples on achievement

Strategies emphasizing feedback

Feedback

No.		Author	Year						Description
566	Teaching	Lysakowski & Walberg	1980	39	4,842	102	1.17		Classroom reinforcement
567	Teaching	Wilkinson	1981	14		14	0.12		Teacher praise
568	Teaching	Walberg	1982	19		19	0.81		Cues and reinforcement
569	Teaching	Lysakowski & Walberg	1982	54	15,689	94	0.97		Cues, participation, and corrective feedback
570	Teaching	Yeany & Miller	1983	49		49	0.52		Diagnostic feedback in college science

NO.	DOMAIN	AUTHOR	YEAR	NO. STUDIES	TOTAL NO.	NO. EFFECTS	MEAN	SE	VARIABLE
571	Teaching	Schmmel	1983	15		15	0.47	0.034	Feedback from computer instruction
572	Teaching	Getsie, Langer & Glass	1985	89		89	0.14		Rewards and punishment
573	Teaching	Skiba, Casey & Center	1985	35		315	0.68		Non-aversive procedures
574	Teaching	Miller	2003	8		8	1.08		Oral negative feedback on learning
575	Teaching	Lyster & Saito	2010	15		28	0.74	0.024	
576	Teaching	Menges & Brinko	1986	27		31	0.44	0.115	Student evaluation as feedback
577	Teaching	Rummel & Feinberg	1988	45		45	0.60		Extrinsic feedback rewards
578	Teaching	Kulik & Kulik	1988	53		53	0.49		Timing of feedback
579	Teaching	Tenenbaum & Goldring	1989	15	522	15	0.72		Cues and reinforcement
580	Teaching	L'Hommedieu, Menges & Brinko	1990	28	1,698	28	0.34		Feedback from college student ratings
581	Teaching	Bangert-Drowns, Kulik, Kulik & Morgan	1991	40		58	0.26	0.060	Feedback from tests
582	Teaching	Wiersma	1992	20	865	17	0.50	0.086	Intrinsic vs extrinsic rewards
583	Teaching	Travlos & Pratt	1995	17		17	0.71	0.010	Knowledge of results
584	Teaching	Azevedo & Bernard	1995	22		22	0.80		Computer-presented feedback
585	Teaching	Standley	1996	98		208	2.87		Music as reinforcement
586	Teaching	Kluger & DeNisi	1996	470	12,652	470	0.38		Feedback
587	Teaching	Neubert	1998	16	744	16	0.63	0.028	Goals plus feedback
588	Teaching	Swanson & Lussier	2001	30	5,104	170	1.12	0.093	Dynamic assessment (feedback)
589	Teaching	Baker & Dwyer	2005	11	1,341	122	0.93		Field independent vs field dependent
590	Teaching	Witt, Wheeless & Aooen	2006	81	24,474	81	1.15		Immediacy of teacher feedback

Frequency/effects of testing

591	Teaching	Kulik, Kulik & Bangert	1984	19	19		0.42	0.080	Practice testing
592	Teaching	Fuchs & Fuchs	1986	22	34	1,489	0.28		Examiner familiarity effects
593	Teaching	Bangert-Drowns, Kulik & Kulik	1991	35	35		0.23		Frequent testing
594	Teaching	Gocmen	2003	78	233		0.40	0.047	Frequent testing
595	Teaching	Kim	2005	148	644		0.39	0.016	Formative assessment
596	Teaching	Kim	2005	148	622		0.39		Performance assessment on achievement
597	Teaching	Lee	2006	12	55		0.36	0.061	Test-driven external testing
598	Teaching	Hausknecht, Halpert, Di Paolo & Moriarty-Gerrard	2007	107	107	134,436	0.26	0.016	Practice and retesting effects

Teaching test-taking

599	Teaching	Messick & Jungeblut	1981	12	12		0.15		Coaching for SAT
600	Teaching	Bangert-Drowns, Kulik & Kulik	1983	30	30		0.25		Training in test-taking skills
601	Teaching	DerSimonian & Laird	1983	36	36	15,772	0.07		Coaching on the SAT-M/V
602	Teaching	Haynie	2007	8	8		0.76		Test-taking on retention learning
603	Teaching	Samson	1985	24	24		0.33	0.039	Training in test-taking skills
604	Teaching	Scruggs, White & Bennion	1986	24	65		0.21		Training in test-taking skills
605	Teaching	Kalaian & Becker	1986	34	34		0.34	0.010	Coaching for SAT
606	Teaching	Powers	1986	10	44		0.21		Coaching for college admission
607	Teaching	Becker	1990	48	70		0.30		Coaching for SAT
608	Teaching	Witt	1993	35	35		0.22		Training in test-taking skills
609	Teaching	Kulik, Bangert-Drowns & Kulik	1994	14	14		0.15		Coaching for SAT

NO.	DOMAIN	AUTHOR	YEAR	NO. STUDIES	TOTAL NO.	NO. EFFECTS	MEAN	SE	VARIABLE
		Providing formative evaluation to teachers							
610	Teaching	Fuchs & Fuchs	1986	21	3,835	21	0.70		Formative evaluation
611	Teaching	Burns & Symington	2002	9		57	1.10	0.079	Use of pre-referral intervention teams
		Response to intervention							
612	Teaching	Tran, Sanchez, Arellano & Swanson	2011	13		107	1.07		Response to intervention programs
		Questioning							
613	Teaching	Redfield & Rousseau	1981	14		14	0.73		Teacher questioning
614	Teaching	Lyday	1983	65		65	0.57		Adjunct questions
615	Teaching	Hamaker	1986	61		121	0.13	0.009	Factual adjunct questions
616	Teaching	Samson, Strykowski, Weinstein & Walberg	1987	14		14	0.26	0.086	Teacher questioning
617	Teaching	Gliessmann, Pugh, Dowden & Hutchins	1988	26		26	0.82		Teacher questioning
618	Teaching	Berkeley, Scruggs & Mastropieri	2009	30		30	0.68		Questioning/strategy instruction in reading
619	Teaching	Gayle, Preiss & Allen	2006	13		13	0.31	0.108	Teacher questioning
620	Teaching	Randolph	2007	18		18	0.38		Response cards to questioning
		Classroom discussion							
621	Teaching	Murphy, Wilkinson, Soter & Hennessey	2011	42		42	0.82		Fostering classroom discussion
		Teacher immediacy							
622	Teaching	Allen, Witt & Wheeless	2007	16	5,437	16	0.16		Immediacy on cognitive outcomes

Strategies emphasizing student perspectives in learning

Time on task

No.	Type	Study	Year				d	SE	Description
623	Teaching	Bloom	1976	11		28	0.75		Time on task
624	Teaching	Fredrick	1980	35		35	0.34		Time on task
625	Teaching	Catts	1992	18		37	0.19		Time on task
626	Teaching	Shulruf, Keuskamp & Timperley	2006	36		36	0.24	0.101	Taking more coursework

Spaced vs mass practice

No.	Type	Study	Year				d	SE	Description
627	Teaching	Lee & Genovese	1988				0.96		Spaced vs massed practice
628	Teaching	Donovan & Radosevich	1999	63		112	0.46		Spaced vs massed practice

Peer tutoring

No.	Type	Study	Year				d	SE	Description
629	Teaching	Hartley	1977	29		50	0.63	0.089	Effects on tutees in maths
630	Teaching	Hartley	1977	29		18	0.58	0.201	Effects on tutors in maths
631	Teaching	Cohen, Kulik & Kulik	1982	65		52	0.40	0.069	Effects on tutees
632	Teaching	Cohen, Kulik & Kulik	1982	65		33	0.33	0.090	Effects on tutors
633	Teaching	Phillips	1983	302		302	0.98		Tutorial training of conservation
634	Teaching	Cook, Scruggs, Mastropieri & Casto	1985	19		49	0.53	0.106	Handicapped as tutors
635	Teaching	Cook, Scruggs, Mastropieri & Casto	1985	19		25	0.58	0.120	Handicapped as tutees
636	Teaching	Mathes & Fuchs	1991	11		74	0.36		Peer tutoring in reading
637	Teaching	Batya, Vaughn, Hughes & Moody	2000	32	1,248	216	0.41		Peer tutoring in reading
638	Teaching	Elbaum, Vaughn, Hughes & Moody	2000	29	325	216	0.67	0.067	One-to-one tutoring programs in reading
639	Teaching	Rohrbeck, Ginsburg-Block, Fantuzzo & Miller	2003	90		90	0.59	0.095	Peer-assisted learning in elementary students

NO.	DOMAIN	AUTHOR	YEAR	NO. STUDIES	TOTAL NO.	NO. EFFECTS	MEAN	SE	VARIABLE
640	Teaching	Erion	2006	32		32	0.82	0.156	Parent tutoring children
641	Teaching	Ginsburg-Block, Rohrbeck & Fantuzzo	2006	28		26	0.35	0.040	Peer-assisted learning
642	Teaching	Kunsch, Jitendra & Sood	2007	17	1,103	17	0.47		Peer-mediated instruction in math with learning disabled students
		Volunteer tutors							
643	Teaching	Ritter, Barnett, Denny & Albin	2009	21	2,180	28	0.26		Adult volunteers
		Mentoring							
644	Teaching	Eby, Allen, Evans, Ng & DuBois	2007	31	10,250	31	0.16	0.04	Mentoring on performance outcomes
645	Teaching	du Bois, Holloway, Valentine & Cooper	2008	43	3,475	43	0.13	0.05	Mentoring on academic outcomes
Strategies emphasizing student meta-cognitive/self-regulated learning									
		Meta-cognition strategies							
646	Teaching	Haller, Child & Walberg	1988	20	1,553	20	0.71	0.181	Meta-cognitive training programs in reading
647	Teaching	Chiu	1998	43	3,475	123	0.67		Meta-cognitive interventions in reading
		Study skills							
648	Teaching	Sanders	1979	28	6,140	28	0.37		Reading-study programs

ID	Type	Author	Year	n	N	count	d	SE	Description
649	Teaching	Kulik, Kulik & Shwalb	1983	57		57	0.27	0.042	Study skills preparation programs
650	Teaching	Crismore	1985	100		100	1.04		Summarizing strategies
651	Teaching	Henk & Stahl	1985	21		25	0.34	0.129	Note-taking
652	Teaching	Rolhelser-Bennett	1987	12	1,968	78	1.28		Memory training
653	Teaching	Runyan	1987	32	3,698	51	0.64		Mnemonic keyword recall program
654	Teaching	Mastropieri & Scruggs	1989	19		19	1.62	0.18	Mnemonic keyword recall program
655	Teaching	Burley	1994	27	7,285	40	0.13		College programs for underprepared
656	Teaching	Hattie, Biggs & Purdie	1996	51	5,443	270	0.45	0.030	Study skills
657	Teaching	Purdie & Hattie	1999	52		653	0.28	0.007	Study skills
658	Teaching	Robbins, Lauver, Le, Davis, Langley & Carlstrom	2004	109	476	279	0.41	0.240	Study skills at college
659	Teaching	Lavery	2005	30	1,937	223	0.46	0.060	Self-regulated learning
660	Teaching	Benz & Schmitz	2009	28		28	0.78		Self-regulated learning
661	Teaching	Sitzmann & Ely	2011	369	90,380	855	0.37		Self-regulation strategies
662	Teaching	Kim, Kim, Lee, Park, Hong & Kim	2008	50		97	0.96		Teaching learning strategies
663	Teaching	Mesmer-Magnus & Viswesvaran	2010	128	13,684	159	0.62		Teaching learning strategies
664	Teaching	Scruggs, Mastropieri, Berkeley & Graetz	2010	35	2,403	94	1.00		Teaching learning strategies to secondary learning disabled students
665	Teaching	Kobayashi	2005	57		131	0.22		Effects of note-taking
666	Teaching	Dignath, Buettner & Langfeldt	2008	30	2,364	263	0.69	0.030	Self-regulation strategies

NO.	DOMAIN	AUTHOR	YEAR	NO. STUDIES	TOTAL NO.	NO. EFFECTS	MEAN	SE	VARIABLE
		Self-verbalization/self-questioning							
667	Teaching	Rock	1985	47	1,398	684	0.51	0.060	Special ed self-instructional training
668	Teaching	Duzinski	1987	45		377	0.84		Self-verbalizing instruction training
669	Teaching	Huang	1991	21	1,700	89	0.58		Student self-questioning
		Student control over learning							
670	Teaching	Niemiec, Sikorski & Walberg	1996	24		24	−0.03	0.149	Student control over learning in CAI
671	Teaching	Patall, Cooper & Robinson	2008	41		14	0.10	0.027	Control over learning on subsequent control
		Student-centred teaching							
672	Teaching	Preston	2007	19		19	0.54	0.149	Student-centred vs teacher-centred approach
		Aptitude-treatment interactions							
673	Teaching	Kavale & Forness	1987	39		318	0.28		Modality testing and teaching
674	Teaching	Whitener	1989	22	1,434	22	0.11	0.070	
		Matching style of teaching							
675	Teaching	Tamir	1985	54		13	0.02		Cognitive preference
676	Teaching	Garlinger & Frank	1986	7	1,531	7	−0.03		Field independence/dependence on achievement
677	Teaching	Sullivan (excluded, see Visible Learning)	1993	42	3,434	42	0.75		Dunn and Dunn learning styles matched to achievement
678	Teaching	Iliff	1994	101		486	0.33	0.026	Kolb learning style matched to achievement

No.	Domain	Author	Year	Number	N	Effects	d	p	Influence
679	Teaching	*Dunn, Griggs, Olson, Beasley & Gorman*	1995	36	3,181	65	0.76		Interventions to enhance matching learning style on achievement
680	Teaching	Slemmer	2002	48	5,908	51	0.27		Learning styles in hyper/technology environments
681	Teaching	Salvione	2007	34	7,093	677	0.28	0.006	Dunn and Dunn learning styles for students
682	Teaching	*Mangino (excluded, see Visible Learning)*	2004	47	8,661	386	0.54		Dunn and Dunn learning styles for adults
683	Teaching	*Lovelace (excluded, see Visible Learning)*	2005	76	7,196	168	0.67		Dunn and Dunn learning styles matched to achievement
		Individual instruction							
684	Teaching	Hartley	1977	51		139	0.16	0.091	Individualization in maths
685	Teaching	Kulik & Kulik	1980	213		213	0.33	0.034	Individualized college achievement
686	Teaching	Horak	1981	60		129	−0.07		Individualization in maths
687	Teaching	Willett, Yamashita & Anderson	1983	130		131	0.17		Individualized science curriculum
688	Teaching	Bangert, Kulik & Kulik	1983	49		49	0.1	0.053	Individualized in high schools
689	Teaching	Waxman, Wang, Anderson & Walberg	1985	38	7,200	309	0.45		Adaptive methods (individual, continuous assessment, periodic evaluation)
690	Teaching	Mitchell	1987	38		39	0.19	0.071	Individualized instruction in mathematics
691	Teaching	Atash & Dawson	1986	10	2,180	30	0.09	0.046	Individualized science curriculum
692	Teaching	Decanay & Cohen	1992	30		30	0.37		Individual instruction in medical education
693	Teaching	Elbaum, Vaughn, Hughes & Moody	1999	19		116	0.43		Special ed in reading

NO.	DOMAIN	AUTHOR	YEAR	NO. STUDIES	TOTAL NO.	NO. EFFECTS	MEAN	SE	VARIABLE
		Psychotherapy programs							
694	Teaching	Baskin, Slaten, Merson, Sorenson & Glover-Russell	2010	83		102	0.38		Psychotherapy on academic outcomes

Implementations emphasizing teaching strategies

NO.	DOMAIN	AUTHOR	YEAR	NO. STUDIES	TOTAL NO.	NO. EFFECTS	MEAN	SE	VARIABLE
		Teaching strategies							
695	Teaching	Rosenbaum	1983	235		99	1.02		Treatment programs for emotionally disturbed students
696	Teaching	O'Neal	1985	31		96	0.81	0.155	With cerebral palsy students
697	Teaching	Baenninger & Newcombe	1989	26		26	0.51		Spatial strategies on spatial outcomes
698	Teaching	Forness & Kavale	1993	268	8,000	819	0.71	0.122	Teaching with low-ability students
699	Teaching	Fan	1993	41	3,219	223	0.56		Metacognitive training on reading comprehension
700	Teaching	Scheerens & Bosker	1997	228		545	0.20	0.030	Various strategies on achievement
701	Teaching	White	1997	222	15,080	1796	0.39	0.046	Cognitive learning strategies in reading with LD
702	Teaching	White	1997	72	8,527	831	0.20	0.039	Cognitive learning strategies in maths with LD
703	Teaching	Marzano	1998	4000	1,237,000	4000	0.65	0.014	Classroom instructional techniques
704	Teaching	Norris & Otera	2000	49		78	0.96		Focused instruction vs minimal exposure to learning in L2
705	Teaching	Swanson & Hoskyn	1998	180	38,716	1537	0.79	0.013	Teaching with low-ability students

No.		Year	Author	No. studies	No. people	No. effects	d	SE	Description
706	Teaching	1999	Xin & Jitendra	14		653	0.89		Word problem-solving in reading
707	Teaching	2000	Swanson	180	180,827	1537	0.79	0.013	Learning strategies for special ed students
708	Teaching	2001	Swanson	58		58	0.82	0.087	Programs to enhance problem-solving
709	Teaching	2007	Seidel & Shavelson	112		1352	0.07		Teaching and learning processes
	Reciprocal teaching								
710	Teaching	1994	Rosenshine & Meister	16		31	0.74		Reciprocal teaching
711	Teaching	2003	Galloway	22	677	22	0.74		Reciprocal teaching on reading comprehension
	Direct instruction								
712	Teaching	1988	White	25		24	0.83	0.133	DI in special ed
713	Teaching	1996	Adams & Engelmann	37		372	0.75	0.020	DI on reading
714	Teaching	2003	Borman, Hewes, Overman & Brown	232	42,618	182	0.21		DI from comprehensive schools reforms
715	Teaching	2005	Haas	10		19	0.55	0.135	Teaching methods in algebra
	Adjunct aids								
716	Teaching	1981	Readence & Moore	16	2,227	122	0.45	0.020	Adjunct pictures in reading
717	Teaching	1982	Levine & Lentz	23	7,182	41	0.55		Text illustrations
718	Teaching	1992	Catts	8		19	0.01	0.067	Adjunct aids
719	Teaching	2006	Hoeffler, Sumfleth & Leutner	26		76	0.46		Instructional animation vs static pictures
	Inductive teaching								
720	Teaching	1983	Lott	24		24	0.06		Inductive teaching in science
721	Teaching	2008	Klauer & Phye	73	3,595	79	0.59	0.035	Inductive teaching

NO.	DOMAIN	AUTHOR	YEAR	NO. STUDIES	TOTAL NO.	NO. EFFECTS	MEAN	SE	VARIABLE
		Enquiry-based teaching							
722	Teaching	Sweitzer & Anderson	1983	68		19	0.44	0.154	Enquiry teaching in science
723	Teaching	Shymansky, Hedges & Woodworth	1990	81		320	0.27	0.030	Enquiry methods in science
724	Teaching	Bangert-Drowns	1992	21		21	0.37		Enquiry teaching effects on critical thinking
725	Teaching	Smith	1996	35	7,437	60	0.17		Enquiry method in science
		Problem-solving teaching							
726	Teaching	Marcucci	1980	33		237	0.35		Problem-solving in maths
727	Teaching	Curbelo	1984	68	10,629	343	0.54	0.037	Problem-solving on science and maths
728	Teaching	Almeida & Denham	1984	18	2,398	18	0.72	0.136	Interpersonal problem-solving
729	Teaching	Mellinger	1991	25		35	1.13	0.060	Increasing cognitive flexibility
730	Teaching	Hembree	1992	55		55	0.33		Problem-solving instructional methods
731	Teaching	Tocanis, Ferguson-Hessler & Broekkamp	2001	22	2,208	31	0.59	0.070	Problem-solving in science
		Problem-based learning							
732	Teaching	Albanese & Mitchell	1993	11	2,208	66	0.27	0.043	PBL in medicine
733	Teaching	Walker & Leary	2008	82		201	0.13		PBL in all subjects
734	Teaching	Vernon & Blake	1993	8		28	-0.18		PBL in college level
735	Teaching	Dochy, Segers, Van den Bossche & Gijbels	2003	43	21,365	35	0.12		PBL on knowledge and skills
736	Teaching	Smith	2003	82	12,979	121	0.31		PBL in medicine
737	Teaching	Newman	2004	12		12	-0.30		PBL in medicine

No.		Author	Year						Description
738	Teaching	Haas	2005	7	1,538	34	0.52	0.187	Teaching methods in algebra
739	Teaching	Gijbels, Dochy, Van den Bossche & Segers	2005	40		49	0.32		PBL on assessment outcomes
740	Teaching	Walker	2008	82		201	0.13	0.025	PBL across disciplines
		Cooperative learning							
741	Teaching	Johnson, Maruyama, Johnson, Nelson & Skon	1981	122		183	0.73		Cooperative learning
742	Teaching	Rolhelser-Bennett	1987	23	4,002	78	0.48		Cooperative learning
743	Teaching	Hall	1988	22	10,022	52	0.31		Cooperative learning
744	Teaching	Stevens & Slavin	1991	4		4	0.48		Cooperative learning
745	Teaching	Spuler	1993	19	6,137	19	0.54		Cooperative learning in maths
746	Teaching	Othman	1996	39		39	0.27		Cooperative learning in maths
747	Teaching	Howard	1996	13		42	0.37		Scripted cooperative learning
748	Teaching	Bowen	2000	37	3,000	49	0.51	0.050	Cooperative learning in high-school chemistry
749	Teaching	Suri	1997	27		27	0.63		Cooperative learning in maths
750	Teaching	Romero	2009	32		52	0.31		Cooperative learning
751	Teaching	Neber, Finsterwald & Urban	2001	12		314	0.13		Cooperative learning with gifted
752	Teaching	McMaster & Fuchs	2002	15	864	49	0.30	0.070	Cooperative learning
		Cooperative vs competitive learning							
753	Teaching	Johnson, Maruyama, Johnson, Nelson & Skon	1981	122		9	0.56		Cooperative with inter-group competition
754	Teaching	Johnson, Johnson & Marayama	1983	98		83	0.82	0.093	Cooperative vs competition
755	Teaching	Johnson & Johnson	1987	453		36	0.59	0.165	Cooperative vs competition

NO.	DOMAIN	AUTHOR	YEAR	NO. STUDIES	TOTAL NO.	NO. EFFECTS	MEAN	SE	VARIABLE
756	Teaching	Hall	1988	18		83	0.28		Cooperative with competition
757	Teaching	Qin, Johnson & Johnson	1995	46		63	0.55		Cooperative vs competition
758	Teaching	Johnson, Johnson & Stanne	2000	158		66	0.55	0.059	Cooperative vs competition
759	Teaching	Roseth, Johnson & Johnson	2008	129	17,000	593	0.46	0.130	Cooperative vs competition
		Cooperative vs individualistic learning							
760	Teaching	Johnson & Johnson	1987	453		70	0.68	0.139	Cooperative vs individualistic
761	Teaching	Hall	1988	15		77	0.26		Cooperative vs individualistic
762	Teaching	Johnson, Johnson & Stanne	2000	158		82	0.88	0.066	Cooperative vs individualistic
763	Teaching	Roseth, Fang, Johnson & Johnson	2006	148		55	0.55	0.060	Cooperative vs individualistic in middle school
		Competitive vs individualistic learning							
764	Teaching	Johnson, Maruyama, Johnson, Nelson & Skon	1981	122		163	0.09		Competitive learning
765	Teaching	Johnson, Johnson & Marayama	1983	98		16	0.45	0.288	Competitive vs individualistic
766	Teaching	Johnson & Johnson	1987	453		12	0.36	0.271	Competitive vs individualistic
767	Teaching	Johnson, Johnson & Stanne	2000	158		12	0.04	0.138	Competitive vs individualistic

Implementations that emphasize school-wide teaching strategies

#		Author	Year						Description
		Comprehensive teaching reforms							
768	Teaching	Borman & D'Agostino	1996	17	41,706,196	657	0.12		Evaluation of Federal Title I programs
769	Teaching	Friedrich	1998	33		50	0.38		Alternative programs for at-risk youth
770	Teaching	Borman, Hewes, Overman & Brown	2003	232	222,956	1111	0.15		Comprehensive school reform
		Various teaching on creative thinking							
771	Teaching	Abrami, Bernard, Borokhovski, Wade, Surkes, Tamim & Zhang	2008	117	20,698	161	0.34	0.005	Interventions on critical thinking skills and dispositions
		Interventions for learning disabled students							
772	Teaching	Swanson, Carson & Sachse-Lee	1996	78		324	0.85	0.065	Programs for learning disabled students
773	Teaching	Swanson, Hoskyn & Lee	1999	180	4,871	1537	0.56	0.017	Between-group designs
774	Teaching	Swanson, Hoskyn & Lee	1999	85	793	793	0.90	0.008	Single-subject designs
		Special college programs							
775	Teaching	Kulik, Kulik & Shwalb	1983	60		60	0.27	0.040	College programs for high-risk students
776	Teaching	Valentine, Hirschy, Bremer, Novillo, Castellano & Banister	2011	33		33	0.07		College programs for high-risk students
777	Teaching	Cohn	1985	48		48	0.20		Innovative teaching vs trad lectures in economics

NO.	DOMAIN	AUTHOR	YEAR	NO. STUDIES	TOTAL NO.	NO. EFFECTS	MEAN	SE	VARIABLE
		Co-/team teaching							
778	Teaching	Murawski & Swanson	2001	6	1,617	6	0.31	0.057	Co-teaching
779	Teaching	Willett, Yamashita & Anderson	1983	130		41	0.06		Co-teaching in science
		Implementations using technologies							
		Computer-assisted instruction							
780	Teaching	Hartley	1977	33		89	0.41	0.062	CAI on achievement
781	Teaching	Aiello & Wolfe	1980	115		182	0.08		CAI in high-school science
782	Teaching	Kulik, Kulik & Cohen	1980	312		278	0.48	0.030	CAI on college
783	Teaching	Burns & Bozeman	1981	40		40	0.40		CAI in mathematics
784	Teaching	Leong	1981	22		106	0.08		CAI in high school maths
785	Teaching	Athappilly, Smidchens & Kofel	1983	134		810	0.10		Modern maths vs trad maths
786	Teaching	Kulik, Kulik & Bangert-Drowns	1983	51		51	0.32		CAI on high-school students
787	Teaching	Kulik, Kulik & Williams	1983	97		97	0.36	0.035	CAI with high-school students
788	Teaching	Willett, Yashashita & Anderson	1983	130		130	0.13		CAI in science
789	Teaching	Kulik et al.	1984	25		25	0.48	0.063	CAI with elementary students
790	Teaching	Bangert-Drowns	1985	74		74	0.33		CAI with pre-college students
791	Teaching	Bangert-Drowns, Kulik & Kulik	1985	42		42	0.26	0.063	CAI in high-school schools
792	Teaching	Clark	1985	42		42	0.09		CAI in schools
793	Teaching	Kulik, Kulik & Bangert-Drowns	1985	32		32	0.47	0.055	CAI with elementary students

794	Teaching	Kulik & Kulik	1986	48		48	0.32	0.061	CAI on college
795	Teaching	Kulik, Kulik & Shwalb	1986	23		23	0.42	0.110	CAI with adults
796	Teaching	Schmidt, Weinstein, Niemic & Walberg	1986	18		48	0.67	0.048	CAI with exceptional children
797	Teaching	Shwalb, Shwalb & Azuma	1986	104		4	0.74	0.069	CAI in Japan
798	Teaching	Gillingham & Guthrie	1987	13		13	1.05		Computer-based instruction
799	Teaching	Kulik & Kulik	1987	199		199	0.31		CAI on achievement
800	Teaching	Mitchell	1987	12		16	0.24	0.093	CAI in mathematics
801	Teaching	Slavin, Cheung, Groff & Lake	2007	12		12	0.23		CAI in reading
802	Teaching	Camnalbur & Erdogan	2008	78	5,096	78	0.95	0.030	CAI in Turkey
803	Teaching	Koufogiannakis & Wiebe	2006	8	408	8	0.09		CAI in informational literacy
804	Teaching	Larwin & Larwin	2011	70	40,125	70	0.57		CAI in post-secondary stats courses
805	Teaching	Means, Toyama, Murphy, Bakia, Jones	2009	51		51	0.24		Online learning on students
806	Teaching	Moran, Ferdig, Pearson, Wardrop & Blomeyer	2008	20		89	0.49		Digital tools on learning
807	Teaching	Li & Ma	2010	46	36,793	85	0.28		Computer technology on maths
808	Teaching	Cheung & Slavin	2011	85	60,721	85	0.16	0.020	Ed technology
809	Teaching	Yun	2010	10	866	10	0.31	0.070	Hypertext glosses on achievement
810	Teaching	Schmid, et al.	2009	231	25,497	310	0.28		Technology in high schools
811	Teaching	Tokpah	2008	31	7,342	102	0.38		CAI in algebra on achievement
812	Teaching	Woolf & Regian	2002	177		177	0.33		Technology in schools
813	Teaching	Zucker, Moody & McKenna	2009	7	401	7	0.41		e-books on achievement

NO.	DOMAIN	AUTHOR	YEAR	NO. STUDIES	TOTAL NO.	NO. EFFECTS	MEAN	SE	VARIABLE
814	Teaching	Sosa, Berger, Saw & Mary	2011	45	9,639	45	0.33		CAI in statistics
815	Teaching	Schenker	2007	46		117	0.24		CAI in statistics
816	Teaching	Zhao	2003	38	1,464	38	0.88		CAI on language learning
817	Teaching	Jahng, Krug & Zhang	2007	20	1,617	20	0.02		Online distance ed
818	Teaching	Keany	2011	85	60,000	85	0.16		Technology on reading achievement
819	Teaching	Niemiec, Samson, Weinstein & Walberg	1987	48		224	0.32		CAI with elementary students
820	Teaching	Cunningham	1988	37		37	0.33		Computer-generated graphics on achievement
821	Teaching	Roblyer, Castine & King	1988	85		85	0.26		CAI on achievement
822	Teaching	Wise	1988	26		26	0.30		CAI in science
823	Teaching	Kuchler	1989	65		65	0.44	0.068	CAI to teach high-school maths
824	Teaching	McDermid	1989	15		15	0.57		CAI on learning disabled and educably mentally retarded
825	Teaching	Bishop	1990	40		58	0.55		Computers in elementary schools
826	Teaching	Wen-Cheng	1990	72		243	0.38	0.037	CAI in elementary and high schools
827	Teaching	Gordon	1991	84		83	0.26	0.030	Computer graphics and maths and problem-solving
828	Teaching	Jones	1991	40		58	0.31		CAI on elementary students
829	Teaching	Kulik & Kulik	1991	248	240	248	0.30	0.029	CAI on achievement
830	Teaching	Liao & Bright	1991	65		432	0.41	0.020	Computer programming on achievement
831	Teaching	Palmeter	1991	37		144	0.48	0.055	CAI/logo on higher cognitive processes

No.	Category	Author	Year				d	SE	Description
832	Teaching	Ryan	1991	40		58	0.31		Microcomputer applications
833	Teaching	Schramm	1991	12	836	12	0.36	0.110	Word processing on writing
834	Teaching	Cohen & Dacanay	1992	37		37	0.41		Computer-based in health education
835	Teaching	Liao	1992	31		207	0.48	0.163	CAI on achievement
836	Teaching	Bangert-Drowns	1993	32		32	0.39		Word processing on writing
837	Teaching	Ouyang	1993	79		267	0.50	0.038	CAI in elementary schools
838	Teaching	Chen	1994	76		98	0.47	0.071	Computer based in maths
839	Teaching	Kulik	1994	97		32	0.35	0.04	CAI on achievement
840	Teaching	Kulik & Kulik	1994	97		97	0.32		CAI in high schools
841	Teaching	Christmann	1995	35	3,476	35	0.23		All education
842	Teaching	Fletcher-Flynn & Gravatt	1995	120		120	0.17		CAI on achievement
843	Teaching	Hamilton	1995	41		253	0.66	0.033	CAI in schools
844	Teaching	Ianno	1995				0.31		CAI on reading of learning disabled
845	Teaching	Cassil	1996	21		349	0.29		Mobile computers on all
846	Teaching	Chadwick	1997	41	8,170	41	0.51		CAI in high-school maths
847	Teaching	Christmann, Badgett & Lucking	1997	27		27	0.21		CAI in high schools
848	Teaching	King	1997	30		68	0.20		CAI college maths
849	Teaching	Christmann & Badgett	1999	11	5,020	11	0.28		CAI in high schools
850	Teaching	Soe, Koki & Chang	2000	17		33	0.27	0.022	CAI in reading
851	Teaching	Wolf & Regian	2000	233		233	0.39		CAI on achievement
852	Teaching	Lou, Abrami & d'Apollonia	2001	100	11,317	178	0.16	0.041	CAI in small groups
853	Teaching	Lou, Abrami & d'Apollonia	2001	22		39	0.31	0.117	CAI in small groups
854	Teaching	Yaakub & Finch	2001	21	2,969	28	0.35		CAI-based technical education instruction

NO.	DOMAIN	AUTHOR	YEAR	NO. STUDIES	TOTAL NO.	NO. EFFECTS	MEAN	SE	VARIABLE
855	Teaching	Akiba	2002	21		21	0.37		CAI on achievement
856	Teaching	Bayraktar	2002	42		108	0.27		CAI in science ed
857	Teaching	Blok, Oostdam, Otter & Overmaat	2002	42		42	0.19		CAI on beginning reading
858	Teaching	Roberts	2002	31	6,388	165	0.69		CAI on achievement
859	Teaching	Torgerson & Elbourne	2002	7		7	0.37		CAI on spelling
860	Teaching	Waxman, Connell & Gray	2002	20	4,400	138	0.39		Technology vs trad teaching on achievement
861	Teaching	Chambers	2003	57	64,766	125	0.51		CAI in elementary and high-school classrooms
862	Teaching	Chambers & Schreiber	2003	25		25	0.40		CAI in elementary and high-school classrooms
863	Teaching	English Review Group	2003	212		43	0.26	0.094	CAI on literacy
864	Teaching	Goldberg	2003	26	1,507	26	0.50		Effects of CAI on writing
865	Teaching	Hsu	2003	25		31	0.43		CAI in statistics
866	Teaching	Kroesbergen & Van Luit	2003	58	10,223	58	0.75		CAI and maths with special ed
867	Teaching	Kulik	2003	12		12	0.88		CAI on college
868	Teaching	Torgerson & Zhu	2003	17		17	0.36		CAI and literacy outcomes
869	Teaching	Waxman, Lin, Michko	2003	29	7,728	167	0.54		CAI on achievement
870	Teaching	Bernard, Abrami, Wade, Borokhovski & Lou	2004	232	3,831,888	688	0.20	0.061	CAI in distance ed
871	Teaching	Lou	2004	71		399	0.15		Small group vs individual learning with CAI on tasks attempted
872	Teaching	Liao	2005	52	4,981	134	0.55		CAI in Taiwan

No.	Domain	Study	Year						Description
873	Teaching	Pearson, Ferdig, Blomeyer & Moran	2005	20		89	0.49	0.078	Technology on reading
874	Teaching	Abrami, Bernard, Wade, Schmid, Borokhovski, Tamin, Surkes, Lowerison, Zhang, Nicolaidou, Newman, Wozney & Peretiatkowics	2006	17		29	0.17		e-learning in Canada
875	Teaching	Sandy-Hanson	2006	23	9,897	23	0.28		CAI on achievement
876	Teaching	Shapiro, Kerssen-Griep, Gayle & Allen	2006	12		16	0.26		PowerPoint in the class
877	Teaching	Timmerman & Kruepke	2006	118	12,398	118	0.24	0.020	CAI with college students
878	Teaching	Onuoha	2007	38	3,824	67	0.26		Computer-based laboratories in science
879	Teaching	Rosen & Salomon	2007	32		32	0.46		Constructivist technology-intensive learning
		Simulations							
880	Teaching	Dekkers & Donatti	1981	93		93	0.33		Simulations and achievement
881	Teaching	Remmer & Jernsted	1982	21		21	0.20		Computer simulations
882	Teaching	Szczurek	1982	58		58	0.33		Simulation games
883	Teaching	VanSickle	1986	42		42	0.43		Instructional simulation gaming
884	Teaching	Sitzmann & Ely	2011	65	4,518	68	0.30	0.060	Computer simulations
885	Teaching	Lee	1990	19		34	0.28	0.114	Simulations on achievement
886	Teaching	McKenna	1991	26		118	0.38	0.070	Simulations in economics
887	Teaching	Armstrong	1991	43		43	0.29		Computers and simulations and games
888	Teaching	Lee	1999	19		19	0.40		Computer simulations
889	Teaching	LeJeune	2002	40	6,416	54	0.34		Computer-simulated experiments in science

NO.	DOMAIN	AUTHOR	YEAR	NO. STUDIES	TOTAL NO.	NO. EFFECTS	MEAN	SE	VARIABLE
		Web-based learning							
890	Teaching	Olson & Wisher	2002	15		15	0.24	0.150	Web-based learning
891	Teaching	Sitzman, Kraiger, Stewart & Wisher	2006	96	19,331	96	0.15		Web-based and traditional classes
892	Teaching	Mulawa	2007	25	3,223	25	0.14	0.099	Web-based learning principles
		Interactive video							
893	Teaching	Clark & Angert	1980	23	4,800	1000	0.65		Media methods on achievement
894	Teaching	Angert & Clark	1982	181		2607	0.51		Technology in Japan
895	Teaching	Shwalb, Shwalb & Azuma	1986	104		33	0.49	0.055	
896	Teaching	Fletcher	1989	24		47	0.50	0.080	Interactive video disk technology
897	Teaching	McNeil & Nelson	1991	63		100	0.53	0.097	Multimedia technologies
898	Teaching	Liao	1999	46		143	0.41	0.073	Hypermedia vs traditional instruction
		Audio-visual methods							
899	Teaching	Kulik, Kulik & Cohen	1979	42		42	0.20		Audio-based teaching
900	Teaching	Cohen, Ebeling & Kulik	1981	65		65	0.15		Visual-based instruction
901	Teaching	Willett, Yamashita & Anderson	1983	130		100	0.02		Visual aids in science
902	Teaching	Shwalb, Shwalb & Azuma	1986	104		6	0.09	0.110	Audio-based teaching in Japan
903	Teaching	Blanchard, Stock & Marshall	1999	10	2,760	10	0.16	0.030	Multi-media using personal and video-game computers
904	Teaching	Baker & Dwyer	2000	8		8	0.71		Use of visual aids in learning

Programmed instruction

		Author	Year	Studies	Sample	N	d	SE	Description
905	Teaching	Hartley	1977	40		81	0.11	0.111	PI in mathematics
906	Teaching	Kulik, Cohen & Ebeling	1980	57		57	0.24		PI with college students
907	Teaching	Kulik, Kulik & Cohen	1980	56		56	0.24		PI in college
908	Teaching	Kulik, Schwalb & Kulik	1982	47		47	0.08	0.070	PI in high schools
909	Teaching	Willett, Yamashita & Anderson	1983	130		52	0.17		PI in science
910	Teaching	Shwalb, Shwalb & Azuma	1986	104		39	0.43	0.028	PI in Japan
911	Teaching	Mitchell	1987	29		29	0.15	0.063	PI in mathematics
912	Teaching	Boden, Archwamety & MacFarland	2000	30		30	0.40	0.146	PI in high schools

Implementations using out-of-school learning

Distance education

		Author	Year	Studies	Sample	N	d	SE	Description
913	Teaching	Machtmes & Asher	1987	19		19	−0.01		Effectiveness of telecourses
914	Teaching	Cavanaugh	1999	19		19	0.13		Interactive distance learning on achievement
915	Teaching	Cavanaugh	2001	19	929	19	0.15	0.106	Interactive distance education
916	Teaching	Bernard et al.	2009	34		74	0.39	0.030	Most interactive distance vs least interactive distance
917	Teaching	Shachar & Neumann	2003	72	15,300	86	0.37	0.035	Distance vs traditional teaching
918	Teaching	Allen, Mabry, Mattrey, Bourhis, Titsworth & Burrell	2004	25	71,731	39	0.10		Distance vs trad classes
919	Teaching	Cavanaugh, Gillan, Kromrey, Hess & Blomeyer	2004	14	7,561	116	−0.03	0.045	Distance in all classes
920	Teaching	Williams	2004	25		34	0.15		Distance in allied health science programs

NO.	DOMAIN	AUTHOR	YEAR	NO. STUDIES	TOTAL NO.	NO. EFFECTS	MEAN	SE	VARIABLE
921	Teaching	Bernard, Abrami, Lou, Wozney, Borokhovski, Wallet, Wade, Fiset	2004	232	3,831,888	688	0.01	0.010	Distance education
922	Teaching	Bernard, Lou, Abrami, Wozney, Borokhovski, Wallet, Wade, Fiset	2004	155		155	−0.02	0.015	Presence or not: asynchronous and synchronous
923	Teaching	Allen, Bourhis, Mabry, Burrell & Timmerman	2006	54	74,275	54	0.09		Distance vs traditional teaching
924	Teaching	Lou, Bernard & Abrami	2006	103		218	0.02		Distance education in undergraduates
925	Teaching	Zhao, Lei, Yan, Lai & Tan	2008	51	11,477	98	0.10	0.090	Distance vs trad classes
		Home-school programs							
926	Teaching	Penuel, Kim, Michalchik, Lewis, Means, Murphy, Korbak, Whaley & Allen	2002	14		14	0.16		Laptop programs between school and home
		Homework							
927	Teaching	Paschal, Weinstein & Walberg	1984	15		81	0.36	0.027	Homework on learning
928	Teaching	Cooper	1989	20	2,154	20	0.21		Homework on achievement
929	Teaching	DeBaz	1994	77	41,828	77	0.39		Homework in science
930	Teaching	Cooper	1994	17	3,300	48	0.21		Homework on learning
931	Teaching	Cooper, Robinson & Patall	2006	32	58,000	69	0.28		Homework from studies 1987–2004

A list of influences on achievement

RANK	INFLUENCE	ES
1	Self-reported grades/Student expectations	1.44
2	Piagetian programs	1.28
3	Response to intervention	1.07
4	Teacher credibility	0.90
4	Providing formative evaluation	0.90
6	Micro-teaching	0.88
7	Classroom discussion	0.82
8	Comprehensive interventions for learning disabled students	0.77
9	Teacher clarity	0.75
10	Feedback	0.75
11	Reciprocal teaching	0.74
12	Teacher–student relationships	0.72
13	Spaced vs mass practice	0.71
14	Meta-cognitive strategies	0.69
15	Acceleration	0.68
16	Classroom behavioural	0.68
17	Vocabulary programs	0.67
18	Repeated reading programs	0.67
19	Creativity programs on achievement	0.65
20	Prior achievement	0.65
21	Self-verbalization and self-questioning	0.64
22	Study skills	0.63
23	Teaching strategies	0.62
24	Problem-solving teaching	0.61
25	Not labelling students	0.61
26	Comprehension programs	0.60
27	Concept mapping	0.60
28	Cooperative vs individualistic learning	0.59
29	Direct instruction	0.59
30	Tactile stimulation programs	0.58
31	Mastery learning	0.58
32	Worked examples	0.57
33	Visual-perception programs	0.55
34	Peer tutoring	0.55
35	Cooperative vs competitive learning	0.54

RANK	INFLUENCE	ES
36	Phonics instruction	0.54
37	Student-centred teaching	0.54
38	Classroom cohesion	0.53
39	Pre-term birth weight	0.53
40	Keller's Master Learning	0.53
41	Peer influences	0.53
42	Classroom management	0.52
43	Outdoor/adventure programs	0.52
44	Home environment	0.52
45	Socio-economic status	0.52
46	Interactive video methods	0.52
47	Professional development	0.51
48	Goals	0.50
49	Play programs	0.50
50	Second/third-chance programs	0.50
51	Parental involvement	0.49
52	Small-group learning	0.49
53	Questioning	0.48
54	Concentration/persistence/engagement	0.48
55	School effects	0.48
56	Motivation	0.48
57	Quality of teaching	0.48
58	Early intervention	0.47
59	Self-concept	0.47
60	Preschool programs	0.45
61	Writing programs	0.44
62	Teacher expectations	0.43
63	School size	0.43
64	Science programs	0.42
65	Cooperative learning	0.42
66	Exposure to reading	0.42
67	Behavioural organizers/adjunct questions	0.41
68	Mathematics programs	0.40
69	Reducing anxiety	0.40
70	Social skills programs	0.39
71	Integrated curricula programs	0.39
72	Enrichment	0.39
73	Principals/school leaders	0.39
74	Career interventions	0.38
75	Time on task	0.38
76	Psychotherapy programs	0.38
77	Computer-assisted instruction	0.37
78	Adjunct aids	0.37
79	Bilingual programs	0.37
80	Drama/arts programs	0.35
81	Creativity related to achievement	0.35
82	Attitude to mathematics/science	0.35
83	Frequency/effects of testing	0.34
84	Decreasing disruptive behaviour	0.34
85	Various teaching on creativity	0.34

RANK	INFLUENCE	ES
86	Simulations	0.33
87	Inductive teaching	0.33
88	Ethnicity	0.32
89	Teacher effects	0.32
90	Drugs	0.32
91	Enquiry-based teaching	0.31
92	Systems accountability	0.31
93	Ability grouping for gifted students	0.30
94	Homework	0.29
95	Home visiting	0.29
96	Exercise/relaxation	0.28
97	Desegregation	0.28
98	Teaching test-taking and coaching	0.27
99	Use of calculators	0.27
100	Volunteer tutors	0.26
101	Lack of illness	0.25
102	Mainstreaming	0.24
103	Values/moral education programs	0.24
104	Competitive vs individualistic learning	0.24
105	Programmed instruction	0.23
106	Summer school	0.23
107	Finances	0.23
108	Religious schools	0.23
109	Individualized instruction	0.22
110	Visual/audio-visual methods	0.22
111	Comprehensive teaching reforms	0.22
112	Teacher verbal ability	0.22
113	Class size	0.21
114	Charter schools	0.20
115	Aptitude/treatment interactions	0.19
116	Extra-curricular programs	0.19
116	Learning hierarchies	0.19
118	Co-/team teaching	0.19
119	Personality	0.18
120	Within-class grouping	0.18
120	Special college programs	0.18
122	Family structure	0.18
123	School counselling effects	0.18
124	Web-based learning	0.18
125	Matching style of learning	0.17
126	Teacher immediacy	0.16
127	Home-school programs	0.16
128	Problem-based learning	0.15
129	Sentence-combining programs	0.15
130	Mentoring	0.15
131	Ability grouping	0.12
132	Diet	0.12
133	Gender	0.12
134	Teacher education	0.12
135	Distance education	0.11

RANK	INFLUENCE	ES
136	Teacher subject matter knowledge	0.09
137	Changing school calendars/timetables	0.09
138	Out-of-school curricular experiences	0.09
139	Perceptual-motor programs	0.08
140	Whole language	0.06
141	Ethnic diversity of students	0.05
142	College halls of residence	0.05
143	Multi-grade/multi-age classes	0.04
144	Student control over learning	0.04
145	Open vs traditional	0.01
146	Summer vacation	−0.02
147	Welfare policies	−0.12
148	Retention	−0.13
149	Television	−0.18
150	Mobility	−0.34

Rankings and effect sizes of program influences from the end-of-chapter exercises

From Chapter 2, Exercise

INFLUENCE	ES	RANK	CLASSIFICATION
Retention (holding back a year)	−0.13	148	Low
Student control over learning	0.04	144	Low
Whole-language programs	0.06	140	Low
Teacher subject matter knowledge	0.09	136	Low
Gender (male compared with female achievement)	0.12	133	Low
Ability grouping/tracking/streaming	0.12	131	Low
Matching teaching with student learning styles	0.17	125	Low
Within-class grouping	0.18	120	Low
Reducing class size	0.21	113	Low
Individualizing instruction	0.22	109	Low
Using simulations and gaming	0.33	86	Medium
Teacher expectations	0.43	62	Medium
Professional development on student achievement	0.51	47	Medium
Home environment	0.52	44	Medium
Influence of peers	0.53	41	Medium
Phonics instruction	0.54	36	Medium
Providing worked examples	0.57	32	Medium
Direct instruction	0.59	29	Medium
Cooperative vs individualistic learning	0.59	28	Medium
Concept mapping	0.60	27	High
Comprehension programs	0.60	26	High
Vocabulary programs	0.67	17	High
Acceleration (for example, skipping a year)	0.68	15	High
Meta-cognitive strategy programs	0.69	14	High
Teacher–student relationships	0.72	12	High
Reciprocal teaching	0.74	11	High
Feedback	0.75	10	High

INFLUENCE	ES	RANK	CLASSIFICATION
Providing formative evaluation to teachers	0.90	4	High
Teacher credibility in eyes of the students	0.90	4	High
Student expectations	1.44	1	High

From Chapter 6, Exercise 4

HIGH INFLUENCES	ES	RANK
How to develop high expectations for each student	1.44	1
Providing formative evaluation to teachers	0.90	4
How to provide better feedback	0.75	10
Teacher–student relationships	0.72	12
How to better teach meta-cognitive strategies	0.69	14
How to accelerate learning	0.68	15
Teaching study skills	0.63	20
Teaching learning strategies	0.62	22
Ways to stop labelling students	0.61	25

MEDIUM INFLUENCES	ES	RANK
Peer influences on achievement	0.53	41
Influence of home environment	0.52	44
How to develop high expectations for each teacher	0.43	62
Integrated curricular programs	0.39	71
Computer-assisted instruction	0.37	77
Decreasing disruptive behaviour	0.34	84
Enquiry-based teaching	0.31	91
Homework	0.29	94
Teaching test-taking and coaching	0.27	98

LOW INFLUENCES	ES	RANK
School finances	0.23	107
Individualized instruction	0.22	109
Reducing class size	0.21	113
Extra-curricular programs	0.19	116
Home-school programs	0.16	127
Ability grouping/tracking	0.12	131
Male and female achievement differences	0.12	133
Student control over learning	0.04	144
Open vs traditional learning spaces	0.01	145

E

Calculating effect sizes

There are many different ways in which to use effect sizes, but here I focus on *progress* – not on comparisons between classes, teaching methods, etc.

Imagine a class of students have been administered a similar, or the same, test relating to the curriculum in February and June. We can use the data from these two tests to calculate an effect size. This effect size helps us to understand the impact of our teaching over this period.

The easiest way in which to calculate an effect size is to use Excel, using the following formula:

$$\text{Effect size} = \frac{\text{Average (post-test)} - \text{Average (pre-test)}}{\text{Spread (standard deviation, or sd)}}$$

Consider this example:

	A	B	C
1	**Student**	**February test**	**June test**
2	David	40	35
3	Anne	25	30
4	Eeofa	45	50
5	Barry	30	40
6	Corrin	35	45
7	Hemi	60	70
8	Juliet	65	75
9	Karmo	70	80
10	Fred	50	75
11	Ginnie	55	85
12			
13	Average	48 = AVERAGE(B2:B11)	59 = AVERAGE(C2:C11)
14	Spread (standard deviation or sd)	15 = STDEV(B2:B11)	21 = STDEV(C2:C11)
15	Average of spread		18 = AVERAGE(B14:C14)
16	Effect size		**0.6** =(C13–B13)/C15

So, to recap, the effect size was calculated as:

$$\text{Effect size} = \frac{58 - 48}{18} = 0.60$$

The interpretation of effect sizes

So now we have the first piece of important information: the class average effect size is 0.60. How should we interpret this? To come up with an independent measure of what expected progress should be, we have used two main considerations.

a. When we look at many major longitudinal databases – the Progress in International Reading Literacy Study (PIRLS); the Program for International Student Assessment (PISA); the Trends in International Mathematics and Science Study (TIMSS); the National Assessment of Educational Progress (NAEP); the National Assessment Program – Literacy and Numeracy (NAPLAN) – they all lead to a similar estimate of an effect size of 0.4 for a year's input of schooling. For example, using NAPLAN (Australia's national assessments) reading, writing, and maths data for students moving from one year to the next, the average effect size across all students is 0.40.

b. The average of 900+ meta-analyses based on 240 million students shows an average intervention of 0.40.

Therefore an effect greater than 0.40 is seen as above the norm and leading towards a more-than-expected growth over a year.

Within a year, it is expected that the progress should be 0.40. So if calculating an effect size over five months, the 0.40 average should still be expected – primarily because teachers often adjust the difficulty of a test to take into account the elapsed time, and because teachers more often create assessments on specific topics within a year's curriculum. So, within a year, the aim is greater than 0.40; over two years, 0.8; over three years, 1.2; and so on.

Individual effect sizes

We can also calculate effect sizes for individual students. When we do this, we assume that each student contributes similarly to the overall variance, then use the pooled spread (standard deviation) as an estimator for each student. We use the following formula:

$$\text{Effect size} = \frac{\text{Individual score (post-test)} - \text{Individual score (pre-test)}}{\text{Spread (standard deviation, or sd) for the whole class}}$$

Let's go back to our example. Remember the average spread for the class was **18**. The effect size for David is:

$$\frac{35 - 40}{18} = -0.28$$

For Anne, it is:

$$\frac{30 - 25}{18} = 0.28$$

And so on . . .

STUDENT	FEBRUARY TEST	JUNE TEST	EFFECT SIZE
David	40	35	−0.28
Anne	25	30	0.28
Eeofa	45	50	0.28
Barry	30	40	0.56
Corrin	35	45	0.56
Hemi	60	70	0.56
Juliet	65	75	0.56
Karmo	70	80	0.56
Fred	50	75	1.39
Ginnie	55	85	1.67

In the above case, there are now some important questions for teachers. Why did Fred and Ginnie make such high gains, and why did David, Anne, and Eeofa make such low gains? The data, obviously, do not ascribe the reasons, but they do provide the best evidence to lead to these important causal explanations. (Note that, in this case, it is not necessarily that it was the struggling students who made the lowest and the brightest who made the highest gains.)

Given that there is an assumption (that each student contributes to the spread similarly), the most important issue is the *questions* that these data create: what possible explanations could there be for those students who achieved below 0.40 and for those who achieved above 0.40? This then allows evidence to be used to form the right questions. Only teachers can seek the reasons, look for triangulation about these reasons, and devise strategies for these students.

There are some things of which you should be aware.

a. Caution should be used with small sample sizes: the smaller the sample, the more care should be taken to cross-validate the findings. Any sample size of fewer than 30 students can be considered 'small'.

b. A key is to look for outlier students. In a small sample, a few outliers can skew the effect sizes and they may need special consideration (with questions including 'Why did they grow so much more than the other students?', or 'Why did they not grow as much as the other students?'); the effect sizes may even need to be recalculated with these students omitted.

Such are the perils of small sample sizes!

Conclusions

The advantage of using the effect-size method is that effect sizes can be interpreted across tests, classes, times, etc. While it makes much sense to use the same test for the pre- and post-test, this is not always necessary. For example, in the longitudinal tests cited above, the tests are different at each time, but they have been built to measure the same dimension at both times. There are some forms of score that are less amenable to interpreting as suggested above: percentiles, stanines, and NCE scores have sufficiently unusual properties that effect sizes as calculated above can lead to misleading results.

Using effect sizes invites teachers to think about using assessment to help to estimate progress, and to reframe instruction to better tailor learning for individual, or groups of, students. It asks teachers to consider reasons why some students have progressed and others not – as a consequence of their teaching. This is an example of 'evidence into action'.

Some (free) references

For more understanding about effect sizes, and how to calculate and interpret them, look at the following.

- Schagen, I., & Hodgen, E. (2009). *How much difference does it make? Notes on understanding, using, and calculating effect sizes for schools*, available online at http://www.education counts.govt.nz/publications/schooling/36097/36098

- Becker, L.E. (2009). Effect size calculators, available online at http://www.uccs.edu/~faculty/lbecker/

- Coe, R. (2002). 'It's the effect size, stupid': what effect size is and why it is important, available online at http://www.leeds.ac.uk/educol/documents/00002182.htm

For more about calculating standard deviation, look online at:

- http://standard-deviation.appspot.com/
- http://easycalculation.com/statistics/learn-standard-deviation.php
- http://simple.wikipedia.org/wiki/Standard_deviation

The Irving Student Evaluation of Accomplished Teaching Scale

Photocopying of this appendix is permitted.

Teacher: _____

Subject: _____

Year level: _____

Please indicate the EXTENT of your disagreement/agreement with the following statements by using the following scale:

STRONGLY DISAGREE	TEND TO DISAGREE	SLIGHTLY AGREE	SOMEWHAT AGREE	USUALLY AGREE	STRONGLY AGREE
1	2	3	4	5	6

This teacher . . .

COMMITMENT TO STUDENTS AND THEIR LEARNING

1. is committed to the learning of all the students in the class.   1 2 3 4 5 6

2. adjusts the lesson if we experience difficulties in learning.   1 2 3 4 5 6

3. enables us to develop confidence and self-esteem in this subject.   1 2 3 4 5 6

4. uses assessment results to provide extra help/extension to appropriate students.   1 2 3 4 5 6

5. creates a positive atmosphere in class in which we feel part of a team of learners.   1 2 3 4 5 6

6. provides time for us to reflect and talk about the concepts that we are learning. 1 2 3 4 5 6

Pedagogy in this subject

7. encourages us to test ideas and discover principles in this subject. 1 2 3 4 5 6

8. develops our ability to think and reason in this subject. 1 2 3 4 5 6

9. encourages us to try different techniques to solve problems. 1 2 3 4 5 6

10. encourages us to place a high value on this subject. 1 2 3 4 5 6

11. tells us what the purpose of each lesson is. 1 2 3 4 5 6

12. knows and caters for the problems that we commonly encounter in learning new topics. 1 2 3 4 5 6

13. helps us to construct an understanding of the language and processes of this subject. 1 2 3 4 5 6

Student engagement with the curriculum

14. challenges students to think through and solve problems, either by themselves or together as a group. 1 2 3 4 5 6

15. makes this subject interesting for me. 1 2 3 4 5 6

16. makes learning this subject satisfying and stimulating. 1 2 3 4 5 6

17. makes this subject come alive in the classroom. 1 2 3 4 5 6

18. shows us interesting and useful ways of solving problems. 1 2 3 4 5 6

19. compared with all other teachers that I have had is the best. 1 2 3 4 5 6

Relationship between subject and the real world

20. helps the class to understand how this subject relates to the real world. 1 2 3 4 5 6

21. helps us to make the links between the different topics of this subject and other aspects of our lives. 1 2 3 4 5 6

22. prepares us for adult life by helping us to see how important this subject will be to our careers and to everyday life. 1 2 3 4 5 6

23. teaches us about the way in which this subject contributes to changes in society, and the way in which society has changed this subject. 1 2 3 4 5 6

24. helps us to realize that this subject is continuously evolving and growing to make sense of the world. 1 2 3 4 5 6

Author index

Subject index

adaptive experts vii, 5, 99–100, 107, 114, 150, 163, 186

approach and avoidance goals 43, 50

assessment *see* feedback from assessment

asTTle 152

average yearly growth 14

backward design 93, 107, 113, 152, 187

capability 93–4, 97, 126, 158

capacity 4, 93

challenge 5, 17, 22, 27–8, 29, 30–1, 35, 39, 41, 49, 51–3, 56, 58, 70, 94, 100–2, 117, 135, 146, 161, 164–5, 168

checklists 6

classroom climate 16, 26, 28, 69–71, 76, 99, 100, 124–5, 138, 140–1, 154, 165

classroom observation 29, 30, 72, 73, 89, 92, 131, 138

coaching 64, 132–3, 152, 154

cognitive acceleration 39, 94

commitment 17, 22, 26, 31, 41, 51, 52–3, 65, 70, 92, 117, 120, 135, 140, 142–3, 167

competence 43, 46, 71, 93

concentration 5, 17, 96, 110–11, 192

conceptual understanding 15, 18, 27, 47, 51, 54, 77–8, 102

confidence 5, 26, 40–1, 46, 51, 53, 83, 104, 110, 120

cooperative learning 78

culture of student 22, 130, 151

curriculum 23, 25, 38, 47, 56–9, 143–4, 151

curriculum resources 56–8

data teams 60–2, 145, 154

degree of implementation 66, 76, 156

deliberate practice 4, 5, 14, 16–18, 41, 60, 66, 78, 96, 107–11, 113, 136, 165

deliverology 156–9

dialogue 5, 39, 39, 60, 72–4, 76, 163–4

direct instruction 65–6, 83–4, 237

disconfirmation 123–4, 135

do your best 27, 164

drivers of change 151–2, 157

effect size 2–3, 10–11, 87

empathy 100, 140–1

engagement 18, 26, 33, 52, 60–1, 65, 70, 72, 91, 110, 112, 120, 139, 192

errors 5, 16, 19–20, 25, 26, 50, 52, 69, 71, 74, 96, 100, 102, 115, 124–5

everything works 2, 13, 158

expectations – parents 22, 140

expectations – school leaders 153–4, 157–8

expectations – students 53–4, 67, 83, 140

expectations – teachers 5, 26, 32, 51, 61, 67, 81–2, 96, 111, 140, 145, 151

expert vs. experienced teachers 24–30

feedback 5, 16–20, 26, 44, 52, 64, 66, 75, 88, 102, 108, 115–37, 159, 227–8

feedback – asking students 130–1

feedback frequency 122

feedback from assessment 125–6, 152, 163

feedback given and received 122–3, 160–1

feedback in motion 98, 135

focus 19–20, 59–60, 64, 86, 153

formative feedback 88, 108, 127–8, 144–5

goal free evaluation 143

goals 14, 27, 40–3, 46–9, 51–2, 77, 93, 95–6, 104–5, 113, 134–5, 154

helping students become their own teachers 5

hinge point (d = 0.40) 3, 11, 12–13, 14, 17

homework 10–13, 149, 165–6